Best of the Best from the

Pacific Rim

Cookbook

Selected Recipes from the
Favorite Cookbooks of Washington, Oregon,
California, Alaska, and Hawaii

Seafood is abundant in Oregon—from the sea and the many lakes and streams. Fresh tuna, salmon, trout, bass, bluegill, catfish, halibut, lingcod, snapper, Dungeness crabs and shellfish can sometimes be bought directly from fishermen.

Best of the Best from the
Pacific Rim
Cookbook

Selected Recipes from the
Favorite Cookbooks of Washington, Oregon,
California, Alaska, and Hawaii

EDITED BY

Gwen McKee

AND

Barbara Moseley

Illustrated by Tupper England

QUAIL RIDGE PRESS
Preserving America's Food Heritage

Recipe Collection ©2009 Quail Ridge Press, Inc.

Library of Congress Cataloging-in-Publication Data

Best of the best from the Pacific Rim cookbook : selected recipes from the favorite
  cookbooks of Washington, Oregon, California, Alaska, and Hawaii / edited by
  Gwen McKee and Barbara Moseley ; illustrated by Tupper England. — 1st ed.
    p. cm..— (Best of the best cookbook series)
  ISBN-13: 978-1-934193-28-0
  ISBN-10: 1-934193-28-3
    1. Cookery, American. 2. Cookery—West (U.S.). 3. Cookery—Alaska. 4.
Cookery—Hawaii.. I. McKee, Gwen. II. Moseley, Barbara.
  TX715.B4856465 2009
  641.5973--dc22   2009003571

ISBN-13: 978-1-934193-28-0 • ISBN-10: 1-934193-28-3
Book design by Cynthia Clark • Cover photo by Greg Campbell
Printed in Canada

First edition, June 2009
On the cover: Grilled Wild Salmon with Fresh Tarragon Butter

QUAIL RIDGE PRESS
P. O. Box 123 • Brandon, MS 39043
info@quailridge.com • www.quailridge.com

CONTENTS

The aurora borealis, or northern lights, provide a rare show over Lynn Canal in Southeast Alaska, where clouds often blot out the sky. Fall, winter and spring are the best seasons for viewing the great lights.

Quest for the Best
Regional Cooking

It seems that everywhere Barbara and I travel, we find that people love to talk about food. Invariably they mention specific dishes that have been an important part of their family's heritage and tradition, and do so with exuberance and pride.

"My mother always serves her fabulous cornbread dressing with our Thanksgiving turkey, and it is simply 'the best.'"

"Aunt Susan's famous pecan pie is always the first to go."

"No family occasion would be complete without Uncle Joe's chicken salad sandwiches."

Well, we heard, we researched, and we captured these bragged-about recipes so that people all over the country . . . and the world . . . could enjoy them.

My co-editor Barbara Moseley and I have been searching for the country's best recipes for three decades, and home cooks everywhere have learned to trust and rely on our cookbooks to bring them fabulous meals their friends and family will love! We always choose recipes based first and foremost on taste. In addition, the ingredients have to be readily available, and the recipes simple, with easy-to-follow instructions and never-fail results.

While touring the country and tasting the local fare, we delight in finding the little secrets that make the big difference. We have eaten buffalo in Wyoming, halibut in Alaska, lobster in Maine, gumbo in Louisiana, each prepared in a variety of creative ways. Finding out about conch in Florida and boysenberries in Oregon and poi in Hawaii . . . . No matter where we venture, this part of our job is always fun, often surprising, and definitely inspiring!

The five states of California, Oregon, Washington, Alaska, and Hawaii have one huge thing in common—the Pacific Ocean! And many of their food dishes are similar for the same reason, because so much comes from the sea. But there are many differences to be sure. In this col-

lection, we have endeavored to bring you recipes that have been created in each state . . . Cracked Dungeness Crab, Northwest Huckleberry Pie, Fisherman's Wharf Garlic Prawns, Oven Kahlua Pig, Alaskaladas . . . . The incredible seafood and the bounty of fresh fruits and vegetables from these states present an overflowing cornucopia of delicious foods. Do what we did . . . dive in!

Gwen McKee

Gwen McKee and Barbara Moseley, editors of BEST OF THE BEST STATE COOKBOOK SERIES

BEVERAGES & APPETIZERS

More than 300,000 tons of grapes are grown annually in California vineyards such as this one in Napa Valley. From these grapes are produced more than seventeen million gallons of wine each year, making California the nation's top wine producer. Washington state is now the second largest wine producer and is ranked among the world's top wine regions.

Country Club Iced Tea

Almost every country club in Hawaii (and some restaurants) make a version of this tea. The trick is to make it with plain ol' black tea, then add fruit juice and lots of fresh mint. Sometimes the juice is pineapple, sometimes it comes from an abundance of lemon trees in the backyard. One kama'āina family made a simple syrup by cooking the sugar first, thereby making it easier to dissolve. There is now a commercial version sold in cans. But fresh is still best.

½ gallon water
12 black tea bags
3 sprigs fresh mint
2 cups sugar

12 ounces pineapple juice
6 ounces lemon juice
Pineapple spears and fresh
  mint sprigs for garnish

In a large pot, bring water to a boil. Steep the tea bags and fresh mint in the hot water. Remove the mint after 3 minutes, but continue to steep the tea until it is very dark. Remove tea bags. Add sugar and juices while tea is still warm. Stir to dissolve sugar. Pour into a gallon container and add water to fill. Refrigerate. Serve with ice and garnishes.

Hawaiian Country Tables (Hawaii)

Instant Russian Tea Mix

This is an old standard that helps get you through long winter nights.

2 cups instant tea with lemon
2 cups sugar
2 cups Tang

1 teaspoon cinnamon
½ teaspoon ground cloves
½ teaspoon nutmeg

Mix ingredients together and store in dry container. Mix 3–4 tablespoons with 8 ounces of boiling water per serving.

Recipes from the Paris of the Pacific—Sitka, Alaska (Alaska)

At their closest, America and Russia are a mere 2.5 miles apart—the distance between Little Diomede Island, Alaska, and Big Diomede Island, Russia. The two islands sit astride the U.S./Russian maritime border in the middle of the Bering Strait. When the Bering Strait freezes, you can walk between the two islands—from America to Russia—and thus, because you would cross the international date line, from today to tomorrow. Or walk from Russia to America and travel from today to yesterday. But don't try it. The frozen Bering Strait can have huge ice ridges as well as open holes of water.

Banana Smoothie

When my kids were young, they voted me "Number 1 Mom" at a family reunion because I let them have shakes for breakfast. See what fresh juices or fruits are available at the grocery store or farmers' market and have fun experimenting with different flavors.

1 small ripe banana, cut into chunks
½ cup fresh orange juice
½ cup canned unsweetened pineapple juice
½ cup plain yogurt

1 tablespoon sugar or honey to taste
Protein powder to taste (optional)
½ cup small or coarsely crushed ice cubes

In a blender, combine banana, orange juice, pineapple juice, yogurt, sugar, protein powder, and ice. Mix at high speed until smooth. Pour into 2 tall, frosty glasses.

Note: If crushing ice cubes is a problem for your blender, eliminate ice cubes, and freeze fruit and yogurt.

Summertime Treats (Oregon)

Tiki Punch

If you are having a small enough party, delight your guests with their own "pineapple glass." When you hollow out the pineapple, take care not to cut through the skin. Use the pineapple for other dishes. It's also a great opportunity to experiment with different garnishes. Recipe serves one.

1 pineapple per guest or couple
1 ounce vodka
½ ounce Galliano liqueur

5 ounces orange juice
5 ounces pineapple juice
Champagne

Combine vodka, Galliano, and juices in a pitcher. Pour into pineapple, approximately ⅔ from the top. Fill with champagne and add garnishes.

Hawaii's Best Tropical Food & Drinks (Hawaii)

Raspberry Liqueur

4 cups raspberries, mashed　　　**3 cups vodka**
½ lemon peel, scraped　　　**¾ cup Simple Syrup**

Mix raspberries, lemon zest, and vodka. Steep 3 weeks; strain and filter. Add Simple Syrup, and age 1 month.

SIMPLE SYRUP FOR LIQUEURS:

It is one of the basic ingredients of many liqueur recipes. It is made by simmering equal volumes of water and sweetener for about 5 minutes. Sweeteners can be cane sugar, brown sugar, or honey. Powdered sugar is not suitable because it has a starch filler and will make a cloudy syrup.

The Alaskan Bootlegger's Bible (Alaska)

Mai Tai

There is much discussion about the origin of the delightful Mai Tai. Whoever invented it, the Mai Tai has become one of the most popular drinks in the islands.

2 ounces light rum　　　**½ ounce amaretto**
1 ounce dark rum　　　**½ ounce lime juice**
1 ounce Triple Sec orange　　　**Crushed ice**
**　liqueur**

Mix the rums, Triple Sec, amaretto, and lime juice in a 7-ounce glass. Add crushed ice and garnish.

Hawaii's Best Tropical Food & Drinks (Hawaii)

HAWAIIBEACHCOMBER.COM

Donn Beach, best known as Don the Beachcomber, is considered to have single-handedly transformed the hospitality industry in Hawaii in the 1940s and 1950s through his creation of the International Market Place, and his successful Polynesian-theme restaurants. Donn invented more than 80 tropical drinks including the Mai Tai, the Zombie, Missionary's Downfall, and the Beachcomber's Daiquiri. The Zombie was considered the most lethal tropical drink ever created, and customers in Donn's bar were limited to two. To protect his recipes, Donn wrote them in code, and his bartenders had to follow coded symbols for the ingredients.

Chocolate Moose Latté

½ ounce chocolate syrup
2 shots of coffee
1 cup steamed milk

1 large scoop of whipped
   cream
6 raisins

Add chocolate syrup, coffee, and steamed milk together in coffee cup. Top with bull-sized (large) scoop of whipped cream and raisins.

Moose in the Pot Cookbook (Alaska)

Café à la Queen of Tonga

Queen Halaevalu Mata'aho, descendant to the throne of Tonga after five hundred years of royalty, was the honored guest for the two-day opening celebration festivities of the Waiakea Village Resort in Hilo, along with her daughter Princess Pilolevu Tuku'aho. In the Queen's honor, Don the Beachcomber concocted the following:

½ cup whipping cream
¼ teaspoon instant coffee
½ teaspoon cocoa
1 drop almond extract
1 light dusting of cinnamon

2 teaspoons coconut syrup*
8 ounces hot Kona coffee
½ ounce gold rum
1 Tahitian vanilla bean

Blend whipping cream, instant coffee, cocoa, almond extract, and cinnamon until granules of coffee dissolve. Whip until stiff peaks form. Into a large cup or glass, add coconut syrup and coffee, and stir until the syrup dissolves. Add rum. Top with a generous dollop of the spiced whipped cream. Add Tahitian vanilla bean and gently stir.

Note: For best results, use Hana Bay Premium Gold Rum.

*A syrup made from coconut milk and sugar. It can be bought in 12-ounce jars.

Hawai'i Tropical Rum Drinks & Cuisine (Hawaii)

Hawaiian Coffee

10 drops almond extract
½ cup crème de cacao
1 cup sugar
½ cup cocoa
1 teaspoon salt

1 pint whipping cream
**3 trays coffee ice cubes made
with Kona coffee (sweetened,
if desired)**

Simmer almond extract, crème de cacao, sugar, cocoa, and salt until well blended. Refrigerate. Whip cream until firm, but not stiff. Fold into coffee mixture. When ready to serve, put ice cubes in punch bowl. Pour in chilled coffee mixture. Makes 30 servings.

Hawaii–Cooking with Aloha (Hawaii)

Café Mocha

**1 (14-ounce) can sweetened
condensed milk**
**1 (4-ounce) Baker's German
sweet chocolate bar**

1 cup whipping cream
Hot brewed coffee

Melt chocolate and sweetened condensed milk in top of double boiler over low heat. Stir occasionally. Cool.

Whip cream until soft peaks form. Fold into cooled chocolate mixture. Cover tightly and refrigerate for up to one week. For each serving, place ¼ cup chocolate mixture in a large coffee cup or mug. Fill with hot brewed coffee. Stir and serve immediately. Serves 10.

Symphony of Flavors (California)

Spiced Mocha Mix

1 cup sugar
1 cup nonfat dry milk powder
½ cup powdered non-dairy
  creamer
½ cup cocoa powder
3 tablespoons powdered
  instant coffee

½ teaspoon ground allspice
¼ teaspoon ground cinnamon
Dash salt
Marshmallows (optional)

In large bowl, combine all ingredients. Store in airtight container. For single serving, place 3 tablespoons mix in mug or cup, and add ¾ cup boiling water. Stir until mixture is dissolved. Top with marshmallows, if desired. Each 2½ cups mix makes 12–14 servings.

McNamee Family & Friends Cookbook (Washington)

Creamy Hot Chocolate

Delicious! This is deluxe!

1 (14-ounce) can sweetened
  condensed milk
½ cup unsweetened cocoa
1½ teaspoons vanilla
  extract

⅛ teaspoon salt
6½ cups hot water
Marshmallows (optional)

In large saucepan, combine sweetened condensed milk, cocoa, vanilla, and salt; mix well. Over medium heat, slowly stir in water; heat through, stirring occasionally. Top with marshmallows, if desired. Makes about 2 quarts.

Sleigh Bells and Sugarplums (Washington)

Spicy Hot Salmon Dip

1 pint canned salmon, drained
 and dark pieces taken out
¼ cup finely chopped onion
¼ cup finely chopped green
 or red pepper
½–1 teaspoon hot horseradish
4–6 shakes Tabasco

1 teaspoon lemon juice
½ fresh jalapeño, chopped or
 1–2 tablespoons canned
½ teaspoon garlic salt
2 tablespoons mayonnaise or
 sour cream or cream cheese

Stir until blended; place in a pretty bowl. Sprinkle with black pepper. Serve with crackers.

Grannie Annie's Cookin' Fish from Cold Alaskan Waters (Alaska)

Salmon Dip

16 ounces smoked salmon
2 tablespoons lemon juice
1 bunch green onions, chopped
½ teaspoon liquid smoke
2–3 teaspoons horseradish

2 (8-ounce) packages cream
 cheese, softened
Pepper to taste
1–2 tablespoons mayonnaise
Red food coloring (optional)

Mix all ingredients in order given. Cover and refrigerate for 1–2 hours before serving. May be served with your favorite crackers or vegetables.

From Our Kitchen to Yours (Washington)

Knock-Your-Socks-Off
Hot Crab Dip

½ cup dry white wine
4 ounces cream cheese, room
   temperature
1 (16-ounce) can water-packed
   artichoke hearts, drained
   and finely chopped
1 cup mayonnaise

1 egg
1 pound fresh crab or
   2 (8-ounce) cans crabmeat
2 ounces blue cheese, finely
   crumbled
Sliced black olives for garnish
   (optional)

Preheat oven to 350°. In a saucepan over low heat, combine white wine and cream cheese and simmer until cheese is creamy. Remove from heat and blend thoroughly with wire whisk. Stir in artichoke hearts, mayonnaise, egg, crabmeat, and blue cheese. Pour into 8x8-inch oven-proof baking dish and bake for 30 minutes at 350°. Garnish with black olives, if desired. Serve with crackers. Yields 10–12 servings.

From Portland's Palate (Oregon)

Aloha Dip

1 (8-ounce) package cream
   cheese, softened
1 cup crushed pineapple,
   drained

1 cup grated coconut
1½ teaspoons ground ginger
1 teaspoon lemon juice
½ cup chopped pecans

Mash cream cheese well. Add remaining ingredients, and stir well. Chill for several hours before serving. Serve with crackers.

Pupus from Paradise (Hawaii)

Hot Chile-Spinach Dip in a Bread Round

1 large round loaf unsliced Shepherd's bread or French bread
2–3 jalapeño chiles, minced
1 (7-ounce) can diced green chiles
1 small onion, chopped
2 tablespoons vegetable oil
2 tomatoes, chopped
1 (10-ounce) package frozen chopped spinach, thawed, drained and squeezed dry
1 tablespoon red wine vinegar
1 (8-ounce) package cream cheese, softened
2 cups grated Monterey Jack cheese
1 cup half-and-half
1 teaspoon cumin
Salt and pepper to taste
Tortilla chips

Preheat oven to 325°. Cut top off bread ¼ of the way down. Carefully scoop out inside, leaving a 1-inch shell. Reserve top.

In a medium skillet over medium heat, cook chiles and onions in oil, stirring, for 4 minutes, or until onions are softened. Add tomatoes and cook mixture, stirring, for 2 more minutes. Stir in spinach, vinegar, cream cheese, Monterey Jack cheese, half-and-half, cumin, salt and pepper, and heat gently.

Pour sauce into bread round, replace top and wrap in heavy foil. Place in a baking pan and bake for 1½ hours.

To serve, place the bread round on a platter and surround with tortilla chips for dipping. The dip may also be served in a chafing dish. Serves 8–10.

California Sizzles (California)

Artichoke Dip

**1 (8-ounce) can artichoke
hearts (water packed)
1 cup mayonnaise**

**1 (4-ounce) can diced chiles
1 cup grated Parmesan cheese**

Dice drained artichokes. Mix all ingredients. Place in oven and bake 20 minutes at 350°. Serve with Wheat Thins or other crisp crackers.

Cooking Treasures of the Central Coast (California)

Artichoke Dip

**1 (14-ounce) can artichoke
hearts (marinated okay)
¾ cup grated mozzarella
cheese
¾ cup grated Cheddar
cheese**

**¼ cup grated Parmesan
cheese
1 cup mayonnaise
1–2 cloves garlic to taste
Tortilla chips**

Drain artichokes well. Place all ingredients in food processor. Blend until smooth. Place in baking dish. Bake at 375° for 20–30 minutes. Serve warm with tortilla chips.

Taste of the Methow (Washington)

Castroville, California, is known as the Artichoke Capital of the World. In 1947, a young woman named Norma Jean was crowned Castroville's first Artichoke Queen. She went on to become actress Marilyn Monroe.

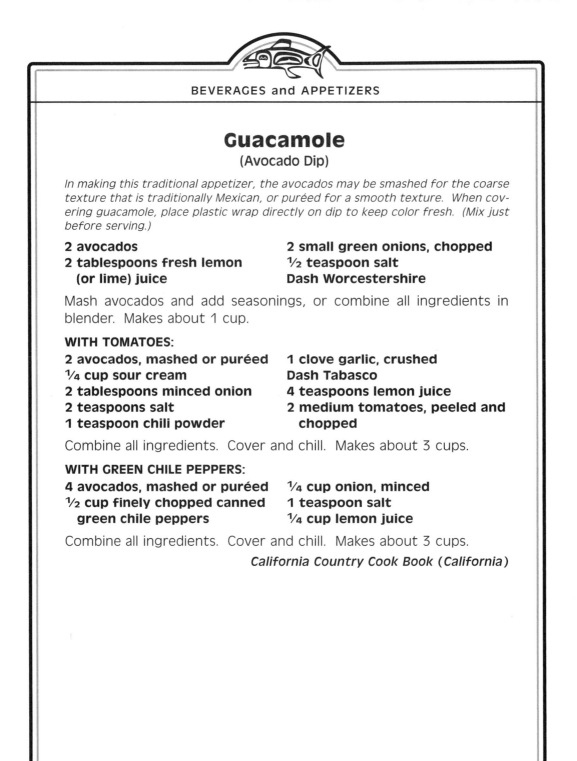

Guacamole
(Avocado Dip)

In making this traditional appetizer, the avocados may be smashed for the coarse texture that is traditionally Mexican, or puréed for a smooth texture. When covering guacamole, place plastic wrap directly on dip to keep color fresh. (Mix just before serving.)

2 avocados	2 small green onions, chopped
2 tablespoons fresh lemon (or lime) juice	½ teaspoon salt
	Dash Worcestershire

Mash avocados and add seasonings, or combine all ingredients in blender. Makes about 1 cup.

WITH TOMATOES:

2 avocados, mashed or puréed	1 clove garlic, crushed
¼ cup sour cream	Dash Tabasco
2 tablespoons minced onion	4 teaspoons lemon juice
2 teaspoons salt	2 medium tomatoes, peeled and chopped
1 teaspoon chili powder	

Combine all ingredients. Cover and chill. Makes about 3 cups.

WITH GREEN CHILE PEPPERS:

4 avocados, mashed or puréed	¼ cup onion, minced
½ cup finely chopped canned green chile peppers	1 teaspoon salt
	¼ cup lemon juice

Combine all ingredients. Cover and chill. Makes about 3 cups.

California Country Cook Book (California)

Papaya Salsa

This salsa is a refreshing complement to the smoky, salty flavor of grilled seafood.

3 cups diced ripe papaya
1 cup diced tomatoes
1 cup finely diced red bell
  pepper
1½ cups diced red onion
½ jalapeño pepper, seeded
  and finely chopped
2 tablespoons extra virgin
  olive oil
2½ tablespoons red wine
  vinegar

6 tablespoons freshly squeezed
  lime juice
2 tablespoons freshly
  squeezed lemon juice
2 teaspoons ground cumin
1 teaspoon freshly ground
  black pepper
Dash Tabasco
1 cup coarsely chopped, loosely
  packed Chinese parsley

Combine all ingredients in a large porcelain or glass bowl. Toss thoroughly. Cover and let stand for 1 or 2 hours. Serve chilled or at room temperature. Makes 1 quart.

Note: Salsa will keep in the refrigerator for up to a week.

Another Taste of Aloha (Hawaii)

In Volcanoes National Park on the Big Island of Hawaii, hiking trails take you where molten lava has destroyed most everything in its path. In time, little specks of green began to spring forth, beginning life's cycle once again. Though walking through this barren area is desolate and a little eerie, it has a special beauty all its own.

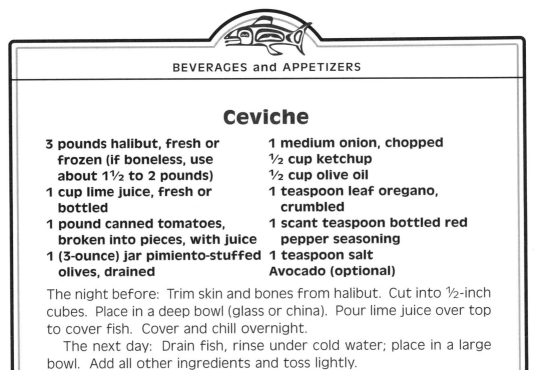

Ceviche

3 pounds halibut, fresh or
frozen (if boneless, use
about 1½ to 2 pounds)
1 cup lime juice, fresh or
bottled
1 pound canned tomatoes,
broken into pieces, with juice
1 (3-ounce) jar pimiento-stuffed
olives, drained

1 medium onion, chopped
½ cup ketchup
½ cup olive oil
1 teaspoon leaf oregano,
crumbled
1 scant teaspoon bottled red
pepper seasoning
1 teaspoon salt
Avocado (optional)

The night before: Trim skin and bones from halibut. Cut into ½-inch cubes. Place in a deep bowl (glass or china). Pour lime juice over top to cover fish. Cover and chill overnight.

The next day: Drain fish, rinse under cold water; place in a large bowl. Add all other ingredients and toss lightly.

May be topped with avocado. Serve with tortilla chips. Serves 10–12.

Variation: Fresh tomato may be added, if desired. Red snapper, salmon or tuna may be substituted for halibut.

California Kosher (California)

Lomi Salmon

1 pound salted salmon
3 large tomatoes, diced
1 onion, chopped

3 stalks green onions, chopped
3 cubes ice, cracked

Soak salted salmon in cold water for one hour. If salmon is very salty, repeat process. Remove skin and bones, and shred salmon with fingers. Place in a bowl and add tomatoes and onions. Chill; add crushed ice just before serving.

Note: Salted salmon was introduced to Hawaiians by Westerners. Lomi salmon is now known as a "traditional" Hawaiian food, which is always served at a lūʻau.

Ethnic Foods of Hawaiʻi (Hawaii)

Smoked Salmon Mousse

12 ounces hard smoked salmon, skinned (not lox)
1 tablespoon plus 2 teaspoons strained, fresh lemon juice
2 tablespoons chopped green onions (white part only)
1 teaspoon dried dill weed (or 2 teaspoons chopped fresh)
¾ cup melted butter, cooled
1 cup sour cream
Capers for garnish (optional)
Fresh dill weed for garnish (optional)

Break up salmon to feel for bone or skin; remove. Put in food processor with chopping blade. Add lemon juice, onions, and dill. Process until smooth. With machine running, slowly pour in cooled, melted butter until it's incorporated. Using rubber spatula, put smoked salmon mixture in a medium-size bowl. Slowly fold in sour cream till completely incorporated. Put in serving dish.

Can be served as spread on crackers, piped with decorative tip on toast rounds, or topped with tiny dollop of whipped cream with caper or sprig of dill.

Note: If using moist smoked salmon, decrease butter and sour cream to ½ cup each.

Coastal Flavors (Oregon)

Smoked Salmon Ball

1 (1-pound) can boneless, skinless smoked salmon
1 (8-ounce) package cream cheese, softened
1 teaspoon horseradish
2 teaspoons grated onion
½ teaspoon liquid smoke
1 tablespoon lemon juice
¼ teaspoon salt
½ cup chopped pecans
3 tablespoons chopped parsley

Drain salmon. Blend with all other ingredients except pecans and parsley, then shape into a ball. Roll ball in chopped nuts and chopped parsley. Chill for several hours and serve with crackers.

Grandma Jean's Rainy Day Recipes (Oregon)

Salmon Pâté

This recipe was developed when we had a mound of leftover grilled salmon. Everyone fights over this pâté, including our grandchildren.

1¾ cups cooked salmon or
   1 (15-ounce) can red salmon, drained
1 tablespoon nonfat mayonnaise
½ cup nonfat plain yogurt
2 cloves garlic, minced
¼ teaspoon Tabasco

1–2 teaspoons dried dillweed
¼ teaspoon (or less) Lite Salt
   (omit if using canned salmon)
¼ cup chopped green onions
2 teaspoons freshly squeezed lemon juice
1 tablespoon chopped fresh `parsley

Remove skin and bones from salmon. Combine all ingredients and mix thoroughly with a fork (not a food processor). Cover and chill in refrigerator. Serve with low-fat crackers or thinly sliced French bread. Makes 2 cups.

The New American Diet Cookbook (Oregon)

Salmon Balls

Canned salmon is fine for these delectable salmon balls, though freshly caught and cooked salmon tastes even better.

1 (1-pound) can salmon
1 (8-ounce) package cream cheese, softened
2 teaspoons lemon juice
1 teaspoon prepared horseradish

3 teaspoons grated onion
¼ teaspoon liquid smoke
¼ teaspoon salt
Chopped pecans or walnuts
Chopped olives (optional)

Drain and clean, as needed, a can of salmon. Combine cream cheese, salmon, lemon juice, grated onion, horseradish, liquid smoke and salt. Mix carefully to a smooth consistency and form into balls. Roll balls in finely chopped nuts, or roll in chopped olives. Refrigerate for several hours before serving. These balls can be successfully frozen.

Alaska Magazine's Cabin Cookbook (Alaska)

Dungeness Crab Puffs

6 ounces Dungeness crab
1 cup mayonnaise
1 cup grated Swiss cheese
½ cup finely chopped onion

1 package frozen puff pastry
 (2 sheets), defrosted
1 whole egg beaten with
 1 teaspoon water

Preheat oven to 400°. Combine crab, mayonnaise, Swiss cheese, and onion in a medium bowl, blending well. Flatten sheets of puff pastry and lightly roll them out. Cut each of the sheets into thirds lengthwise, and then into fourths along the short side, making a total of 12 squares per sheet. Brush lightly with beaten egg and water. Put a teaspoon of filling in center of each square. Fold squares in half diagonally, and seal by pressing tines of a fork around the edges. Brush tops with more of the beaten egg mixture. Place puffs on a baking sheet lined with baking parchment (or a non-stick baking sheet) and bake for 10–12 minutes, or until puffed and golden brown. Let cool for 4 minutes or so before serving. Makes 24 appetizers.

All About Crab (Oregon)

Halibut Puffs

½ pound mashed, cooked
 halibut
1 (8-ounce) package cream
 cheese, softened
½ teaspoon salt

2 teaspoons minced onion
¼ teaspoon garlic powder
40 wonton skins
1 egg, slightly beaten
Vegetable oil

Mix mashed halibut, cream cheese, salt, onion, and garlic powder. Brush a wonton skin with egg. Place heaping teaspoonfuls of halibut mixture in center of wonton skin. Top with another wonton skin, press edges to seal. Brush a dab of egg on center of each side of puff. Make a pleat on each edge, pressing to seal. Repeat with remaining wonton skins. Fry puffs in vegetable oil until golden brown (about 2 minutes), turning 2 or 3 times. Drain and serve with desired sauce.

Just for the Halibut (Alaska)

Cheese Puffs
with Smoked Salmon Filling

If you don't have time to make the Puffs, spread the Salmon Filling on crackers.

SALMON FILLING:

6–7 ounces smoked salmon, bones removed
1 (8-ounce) package cream cheese
1 tablespoon lemon juice

1 tablespoon grated onion
2 tablespoons mayonnaise
1 tablespoon horseradish
2 tablespoons chopped parsley

Place all ingredients in food processor and blend until smooth.

PUFFS:

1 cup water
½ cup butter or margarine, cut into small pieces

1 cup all-purpose flour, sifted
4 eggs
¾ cup grated Cheddar cheese

Preheat oven to 400°. In a medium saucepan, bring water and butter to a boil over medium heat. Remove from heat. Add all the flour at once and beat vigorously until mixture is smooth, forming a ball. Return to heat and beat vigorously for 1–2 minutes. Remove from heat and add eggs, 1 at a time, beating well to incorporate until smooth and velvety. Add cheese. Spoon about 1½ teaspoons of batter (or pipe with a pastry bag with no tip attached) onto greased cookie sheet (can use parchment). Makes approximately 50.

Bake 10 minutes. Open oven door slightly and keep ajar, using a wooden spoon, and bake an additional 15 minutes. (This allows steam to escape from oven.) Remove from oven and pierce each puff with a thin, sharp knife to let steam escape. Turn off oven; return puffs to oven for 30–45 minutes to dry out, leaving door ajar. Remove from oven; split and fill puffs with Salmon Filling. May be reheated briefly in a 350° oven to crisp before filling and serving.

Wandering & Feasting (Washington)

Tiropetes

8 ounces phyllo dough
1 cup butter, melted

Four-Cheese Filling

Let the wrapped phyllo stand at room temperature. Unwrap, cover with wax paper and a damp towel to prevent drying. Place 1 sheet of phyllo at a time on the work surface and brush with melted butter. Cut the phyllo horizontally into 5 strips. Place a small spoonful of Four-Cheese Filling at the end of a strip, fold the phyllo over the filling about ½ inch and roll up; the finished roll should resemble a cigar. Place on a baking sheet and brush with additional melted butter. Repeat with the remaining phyllo, filling and melted butter. Bake at 375° for 20 minutes or until golden brown. Tiropetes may be frozen before baking; use wax paper between layers to prevent sticking together.

FOUR-CHEESE FILLING:
4 eggs
8 ounces feta cheese,
   crumbled
8 ounces dry curd cottage
   cheese

4 ounces bleu cheese, crumbled
¼ cup grated Parmesan or
   Romano cheese
⅛ teaspoon pepper

Beat the eggs in a large mixer bowl. Add the cheeses and pepper and mix well. Note that there is no salt required; the cheeses provide enough. Yields 100.

La Jolla Cooks Again (California)

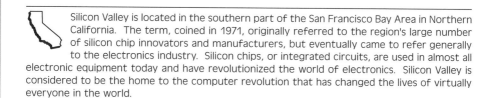

Silicon Valley is located in the southern part of the San Francisco Bay Area in Northern California. The term, coined in 1971, originally referred to the region's large number of silicon chip innovators and manufacturers, but eventually came to refer generally to the electronics industry. Silicon chips, or integrated circuits, are used in almost all electronic equipment today and have revolutionized the world of electronics. Silicon Valley is considered to be the home to the computer revolution that has changed the lives of virtually everyone in the world.

Apricot Almond Brie

Probably my favorite appetizer, and definitely the one I use most often. Serve with a glass of white wine and your guests will never know it took you less than ten minutes to put together.

1 (8- to 10-ounce) wedge Brie cheese
1 tablespoon Grand Marnier liqueur

½ cup apricot preserves
1 tablespoon toasted sliced almonds

Remove top rind from cheese. Place cheese on serving plate. In a small saucepan, combine liqueur with preserves and heat until hot, but do not boil. Spoon some of the sauce over cheese (save remainder for later). Sprinkle almonds over top. Serve with butter crackers.

Six Ingredients or Less (Washington)

Tapenade

This is a delicious spread for crackers and thinly sliced bread. Also good mixed with steamed or water sautéed vegetables and as a spread for sandwiches. Tapenade is so good, you'll wonder why you never made it before.

1 can pitted black olives, 6 ounces dry weight
5 anchovy fillets
½ cup plumped sun-dried tomatoes, finely chopped
1 tablespoon finely chopped parsley
1 tablespoon finely chopped basil
1 tablespoon minced garlic
2 tablespoons lemon juice

2 tablespoons virgin olive oil
2 tablespoons capers
½ teaspoon Canned Fire, or ¼ teaspoon cayenne
1 teaspoon Bouquet Garni, or ¼ teaspoon each of the following dried herbs: oregano, marjoram, basil, and tarragon
3 tablespoons mayonnaise

Chop olives, anchovies, tomatoes, parsley, and basil in processor using pulsing technique so that ingredients are chopped and not puréed, or mince by hand. Press garlic into olive mixture. Add rest of ingredients and mix well.

Serve with assorted crackers, thinly sliced sourdough bread, crostini, or sliced carrots and celery. Makes 1½ cups.

The Organic Gourmet (California)

Caponata

Caponata is a most requested recipe. Even people who hate eggplant love it, as long as you tell them it has eggplant in it after they have tasted it.

2 small eggplants, peeled and cut into 1-inch cubes
Olive oil
2 onions, coarsely chopped
1 cup celery, cut into ½-inch pieces
3 cloves garlic, chopped
1 large can whole pear-shaped tomatoes
1 (8-ounce) can tomato sauce or purée
½ teaspoon caper juice

½ teaspoon basil
½ teaspoon oregano
½ teaspoon Italian seasoning
½ teaspoon seasoned salt
1 tablespoon sugar
1 tablespoon wine vinegar
1 cup ripe green olives, coarsely chopped
1 cup ripe black olives, coarsely chopped
½ cup seedless raisins
2 tablespoons capers

Salt eggplant and let sit about 1 hour for bitter liquid to drain. Rinse eggplant to remove extra salt. Pat dry.

In a large nonstick pan, sauté eggplant in olive oil until browned. Do eggplant in batches to prevent crowding. You only need about 2 tablespoons oil per batch. Remove to casserole dish. Sauté onions in oil for a short while, until soft. Add to casserole dish. Add to sauté pan the celery, garlic, tomatoes, tomato sauce, caper juice, basil, oregano, Italian seasoning and seasoned salt. Cook sauce for 20 minutes, dissolve sugar in wine vinegar and add to sauce. Meanwhile, add olives, raisins and capers to eggplant. Pour sauce over the mix. Bake at 375° for about 1 hour or more, or until thick and everything looks soft. Chill and serve. Makes about 2 quarts.

Note: Serve with assorted specialty crackers such as Water Crackers or Euphrates or as an antipasto. Caponata also makes a wonderful pizza topping, or if you add more tomatoes and sauce, and don't cook it down too much, it is wonderful on pasta.

Caponata is better after it sits for a few days. It keeps well in the refrigerator and freezes beautifully. You can substitute fresh herbs for the dry, but in much larger quantities. If you cannot find green olives, use all black. (Cosentino's market carries the green ones). Recipe can be doubled easily. Cook for a little longer.

Dining Door to Door in Naglee Park (California)

Jalapeño Roll-Ups

This mixture also works well for a dip with crackers, chips or veggies.

1 (8-ounce) package cream
cheese, softened
1 cup sour cream
1 (4-ounce) can jalapeño
peppers, diced
1 (6-ounce) can black olives,
drained and finely chopped

2 cups grated Cheddar cheese
¾ cup finely chopped onions
1 tablespoon Worcestershire
Seasoned salt to taste
1 teaspoon garlic salt
½–1 teaspoon Tabasco
6–8 burrito-size tortilla shells

Mix together softened cream cheese and sour cream. Add remaining ingredients except tortilla shells; mix well. Spread onto tortilla shells. (It should be spread thin.) Roll shells tightly. Wrap each in plastic wrap and let set at least 5 hours or overnight. Slice and serve with choice of salsa.

Pig Out (Oregon)

Mediterranean Wrap-Ups

1 cup mixed nuts (almonds,
cashews, and pecans are
best)

1 (8-ounce) package pitted
dates
1 pound bacon, cut in half

Slip the nuts into the pitted dates. Wrap each date with ½ strip of bacon and secure with a toothpick. Broil until the bacon is cooked. Serve warm or cold.

Extraordinary Cuisine for Sea & Shore (Washington)

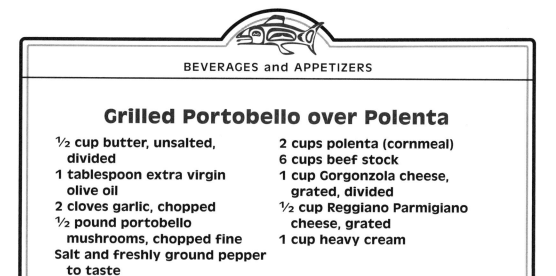

Grilled Portobello over Polenta

½ cup butter, unsalted,
  divided
1 tablespoon extra virgin
  olive oil
2 cloves garlic, chopped
½ pound portobello
  mushrooms, chopped fine
Salt and freshly ground pepper
  to taste

2 cups polenta (cornmeal)
6 cups beef stock
1 cup Gorgonzola cheese,
  grated, divided
½ cup Reggiano Parmigiano
  cheese, grated
1 cup heavy cream

In a medium-size skillet add 1 tablespoon butter, olive oil, chopped garlic, and mushrooms and sauté over medium heat for 4–6 minutes, or until done. Season lightly with salt and pepper. Preheat oven to 350°.

Put cornmeal in a large pot; slowly whisk in beef stock. Add salt to taste and bring cornmeal to a boil. Lower heat to a simmer, and cook cornmeal for approximately 25 minutes, stirring often until mixture thickens. Slowly add 3 tablespoons butter, ⅔ cup Gorgonzola, and Reggiano Parmigiano to polenta, stirring briskly to melt and combine ingredients. Add cream and stir briskly with a wooden spoon. Continue cooking for another 10 minutes or so until cornmeal has thickened. Stir in a couple of tablespoons of water if mixture becomes difficult to stir.

Pour cooked polenta into a well-buttered baking dish, spreading polenta with a plastic spatula to form a layer of uniform thickness. Place polenta in fridge for 20–30 minutes, until cooled. Using a cookie cutter or sturdy glass, cut firm polenta into 3- to 4-inch circles.

Place polenta circles on greased baking dish. Place some sautéed mushrooms on each circle and add a bit of grated Gorgonzola cheese. Place baking dish in preheated oven and bake for 15 minutes. Remove from oven and allow to cool for several minutes before serving. Serves 6.

Cooking with Mushrooms (California)

Chicken Bites in Creamy Garlic-Almond Sauce

CREAMY GARLIC-ALMOND SAUCE:

1 tablespoon vegetable oil

3 tablespoons minced garlic

1 (1-inch) piece fresh ginger, peeled and minced

⅔ cup slivered almonds

2–3 tablespoons water

In frying pan, combine oil, garlic, and ginger. Sauté on low heat, uncovered, until garlic is very tender, about 5–6 minutes, stirring often. Transfer to blender, add almonds and 2 tablespoons water, and pulse to purée, adding more water, if necessary.

CHICKEN BITES:

2 pounds skinned, boned chicken breasts, cut in 1-inch pieces

Salt and pepper to taste

2 tablespoons vegetable oil

1½ cups heavy cream

Chopped parsley and slivered almonds, for garnish

Season chicken pieces with salt and pepper. Heat oil in a frying pan on medium heat; add chicken and sauté, tossing until golden, about 5 minutes. Pour in Creamy Garlic-Almond Sauce and cream; simmer, stirring occasionally, until sauce thickens, 2–3 minutes. Transfer mixture to bowl and garnish with parsley and almonds. Serve with toothpicks and plenty of napkins.

Northwest Garlic Festival Cookbook (Washington)

Fiery Pupu Wings

2½ pounds chicken wings,
   cut at joints (or drumettes)

Oil for frying

MARINADE:

2 cloves garlic, minced
1 tablespoon sesame seed oil
1 tablespoon brown sugar
1 tablespoon soy sauce
1 tablespoon dry sherry
2 teaspoons sake (rice wine)

2 teaspoons fresh grated ginger
1 teaspoon cayenne pepper
1 teaspoon salt
Pinch freshly ground black
   pepper and red pepper flakes

In a small bowl, combine chicken with Marinade ingredients. Marinate 2 hours.

BATTER:

½ cup flour
½ cup cornstarch

2 large eggs, beaten
¾ cup water

In a wok or deep fryer, heat oil. In a mixing bowl, combine Batter ingredients. Dip drained chicken into batter; deep-fry until golden.

SAUCE:

¼ soy sauce
2 tablespoons brown sugar
2 tablespoons rice wine vinegar
2 tablespoons sesame seed oil
2 cloves garlic, minced

2 teaspoons minced fresh
   ginger
2 stalks green onions, chopped
1 teaspoon Thai chili garlic
   paste

In a mixing bowl, combine Sauce ingredients. Drizzle over chicken. Serves 8.

Dd's Table Talk II (Hawaii)

pū pū [poo-poo] – The Hawaiian term for any hot or cold appetizer, which can include a wide range of items such as macadamia nuts and won tons.

Pacific Rim Rumaki

½ chicken liver
Sprinkling soy sauce
½ water chestnut

½ strip bacon
1 (1-inch) square of pineapple or
    papaya (optional)

Sprinkle the liver with soy sauce. Wrap the liver and water chestnut in the bacon strip. Securely hold in place with small bamboo skewer (leaving room on top for fruit, if used). Place on a metal rack or baking sheet (to catch the drippings) in a 400° oven, until bacon is crisp, about 15–20 minutes. If you cook rumaki over charcoal, turn skewer while cooking so each side is cooked evenly. Serves 1.

The California Cookbook (California)

Prawns Genovese

Impress your guests with an appetizer that will be remembered long after the evening is over. This easy-to-make and flavorful dish is a great beginning to a memorable meal.

3 tablespoons extra virgin
    olive oil
8 large prawns, shelled and
    deveined
1 tablespoon minced shallots
½ teaspoon minced garlic
¼ cup dry white wine

1½ tablespoons capers
3 tablespoons diced tomatoes
Juice of 1 lemon
1 tablespoon chopped parsley
1 tablespoon butter
Salt and pepper to taste

In a medium-size sauté pan, preheat olive oil over medium-high heat. Add prawns and lightly cook both sides. Add shallots and garlic. When garlic begins to brown, deglaze with wine. Add capers, tomatoes, lemon juice, and parsley. Cook until prawns lose their translucency. Take pan off heat and whisk in butter. Season to taste with salt and pepper. Serves 2.

LaConner Palates (Washington)

BREAD and BREAKFAST

This sign marks the route of the historic Oregon Trail through La Grande. Wagon trains rested here and prepared for the treacherous climb over the Blue Mountains, considered to be the most difficult portion of the journey—steeper and more rugged than the pass through the Rockies.

Green Chile-Cheese Cornbread

½ cup canola oil, divided
1 cup yellow cornmeal
1 cup unbleached white flour
1 teaspoon baking soda
1 teaspoon baking powder
¼ teaspoon salt
1 cup buttermilk

1 egg
1 (4-ounce) can green chiles, chopped
1 cup whole-kernel corn, cut off the cob or frozen
1 cup grated Cheddar cheese

Preheat the oven to 400°. Pour ¼ cup of oil into a 10-inch cast-iron skillet and place in the oven to heat. Combine dry ingredients in a bowl and stir. Add milk, remaining ¼ cup oil, egg, chiles, corn, and cheese; mix well. Pour batter into heated skillet and reduce oven heat to 375°. Bake for 30 minutes until golden brown and done in the center. Yields 6–8 servings.

Drop the Hook, Let's Eat (Alaska)

Skillet Sun-Dried Tomato & Cheddar Bread

2 cups yellow cornmeal
2 cups all-purpose flour
¼ cup granulated sugar
2 tablespoons baking powder
1 jalapeño, seeded, finely diced

1 cup Cheddar cheese, grated
½ cup sun-dried tomatoes, chopped, drained of oil
2 eggs
2 cups milk
⅔ cup peanut oil

Combine all dry ingredients in a medium mixing bowl. Stir in jalapeño, Cheddar, and chopped tomato.

In a separate bowl, whisk together eggs and milk in the peanut oil. Lightly oil and heat an 8-inch cast-iron skillet until very hot. Pour in batter and bake at 400° for approximately 40 minutes. If using an 8-inch baking pan, add additional 20 minutes to the cooking time. Yields 8–10 servings.

The Great Vegetarian Cookbook (California)

Bruschetta
"The original garlic bread"

2 cloves garlic (1 minced, 1 cut)
3 Roma tomatoes, diced
Extra virgin olive oil (about
  ¾ cup)

Salt and pepper to taste
10 fresh basil leaves, finely
  chopped
4 slices Tuscan country bread

Mix together minced garlic, tomatoes, olive oil, salt, pepper, and basil. Set aside. Grill both sides of the bread. Rub one side of the bread with a garlic clove. Then add tomato mixture. Grill again for 30 seconds. Garnish with basil leaf. Buon Appetito!

International Garlic Festival® Cookbook (California)

Cheddar Pecan Crackers

½ cup all-purpose flour
¾ cup finely ground
  toasted pecans
½ teaspoon salt
¼ teaspoon ground black
  pepper
¼ teaspoon cayenne

2 tablespoons cold unsalted
  butter, cut up
¼ pound sharp Cheddar
  cheese, grated
2 tablespoons cold water
Kosher salt for sprinkling
  (optional)

Heat oven to 350°. In food processor, pulse flour, pecans, ½ teaspoon salt, black pepper, and cayenne. Add butter; pulse until mixture resembles coarse meal. Add grated cheese; pulse until pieces are no longer visible. With machine running, gradually add cold water; process until dough comes together.

Transfer to a lightly floured surface; divide dough into 2 equal parts. Roll out each into a ¼-inch thickness. Sprinkle very lightly with kosher salt (optional). Cut dough into 2½-inch rounds or other desired shape; transfer to ungreased baking sheet. Bake for 15 minutes until centers are firm to touch. Do not overbake. Cool on wire rack. Store in airtight containers. Makes 16.

Great Recipes from Redeemer's Fellowship (Oregon)

Country Gravy and Biscuits

MILK GRAVY:

¼ pound sausage, bacon,
    ham, or hamburger
4 tablespoons drippings

4 tablespoons flour
2 cups milk
Salt and pepper

In a skillet, brown meat and drain grease, saving 4 tablespoons of drippings. Add flour to drippings and meat in skillet. Let this mixture bubble for 3 minutes, then add milk. Stir constantly until well thickened. Season and serve hot gravy over biscuits or mashed potatoes.

BISCUITS:

2 cups flour
3 teaspoons baking powder
1 teaspoon salt

6 tablespoons shortening
¾ cup milk

Mix dry ingredients; cut in shortening; add milk; knead lightly about 10 times. Pat to ½-inch thick, and cut into biscuits. Place in pan so that biscuits are not touching. Bake in preheated 400° oven until golden, about 15 minutes.

Variation: Buttermilk biscuits can be made by adding ¼ teaspoon each baking powder and baking soda and ¾ cup buttermilk in place of sweet milk.

Sleigh Bells and Sugarplums (Washington)

Mount St. Helens is an active volcano in the Cascade Range in Skamania County, Washington, 96 miles south of Seattle and 53 miles northeast of Portland, Oregon. Its eruption in 1980 was the deadliest and most destructive volcanic event in the history of the United States. Fifty-seven people were killed; 250 homes, 47 bridges, and 185 miles of highway were destroyed.

Buttermilk Cinnamon-Nut Bread

4 cups unbleached flour
2 teaspoons baking soda
1 teaspoon salt
½ cup vegetable oil
2½ cups sugar, divided

2 cups buttermilk
2 eggs
2 tablespoons chopped walnuts
1 tablespoon cinnamon

Mix flour, soda, and salt. Combine oil and 1½ cups sugar. Add butter-milk and eggs. Mix well. Stir into dry ingredients; add nuts. Pour batter into 2 loaf pans. Mix cinnamon and leftover sugar. Sprinkle over batter. Swirl batter with a knife. Bake at 350° for 40–45 minutes.

Upper Kenai River Inn Breakfast Cookbook (Alaska)

Liberty Lake Huckleberry Bread

3 cups flour
2 teaspoons baking powder
1 teaspoon baking soda
½ teaspoon salt
1⅓ cups sugar
⅔ cup shortening
4 eggs

½ cup milk
1½ teaspoons lemon juice
1 cup crushed pineapple
2 cups huckleberries
1 cup chopped nuts
½ cup coconut

Sift dry ingredients. Cream shortening and eggs. Add sifted mixture, milk, lemon juice and pineapple; beat well. Stir in huckleberries, nuts and coconut. Bake in 2 small greased loaf pans or 1 greased 9x13-inch pan for approximately 45 minutes at 350°.

Liberty Lake Community Cookbook (Washington)

Cranberry Apple Nut Bread

3 eggs
1 teaspoon vanilla
¾ cup vegetable oil
½ cup milk
3 cups flour
1¾ cups sugar
1 teaspoon baking soda

1 teaspoon salt
½ teaspoon cinnamon
3 cups diced Granny Smith
   apples
1 cup chopped walnuts
1½ cups cranberries (Alaskan
   low-bush)

Mix liquids together in one bowl and dry in another. Gradually add dry to liquid until mixed, and beat on low speed for 3 minutes. Stir in apples and nuts. Last, fold in cranberries. Spoon into sprayed loaf pans (any size) to about ½ full. Bake at 350° for about 1 hour, or until browned, and bread pops back when touched. Spoon Glaze over top, if desired. Yields 16 servings.

GLAZE:

1 cup powdered sugar

2 tablespoons lemon juice

Recipe from Alaskan's Lazy Daze B & B, North Pole
Favorite Recipes from Alaska's Bed and Breakfasts (Alaska)

The Yogi's Banana Bread

Discovered in the '70s by a Yogi in Bellingham who taught it during a meditation.

1 cup brown sugar
½ cup butter, softened
2 eggs
3 or 4 very ripe bananas
2 cups flour
1 teaspoon baking powder
½ teaspoon salt

½ teaspoon baking soda
1 teaspoon cinnamon
1 teaspoon cloves
1 teaspoon nutmeg
1 cup frozen blueberries
1 cup chopped cashews

Mix brown sugar, butter, eggs, and bananas in food processor. Add flour, baking powder, salt, baking soda, cinnamon, cloves, and nutmeg; blend thoroughly. Add blueberries and cashews, and blend very lightly. Bake in well-greased loaf pan at 325° for about 1 hour. Test with a knife to see if it's done in the middle. Remove from pan and set on wire rack to cool. Slice and serve.

The Colophon Cafe Best Recipes (Washington)

Lingonberry Loaf
Alaska Low-Bush Cranberries

This makes a good loaf in appearance and taste.

2¼ cups all-purpose flour
2¼ teaspoons baking powder
¼ teaspoon baking soda
¾ teaspoon salt
3 teaspoons shortening
¾ cup sugar
1 egg, beaten
¾ cup orange juice
½ cup chopped walnuts
1 cup lingonberries
½ cup minced pineapple

Grease and flour 9x5x3-inch loaf pan. Sift flour; measure and resift 3 times with next 3 ingredients. Cream shortening and sugar well; add egg and beat until smooth and fluffy. Add orange juice and sifted dry ingredients alternately in 3 portions, beating smooth after each. Fold in nuts, lingonberries, and pineapple. Turn into prepared pan and let set for 15 minutes. Cover with another pan and bake for 20 minutes in 350° oven. Remove top pan and bake for 50 minutes longer.

TOPPING:
½ cup orange juice
¾ cup sugar
2 tablespoons grated orange rind
½ teaspoon vanilla
½ teaspoon rum extract or 1 tablespoon rum

Mix Topping and spoon over hot loaf while still in pan. Remove warm loaf; cool on rack. Wrap in plastic wrap or aluminum foil.

Editors' Extra: You may substitute cranberries where lingonberries are not available.

Pioneers of Alaska Auxiliary #8 (Alaska)

Quick Gingerbread

½ cup margarine
½ cup sugar
1 egg
¾ cup dark molasses
2¼ cups flour
1 teaspoon ginger

1 teaspoon cinnamon
¼ teaspoon cloves
1 teaspoon soda
½ teaspoon salt
1 cup sour milk or buttermilk

Cream margarine, sugar, and egg. Beat in molasses for 1 minute. Blend in dry ingredients and milk alternately for 2 minutes or until batter is smooth. Bake in greased 9x9x2-inch pan at 350° for 35–40 minutes.

The Miller Cookbook (Oregon)

Chunky Monkey Muffins

1 cup walnuts

Preheat oven to 350°. Toast walnuts in oven, then coarsely chop and set aside. Prepare muffin papers for 16 muffins. Set pans aside.

CREAM CHEESE FILLING:

4 ounces cream cheese,
  softened
2 tablespoons powdered sugar

Pinch salt
½ cup semisweet chocolate
  chips

Combine and cream well soft cream cheese, powdered sugar, and salt. Blend in chocolate chips. Set aside.

MUFFIN BATTER:

2 cups all-purpose flour
1 cup sugar
½ teaspoon salt
1 teaspoon baking powder
1 teaspoon baking soda

2 tablespoons salad oil
1 large egg
½ cup orange juice
2 large bananas, peeled
1 teaspoon vanilla

In a bowl, sift dry ingredients. Add chopped nuts. Set aside. In mixer bowl, blend oil, egg, orange juice, bananas, and vanilla. Slowly add dry ingredients and blend. Divide batter evenly between prepared muffin cups, reserving a small amount. Top each muffin with a teaspoon of Cream Cheese Filling and press down slightly. Put a small amount of reserved batter on top of each muffin to cover cream cheese. Bake at 350° for 20–25 minutes.

Recipe by Kangaroo House B&B, Orcas Island
Another Taste of Washington State (Washington)

Alegra's Six Week Muffins

These are the best bran muffins I have ever tasted.

1 (15-ounce) box Raisin Bran
3 cups sugar
5 cups flour
5 teaspoons baking soda

2 teaspoons salt
4 eggs, beaten
1 cup oil
1 quart buttermilk

In a very large bowl, mix Raisin Bran, sugar, flour, baking soda, and salt. Add eggs, oil, and buttermilk. This batter will keep up to six weeks in the refrigerator. As you are ready to use it, fill muffin tins ⅔ full and bake at 400° for 15–20 minutes depending on tin size. Yields 4–5 dozen.

The Lazy Gourmet (California)

Washington State Apple Muffins

2 cups sugar
½ cup vegetable oil
2 eggs
2 teaspoons vanilla
2 cups flour

2 teaspoons baking soda
2 teaspoons cinnamon
1 teaspoon salt (optional)
4 cups chopped apples

In large bowl, beat sugar, vegetable oil, eggs, and vanilla. Slowly stir in dry ingredients just until flour is moistened. Fold in chopped apples. Fill greased muffin tins ⅔ full. Bake at 400° for approximately 20 minutes. Makes 8 muffins.

Recipe by The Guest House B&B, Seattle
Another Taste of Washington State (Washington)

Breakfast Scones

2 cups flour
½ teaspoon baking soda
2 teaspoons baking powder
¾ teaspoon nutmeg
½ teaspoon salt

1 stick butter (½ cup)
1 egg yolk
¾ cup buttermilk
2 tablespoons sugar
1 cup raisins

Preheat oven to 375°. In a food processor, combine flour, baking soda, baking powder, nutmeg, and salt. Add butter in small pieces, mixing until it's a grainy cornmeal consistency. Remove and put in a bowl.

Whip together egg yolk and buttermilk. Add sugar and raisins. Add this to flour mixture. Knead 10–12 times. It will be very sticky, so flour hands well. Flatten into a mound 6 inches in diameter. Cut into wedges. It will yield 6 nice-size scones. Scoop onto cookie sheet. Bake 20–25 minutes or until golden brown.

Recipe from Tomales Country Inn
The Coastal Cook of West Marin (California)

Apricot-Pecan Scones

No collection of brunch recipes would be complete without scones! These are quick to assemble, delicate in texture and full flavored.

1 cup flour
1 cup whole-wheat pastry
   flour
1 tablespoon baking powder
6 tablespoons sugar

6 tablespoons cold butter
½ cup snipped apricots
½ cup chopped pecans
2 eggs
¼ cup half-and-half

Preheat oven to 375°. Combine flours, baking powder, and sugar. Cut in the butter. Stir apricots and pecans into flour mixture. Beat eggs and half-and-half together. Stir into flour mixture. Gather into a ball and turn out onto a lightly floured counter. Knead gently a few times. Roll out to ½ to ¾ inch thick and cut with biscuit cutter. Place scones on a lightly buttered (or parchment covered) baking sheet and bake for 12–15 minutes in the preheated oven. Serve warm from oven with butter and honey. Makes 8–10 scones.

Note: For an alternative shape, drop by spoonful onto lightly buttered baking sheet. Bake as directed.

Thyme & the River, Too (Oregon)

Sticky Orange Rolls

Refrigerator biscuits
  (whatever is on sale)

Orange juice
Sugar cubes

Place biscuits side by side in baking pan with edges. Pour orange juice into shallow bowl. For each biscuit, dip a sugar cube into the orange juice, holding it down briefly so it will absorb some juice, then push it lightly but firmly into the dough. Bake according to package directions or until rolls are nicely browned.

Seasoned with Words (Oregon)

Overnight Brunch Rolls

Easy, exciting, tender rolls—your guests and family will think you've been up all night making and baking.

1 (15-ounce) package frozen
  dinner rolls
1 small package butterscotch,
  lemon or other desired flavor
  pudding mix (not instant)

½ cup brown sugar
½ cup butter, melted
½ teaspoon cinnamon
  (optional)
½ cup chopped nuts

The night before serving, arrange frozen dinner rolls in greased Bundt pan. Sprinkle dry pudding over top; then brown sugar. If using cinnamon, mix with melted butter. Pour melted butter (or butter and cinnamon mixture) over top and sprinkle with nuts. Cover with towel; set on counter overnight. Pop in oven next morning at 350° for 25–30 minutes. Cool 5 minutes in pan; then flip over onto serving plate.

Sleigh Bells and Sugarplums (Washington)

Butterscotch Toast

A quick "sweet bread" for breakfast.

¼ cup chopped walnuts
¾ cup brown sugar
1 teaspoon water

⅓ cup soft margarine
¼ teaspoon nutmeg
Bread slices

Mix first five ingredients well and store in fridge and use as needed. Spread on bread slices and toast or broil in oven till brown and crunchy.

All-Alaska Women in Timber Cookbook (Alaska)

Mendocino Streusel Coffee Cake

If you're looking for a light coffeecake with, as professional bakers would say, just the right "crumb," this is it. From Margaret Fox of Mendocino's Café Beaujolais, named more than once the best place to eat breakfast in California.

STREUSEL:

¾ **cup packed brown sugar**   3 **tablespoons cocoa powder**
1 **tablespoon ground cinnamon**   1 **cup finely chopped walnuts**
2 **tablespoons fine instant**
   coffee powder

Stir brown sugar with cinnamon, coffee powder, cocoa, and walnuts; set aside.

COFFEECAKE:

2¾ **cups all-purpose flour**   2 **teaspoons vanilla extract**
1½ **teaspoons baking**   1½ **cups granulated sugar**
   powder   3 **eggs**
1½ **teaspoons baking soda**   1 **pint sour cream**
½ **teaspoon salt**   **Confectioners' sugar**
12 **tablespoons (1½ sticks)**
   butter, room temperature

Heat oven to 375°. Have ready a buttered and floured 10-inch Bundt pan, or coat it with a nonstick cooking spray. Stir flour with baking powder, baking soda, and salt; set aside. Beat butter with an electric mixer until light and fluffy. Add vanilla and sugar; beat mixture 3 minutes. Add eggs and beat at high speed 5 minutes, until mixture is light and creamy. Alternately add flour mixture in 3 additions, using lowest speed of mixer, and sour cream in 2 additions, beating only until smooth after each addition.

Spread a thin layer of batter in bottom of prepared pan. Sprinkle with ⅓ of Streusel mixture. Continue making these layers until there are 4 of batter and 3 of Streusel. The top layer should be batter and it should be thin. Bake coffeecake until a toothpick inserted in center comes out clean, about 1 hour. Take it out of oven to a rack and let cool 5 minutes in pan. Turn cake out of pan and sprinkle with sifted confectioners' sugar before serving. Yields 12–16 servings.

Jan Townsend Going Home (California)

Sunrise Coffee Cake

NUT TOPPING:

2 teaspoons cinnamon   ½ cup chopped nuts

Mix Topping ingredients together; set aside.

COFFEE CAKE:

½ cup margarine   ½ teaspoon baking soda
1 cup sugar   ½ teaspoon salt
1 teaspoon vanilla   ¾ cup sour cream
2 eggs   ½ cup orange juice
2 cups sifted flour   1 tablespoon grated orange rind
1 teaspoon baking powder

Cream margarine, sugar, and vanilla. Beat in eggs, 1 at a time. Sift flour, baking powder, baking soda, and salt. Stir alternately with sour cream and orange juice. Fold in orange rind. Spoon half of batter into greased 9-inch-square pan. Top with half of Nut Topping. Repeat layer. Bake at 375° for 40 minutes or until done.

Nautical Niceaty's from Spokane Yacht Club (Washington)

Wonders

3 eggs   3 tablespoons melted
3 tablespoons sugar   shortening
½ teaspoon salt   2 cups self-rising flour

Beat eggs very light; add sugar and salt, then shortening and flour to make a batter stiff enough to roll. Roll very thinly on a floured surface; cut in 3-inch squares. Make several slits to form "fingers" in each square to ½ inch of edge. Fry in deep hot fat (375° to 385°) until golden brown. Drain on paper towels. When cool, dust with powdered sugar.

The 'Hole Cake Doughnut Book (Oregon)

Berry Stuffed French Toast— San Francisco Style

Is this French toast or a bread pudding? This dish is so rich, yet light, we think it may even be an improvement on bread pudding. Note that like a bread pudding, the longer it is allowed to soak before baking, the fuller the flavor.

12 slices San Francisco
   sourdough bread
8 ounces low-fat cream
   cheese
1 cup berries, your choice,
   fresh or frozen

10 eggs
⅓ cup maple syrup
2 cups low-fat milk

Remove crusts from bread and cut into cubes. Oil a 9x13-inch baking dish. Spread half of bread cubes over bottom of pan. Cut cream cheese into cubes and distribute over bread layer. Spread berries over cream cheese. Place remaining bread cubes over top.

Beat eggs, maple syrup and milk together well. Pour over bread. Cover with foil and refrigerate overnight. Press down on foil to make sure all bread is soaked.

In the morning, preheat oven to 350°. Bake, covered with foil, 30 minutes, then remove foil and bake an additional 30 minutes until center is set and top is lightly browned. Let stand 10 minutes before slicing. Serve with Berry Sauce.

BERRY SAUCE:
1 cup water
1 cup sugar
2 tablespoons cornstarch

1 cup berries, fresh or frozen
1 tablespoon butter

Stir water, sugar, cornstarch, and berries over medium heat until thickened. Add butter and stir until melted. Pour over individual pieces of French toast with a twist of lemon for decoration. Serves 6.

Mendocino Mornings (California)

Peg's Kid-Pleasin' French Toast

½ cup creamy peanut butter
¼ cup honey
8 slices bread

4 eggs
1 cup milk
Butter

Mix peanut butter and honey. Spread on 4 slices of bread and top with remaining bread. Trim crusts. Beat eggs and milk. Cut sandwiches into 3 slices. Dip each piece in milk mixture. Cook on hot buttered griddle until browned on each side. Can sprinkle with powdered sugar. It is also good served with honey for dipping.

Upper Kenai River Inn Breakfast Cookbook (Alaska)

Oatmeal Pancakes

2 cups quick or rough-cut oats
½ teaspoon baking soda
2½ cups buttermilk
1 cup flour

2 teaspoons baking powder
½ teaspoon salt
⅓ cup oil
2 eggs, beaten

Mix oats, baking soda, and buttermilk; let stand 5 minutes (if using rough cut, soak longer). Stir in flour, baking powder, salt, oil, and eggs; mix well. Drop ⅓ cup batter on medium-hot griddle. (Batter is thick, so pancakes need to "bake," versus fry like regular pancakes.) Cook until bubbles burst, then cook on other side.

Recipes from the Paris of the Pacific—Sitka, Alaska (Alaska)

EDWARD Z. YANG

Sourdough bread has long been a symbol of San Francisco since Isadore Boudin opened his North Beach bakery in 1849. The bread's tangy taste comes from a special yeast starter, though some claim that San Francisco's air gives the yeast a characteristic flavor that cannot be exported. Since 1849 they have been using the same sourdough culture, which they call a "Mother dough" and the same recipe. So important is their "Mother Dough," it was heroically saved by Louise Boudin during the Great San Francisco Earthquake of 1906.

Hazelnut Buttermilk Pancakes with Blackberry Butter

These wonderfully dense pancakes, loaded with bits of roasted hazelnuts, are served with warm Blackberry Butter. The Blackberry Butter can be made days ahead and the pancake batter the night before. Blackberry Butter makes a great gift, too, tucked into a basket of homemade biscuits.

PANCAKES:

1 package active dry yeast
½ cup warm water
2½ cups buttermilk
3 eggs
2 cups all-purpose flour

3 tablespoons sugar
1 tablespoon baking soda
1 teaspoon salt
¼ cup finely ground, toasted hazelnuts

In a large bowl dissolve yeast in warm water. Add buttermilk and remaining ingredients and mix well. Cover and place in refrigerator overnight. In the morning stir in more buttermilk if batter seems too thick. Heat a lightly greased griddle and cook pancakes on one side until bubbles rise to the surface and pop. Turn pancakes over and cook for 2–3 more minutes. Serve with Blackberry Butter. Serves 4.

BLACKBERRY BUTTER:

8 tablespoons (½ cup) unsalted butter
1 cup sugar

2 cups fresh blackberries (or 1 pound frozen and thawed, puréed and seeded)

Melt butter and stir in sugar and blackberries. Remove from heat and stir until sugar is dissolved. Taste for sweetness. More sugar may need to be added depending on sugar content of blackberries. Store in refrigerator (good for up to 2 weeks). Makes 2 cups.

Variations: May substitute raspberries or strawberries for blackberries.

Dungeness Crabs and Blackberry Cobblers (Oregon)

Cottage Pancakes

These pancakes are very light.

3 eggs, separated
1 whole egg
1 cup cottage cheese, small
 curd (or ricotta cheese)

¼ cup flour
¼ teaspoon salt
1 apple, grated
Margarine or butter for frying

Beat 3 egg whites until stiff; set aside. Place whole egg and egg yolks in bowl with cottage cheese, flour, salt, and apple. Blend well. Fold in egg whites. Heat butter or margarine in skillet. Drop batter by table-spoonfuls into skillet and fry until golden brown. Turn only once.

Apples Etc. Cookbook (California)

Banana Pecan Pancakes

This batter is wonderfully versatile. In this recipe, the bananas and pecans give a distinctively appealing texture and flavor.

2 bananas
2 eggs
3 cups buttermilk
3 tablespoons butter, melted
2 cups unbleached flour
1 teaspoon baking soda

½ teaspoon salt
1 cup cornmeal
½ cup bran
1 tablespoon honey
½ cup pecans, sautéed in
 butter until golden

In a medium mixing bowl, mash bananas with fork until lumps are mostly worked out. Add eggs, buttermilk, and melted butter; mix thoroughly. In separate bowl, sift flour with baking soda and salt. Stir in cornmeal and bran; add dry ingredients to banana mixture, stirring until moistened. Add honey and pecans (that have been sautéed in butter until golden). Prepare as any other pancake.

Christmas in Washington Cook Book (Washington)

Bayfield Eggs

1½ pounds sausage
12 eggs
¾ pound shredded Cheddar
  cheese, divided
½–1 cup chopped green
  onions

½ green pepper, chopped
Small can sliced mushrooms,
  drained
½ teaspoon salt
½ teaspoon pepper
½ pint whole cream

Fry sausage and drain well. Grease 9x13-inch pan. Break eggs into pan. Poke the yolks. Top with all the sausage, ½ cheese, all the onions, green pepper, and mushrooms. Sprinkle with salt and pepper. Cover all with cream and remaining cheese. Refrigerate overnight. Bake at 350° for 1 hour. Serves 8.

Sharing Our Best (Alaska)

English Muffin Breakfast Casserole

1 pound hot pork sausage
3 English muffins, cut in halves
8 eggs
2½ cups milk
2 tablespoons chopped onions
2 tablespoons chopped green
  pepper

2 teaspoons prepared mustard
½ teaspoon salt
¼ teaspoon black pepper
2 cups grated sharp Cheddar
  cheese, divided

Brown, drain, cool, and crumble pork sausage. Place muffins, split-side-down, in a 9x13-inch buttered glass baking dish. In another bowl, whisk together eggs, milk, onions, green pepper, mustard, salt, and pepper until well mixed. Fold into the egg mixture the crumbled sausage and ½ cup of the grated cheese. Pour the egg mixture over the muffins. (The muffins will be floating.) Cover and refrigerate overnight (at least 12 hours).

To bake, preheat oven to 325°. Remove the casserole from the refrigerator, top with the remaining cheese, and bake for 55–65 minutes. The casserole will be set when done. Serve hot. Serves 6–8.

San Ramon's Secret Recipes (California)

Breakfast Sausage Soufflé

This makes a wonderful breakfast for company and has become something of a tradition for Christmas breakfast.

8 slices bread, cubed
1½ pounds sausage, browned
Sliced mushrooms
1 cup chopped onion
2 cups shredded sharp Cheddar
  cheese

4 eggs
3 cups milk, divided
¾ teaspoon dry mustard
1 can cream of mushroom soup,
  condensed

Cube bread and spread on bottom of a greased 9x13-inch pan. Brown sausage, adding mushrooms and onions just before done. Drain. Layer sausage mixture and cheese over bread. Beat together eggs, 2½ cups milk, and dry mustard. Pour over bread, sausage and cheese; stir lightly until mixed. Refrigerate overnight. Just before baking, combine mushroom soup and ½ cup milk. Pour over casserole. Bake at 300° for 1½ hours.

Harvest Feast (Washington)

Breakfast-On-The-Run Bar

Great with a hot drink of your choice.

1 egg, slightly beaten
½ cup peanut butter
¼ cup honey
2 tablespoons molasses

⅓ cup instant nonfat dry milk
3 cups whole-wheat and bran
  cereal with raisins, apples and
  almonds

Combine egg, peanut butter, honey, and molasses; mix well. Add dry milk and mix until well blended. Add cereal and mix until evenly coated. Press firmly into greased 8-inch-square pan. Bake at 325° for 20 minutes. Cool; cut into 6 bars.

Variation: Can use egg substitute and plain cereal with bits of dried fruit and nuts of choice.

Pig Out (Oregon)

Moose Racks

1 pound thinly sliced bacon
1 tablespoon sesame seeds

1 cup brown sugar

Preheat oven to 375°. Line an 11x15-inch baking pan with foil. Cut bacon strips in half and arrange in prepared pan in a single layer. Bake for 10 minutes, then turn and sprinkle with sesame seeds and brown sugar. Return to oven and bake another 10 minutes. Remove to a slightly greased platter to cool. Makes about 36 slices.

Moose Racks, Bear Tracks, and Other Alaska Kidsnacks (Alaska)

Sunshine Pie

2 cups or 1 (15-ounce) carton
  low-fat ricotta cheese
3 eggs
⅔ cup sugar
2 tablespoons all-purpose flour
2 tablespoons orange juice

2 teaspoons grated fresh
  orange rind
1 teaspoon orange extract
¼ teaspoon lemon extract
1 (9-inch) deep dish pie shell,
  uncooked

Preheat oven to 350°. Beat ricotta cheese in a large bowl with an electric mixer on high speed for 1 minute. Add eggs, sugar, flour, orange juice, orange rind, orange extract, and lemon extract; blend well with electric mixer. Pour into uncooked pie shell and bake for 50 minutes, until a knife inserted comes out clean. Refrigerate overnight; serve chilled the next morning.

A serving suggestion: A small slice (10 servings per pie) on a plate with fresh fruit is a perfect addition to your breakfast menu, or a large slice (6 servings per pie) can be served as your main breakfast dish.

Recipe from Skyline B&B, Homer
Favorite Recipes from Alaska's Bed and Breakfasts (Alaska)

Papaya Jelly

½ package unflavored
  gelatin
½ cup cold water
½ cup sugar

1 cup boiling water
1 cup papaya pulp
Juice of 1 lemon

Soak gelatin in cold water 5 minutes. Dissolve sugar in boiling water; add gelatin and strain. When cool, add papaya and lemon juice. Place on ice (refrigerate) to harden.

How to Use Hawaiian Fruit (Hawaii)

Apricot Pepper Jelly

¼ cup jalapeño peppers, with
  stems and seeds removed
3 cups assorted bell peppers,
  cut into thin slices
2 cups apple cider vinegar

1½ cups dried apricots, cut
  into thin strips
6 cups sugar
1 teaspoon vegetable oil
1 pouch liquid pectin

Process jalapeño peppers in blender until fine. Combine bell peppers, vinegar, jalapeño peppers, dried apricots, and sugar in a large saucepan. Bring to a boil. Add oil to prevent foam from forming. Boil for 10 minutes. Remove from heat. Stir in pectin. Place in sterilized canning jars and process in boiling water bath for 10 minutes. Yields 6 half-pints.

Sounds Tasty! (California)

WWW.WAYFARING.INFO

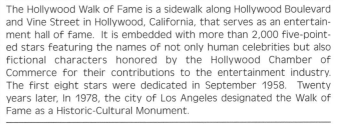

The Hollywood Walk of Fame is a sidewalk along Hollywood Boulevard and Vine Street in Hollywood, California, that serves as an entertainment hall of fame. It is embedded with more than 2,000 five-pointed stars featuring the names of not only human celebrities but also fictional characters honored by the Hollywood Chamber of Commerce for their contributions to the entertainment industry. The first eight stars were dedicated in September 1958. Twenty years later, In 1978, the city of Los Angeles designated the Walk of Fame as a Historic-Cultural Monument.

Apples with Granola and Cider Cream

Cinnamon-sugar mixture, to taste
4 large apples (reds, goldens, Braeburn or Fuji)
½ cup dried cranberries
4 cups granola
8 tablespoons melted butter, plus extra for buttering dish

Generously butter 9x9-inch glass pan or 8 large ramekins. Sprinkle bottom of pans with cinnamon-sugar, reserving some for later use. Peel, halve, and core apples. Maintain shape of apple half and place in dish. Sprinkle tops of apples with more cinnamon-sugar and dried cranberries. Pour ½ cup granola on each apple half. Pour melted butter onto granola. Cover with foil and bake at 350° for 45–60 minutes. Serve apples topped with Cider Cream and a dash of cinnamon. Makes 8 servings.

CIDER CREAM:
1 cup apple cider
1 cup whipping cream

Boil cider until reduced to ¼ cup. Cool. Beat cream until stiff. Blend in cider syrup.

Recipe by Autumn Pond Bed & Breakfast, Leavenworth
Another Taste of Washington State (Washington)

SOUPS, CHILIS, & STEWS

Grand Coulee Dam, positioned deep in the Columbia River Gorge of Central Washington, is one of the world's largest producers of hydroelectric power and is second only to the Great Wall of China as the largest man-made structure in the world.

Mooseball Soup

MOOSEBALLS:

½ cup bread crumbs
½ teaspoon salt
1½ pounds ground moose
   meat (or ground beef)

1 egg
½ teaspoon thyme
1 small onion, chopped very
   fine

Mix bread crumbs, salt, ground meat, egg, thyme, and onion until well blended. Shape into 1-inch balls. Place in a Dutch oven and brown; remove and drain.

SOUP:

1 onion, chopped
¾ cup sliced, fresh mushrooms
   or 1 small can mushrooms
1 tablespoon olive oil

2 cans beef broth
1 can stewed tomatoes
5 red potatoes with skins left
   on, cubed

In the same sauté pan used for meatballs, sauté onion and mushrooms in olive oil. Add beef broth, stewed tomatoes, and potatoes. Bring to a simmer and add the browned Mooseballs. Simmer until potatoes are done, 30–40 minutes; or if you are doing this on the wood stove, simmer all day until you have the snow shoveled and the wood chopped.

Grannie Annie's Cookin' on the Wood Stove (Alaska)

Super Taco Soup

8 ounces ground beef
½ cup chopped onion
1½ tablespoons flour
2 cups water
1 (17-ounce) can whole kernel
   corn, drained
1 (16-ounce) can kidney beans

1 (16-ounce) can tomatoes
2 tablespoons taco seasoning
1 tablespoon mild taco sauce
1 teaspoon seasoned salt
¼ teaspoon garlic powder
Salt to taste

Brown ground beef and onion in skillet, stirring frequently; drain. Add flour, stirring until dissolved. Add water. Pour into large saucepan. Add corn, beans, tomatoes, taco seasoning, taco sauce, seasoned salt, garlic powder, and salt. Bring to a boil; reduce heat. Simmer for 20 minutes, stirring occasionally. Ladle into serving bowls. Garnish with shredded Cheddar cheese, sliced green onions, crushed tortilla chips, and sour cream. Yields 8 servings.

California Gold (California)

Colony Chicken Soup

An old favorite—the sauerkraut makes it special.

2½ pounds chicken pieces
6 cups water
4 teaspoons chicken base, or
  4 chicken bouillon cubes
1 cup chopped celery
1 cup grated carrots
1 cup chopped onions

¼ cup butter, melted
¼ cup flour
1½ cups half-and-half or milk
¼ teaspoon white pepper
2 cups sauerkraut, rinsed,
  drained, and chopped

In a large kettle, simmer chicken in water to which chicken base or bouillon cubes have been added, being careful not to boil. When chicken is cooked through and tender, about 30–45 minutes, remove chicken. When cool, skin, debone, and cut into bite-size pieces and set aside to add later. Degrease broth.

Add celery, carrots, and onions to chicken broth. Simmer about 12 minutes or until tender. Mix melted butter and flour. Gradually add to broth, stirring well. Add half-and-half and white pepper. Stir frequently until soup is very hot and slightly thickened. Add sauerkraut and chicken pieces. Simmer on very low heat for a few minutes before serving. The flavor of this delicious soup becomes even better when served the second day. Serves 8–10.

Albertina's Exceptional Recipes (Oregon)

The Oregon Trail is the longest of the overland routes used in the westward expansion of the United States. Used between 1840 and 1860, it was about 2,000 miles long, starting in Missouri and ending in Oregon.

Portuguese Bean Soup

There must be as many versions of this popular Honolulu soup as there are varieties of hibiscus on the city's streets. Local politicians, musicians, and schoolteachers swear by their family recipes, and often cook and sell bean soup for charity fund raisers. Basically it is a bean soup, brought from Portugal by the first Portuguese immigrants. It combines beans, ham hocks, and cabbage in a thick tasty soup. One might call it a "minestrone" of the Hawaiian Islands, meaning that this and that can be added to a basic recipe.

1 pound dried small red or kidney beans (or combination)
2 quarts water
1 medium onion, sliced
2 ham hocks
Salt and pepper to taste
1 (8-ounce) can tomato sauce
2 medium-sized potatoes, peeled and diced
2 stalks celery, diced
1 small cabbage, chopped or thinly sliced
½ cup uncooked, small elbow macaroni
½ pound Portuguese or any hot-style sausage, thinly sliced

Cover beans with water and soak overnight. Drain and place beans in a soup pot. Cover with 2 quarts of water. Add onion, ham hocks, salt and pepper. Cover and simmer for one hour, stirring now and then.

Remove cover and take out the ham hocks. Add tomato sauce, potatoes, and celery. Remove ham from bones and dice. Return to the pot and simmer, uncovered, for 20 minutes. Add remaining ingredients and continue to cook for an additional 30 minutes. If the soup is too thick for your taste, thin with water or white wine. Garnish with minced parsley or watercress. Serves 6–8.

Honolulu Hawaii Cooking (Hawaii)

Baked Ripe Olive Minestrone

A popular favorite at our house. It makes a lot and freezes well for future use. This recipe is from the old Palo Alto Times.

1½ pounds lean beef stewing meat
1 cup coarsely chopped onion
1 teaspoon minced garlic
1 teaspoon salt
¼ teaspoon pepper
2 tablespoons olive oil
3 (10½-ounce) cans beef broth
2 cans water
1½ teaspoons Italian herb seasoning

1 (1-pound) can tomatoes (undrained)
1 (15¼-ounce) can kidney beans (undrained)
1¾ cups pitted canned ripe olives
1 cup liquor from ripe olives
1½ cups thinly sliced carrots
1 cup small seashell macaroni
2 cups sliced zucchini
Grated Parmesan cheese

Preheat oven to 400°. Cut beef into 1¼-inch cubes. Mix together beef, onion, garlic, salt and pepper in a Dutch oven. Add olive oil and stir to coat meat evenly. Brown, uncovered, in preheated oven about 40 minutes, stirring once or twice.

Reduce heat to 350°. Add broth, water and Italian seasoning. Cover and cook 1 hour until meat is almost tender. Remove from oven and stir in tomatoes, kidney beans, ripe olives, canned ripe olive liquor, carrots, and macaroni. Sprinkle zucchini on top. Cover and return to oven to bake 40–45 minutes longer, until macaroni is tender. Serve with grated Parmesan cheese. Makes about 3½ quarts.

Seasons: Food for Thought and Celebration (California)

Virtually all U.S. commercial olive production is concentrated in California's Central Valley. The California Mission Olive is a variety unique to the United States. Although its origin was believed to be Spanish, tests at the University of Spain at Cordoba were unable to link it to any of the 700 varieties documented there. The roots of the California Mission Olive are in the orchards of the Jesuit and Franciscan missions founded several centuries ago throughout California. California Mission Olives are unique in that they are suitable for both the pressing of oil (for olive oil) and the curing of table olives.

Pea Soup

The secret to this soup is a good stock. Make it with the bone that's left from the Easter ham, or whenever you cook a whole or half ham. I have used smoked pork hocks, but the best stock is really from a ham bone. I learned to make this soup from my mom when I was quite young.

STOCK:

1 ham bone (shank)
1 large onion
2 medium carrots

1 bay leaf
½ tablespoon crushed, black peppercorns

Remove the rest of the usable ham from the bone and reserve. Cut onion into quarters. Chop carrots in large pieces. Put bone, onion, and carrot into stockpot and cover with cold water. Add bay leaf and peppercorns; simmer for 3 hours. Strain Stock. Return strained Stock to soup pot; bring to boil.

1 package split peas (green or yellow)
1 onion, diced
1–2 carrots, diced

½–1 cup diced ham, from ham bone
Freshly ground black pepper to taste

Add peas, onion, carrots, and ham to stock. Simmer 1½ hours, or until peas are cooked. Serve with a good bread and freshly ground black pepper.

Liberty Lake Community Cookbook (Washington)

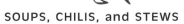

Baked Potato Soup

A make-ahead recipe.

4 large baking potatoes
½ cup margarine
½ cup flour
1 teaspoon garlic salt
½ teaspoon pepper
½ teaspoon onion powder

6 cups 1% low-fat milk
1 cup grated Cheddar cheese
⅓ pound bacon, cooked and
** crumbled**
2 green onions, chopped

Bake potatoes at 400° for 1 hour. Cool. Peel and cut into cubes. Freeze in Ziploc bag.

Thaw potatoes. Melt margarine in a saucepan and add flour, garlic salt, pepper, and onion powder. Add milk and stir constantly until soup comes to a boil and begins to thicken. Add potato cubes and simmer on low heat for at least 30 minutes, longer if desired. Serve topped with cheese, bacon, and green onions. Serves 6.

Note: Amount of milk may vary according to your liking. As the soup simmers, it will thicken, and you may need to add more milk before serving.

What's for Dinner? (Oregon)

Gazpacho Soup

This is a wonderful cold soup for warm summer days.

4 medium ripe tomatoes,
** peeled and chopped**
2 cloves garlic, mashed
1 medium cucumber, chopped
1 large green pepper, chopped
1 large red pepper, chopped
1 cup minced onion
¼ cup olive oil

2 cups tomato juice
¼ cup wine vinegar
Dash of Tabasco
1 cup ice water
Salt and pepper
Croutons for garnish
Chopped chives for garnish

Mix all ingredients in a large bowl and refrigerate 3 hours or longer. You may want to add more vinegar. Pour into chilled bowls and serve with croutons and chopped chives. Serves 6.

Heavenly Fare (Washington)

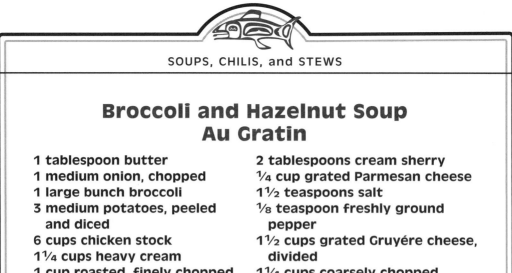

Broccoli and Hazelnut Soup
Au Gratin

1 tablespoon butter
1 medium onion, chopped
1 large bunch broccoli
3 medium potatoes, peeled
 and diced
6 cups chicken stock
1¼ cups heavy cream
1 cup roasted, finely chopped
 hazelnuts

2 tablespoons cream sherry
¼ cup grated Parmesan cheese
1½ teaspoons salt
⅛ teaspoon freshly ground
 pepper
1½ cups grated Gruyére cheese,
 divided
1¼ cups coarsely chopped
 hazelnuts, divided

Melt butter in a 4- to 6-quart kettle; sauté onion until softened, about 3 minutes. Cut broccoli into florets and thinly slice tender upper portion of the stems. Add to kettle along with potatoes and chicken stock. Cover and simmer until potatoes and broccoli are tender, about 25 minutes. Purée mixture in several batches in food processor. Return purée to kettle and stir in cream, roasted hazelnuts, sherry, Parmesan cheese, salt, and pepper to taste. Gently heat.

   To serve, ladle 8-ounce servings into broiler-safe dishes. Sprinkle each with ½ ounce grated Gruyére cheese and ½ ounce coarsely chopped hazelnuts. Place under broiler until cheese is melted and hazelnuts are browned, about 1 minute. Instead of broiling, you might use a small propane torch to brown the hazelnuts. Yields 10 (1-cup) servings.

Kay's Kitchen (Alaska)

Today the two main groups of Eskimos are the Inuit of northern Alaska, Canada, and Greenland, and the Yupik, from western Alaska, South Central Alaska along the Gulf of Alaska coast, and the Russian Far East. A third group, the Aleut, is related. Aleuts are the indigenous people of the Aleutian Islands of Alaska, United States and Kamchatka Krai, Russia.

Chilled Avocado Soup

There are many versions of avocado soup in California, some served chilled, some hot. Some include cream, which I find eclipses the flavor of the avocado. To my palate, this creamy but creamless version, bright, tangy, and mildly spicy, with the edge of sweetness that avocados have, is the best.

2 tablespoons olive oil
1 small yellow or white onion, minced
3 serrano chiles, minced
2 garlic cloves, minced
3 ripe Haas avocados

3½ cups chicken stock
2 tablespoons fresh lime juice
3 tablespoons minced cilantro leaves
Kosher salt
Black pepper in a mill

Heat olive oil in a small skillet over medium heat; add onions and sauté until limp and fragrant, about 10 minutes. Add serranos, sauté 5 minutes, then add garlic and sauté 2 minutes more. Remove from heat and let cool slightly. Cut avocados in half and remove pits. Scoop out flesh and place in blender or food processor. Add half the stock and onion mixture, and purée. Transfer to a large container, stir in remaining stock, and refrigerate until soup is well chilled, at least 3 hours.

To serve, stir in lime juice and half the cilantro, season with salt and pepper, and ladle into chilled soup bowls. Sprinkle remaining cilantro over each portion and serve immediately. Serves 4–6.

VARIATIONS:

With Cherry Tomato Salsa: Cut 1 cup cherry tomatoes into quarters, and toss with 2 tablespoons minced onion, 1 minced serrano chile, juice of half of lime, and kosher salt and black pepper to taste. Spoon a little salsa over each portion of soup.

With Bay Shrimp: Toss 8 ounces cooked bay shrimp with juice of 1 lime and 1 tablespoon minced onion. Divide among chilled soup bowls and ladle soup on top.

With Bacon and Bleu Cheese: Fry 4 strips bacon until crisp, drain on absorbent paper, then crumble and scatter some over each serving of soup. Crumble 2 ounces of bleu cheese and scatter it over the soup.

California Home Cooking (California)

Cioppino

Traditionally served on Friday nights in North Beach's Italian restaurants, this fish soup is loaded with the catch of the day in a rich tomato stock. Crusty sourdough bread is essential for soaking up all the delicious broth.

¼ cup olive oil
1 large red onion, thinly sliced
1 large leek, white part only, washed and chopped
1 shallot, minced
3 garlic cloves, minced
1 fennel bulb, trimmed and thinly sliced
1 bay leaf
⅛ teaspoon saffron threads
3 tablespoons minced flat-leaf parsley
Salt and freshly ground pepper to taste

6 tomatoes, peeled, seeded, and chopped
1 cup fish stock or clam broth
1 cup dry white wine
2 pounds fresh white fish, such as sea bass or monkfish
8 ounces shrimp
1 live Dungeness crab, cleaned and sectioned*
8 ounces bay scallops
8 ounces mussels, scrubbed and debearded, or cherrystone clams

In a soup pot over medium heat, heat olive oil and sauté onion, leek, shallot, garlic, fennel, bay leaf, saffron, and parsley for 8–10 minutes, or until vegetables are tender. Add salt and pepper. Add tomatoes and cook for 3 minutes. Add fish stock or clam broth and wine. Simmer for 15 minutes. Add fish and shellfish and simmer 5–10 minutes, or until shrimp is pink, the fish is firm, and mussels or clams have opened. Do not overcook, or fish will be tough. Discard any clams or mussels that do not open. Serves 6.

*To clean and section Dungeness crabs, keep the crabs in a paper bag in the refrigerator until cooking. To stun the crabs, approach one from behind, grasp the legs and the claw on each side with each hand, and crack the center of the underside of the shell with a sharp blow against the hard edge of a table or counter. Pull the top shell off the crab and remove the gray gills and green tomalley (crab liver). To make serving easier, use a large cleaver to cut the crabs in half, then cut the body into portions, each with a leg. Crack the shells with a nutcracker or hammer.

San Francisco Flavors (California)

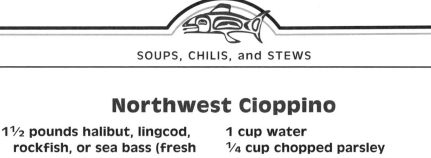

Northwest Cioppino

1½ pounds halibut, lingcod,
   rockfish, or sea bass (fresh
   or frozen)
2 cups sliced onions
2 cloves garlic, finely minced
¼ cup oil (olive or canola)
1 can (1 pound 12 ounces)
   Italian stewed tomatoes,
   undrained
1 cup (8 ounces) tomato sauce
1 cup water
¼ cup chopped parsley
2 teaspoons salt
1 teaspoon basil
½ teaspoon oregano
¼ teaspoon pepper
1 dozen clams (in shells),
   washed
1 cup cooked, peeled shrimp

Cut fish into 1½-inch chunks. Cook onions and garlic in oil till onion is tender but not brown. Add tomatoes, sauce, water, and all spices. Cover and simmer 30 minutes. Add fish chunks; cover and simmer 10–20 minutes. Add clams in shell and shrimp; cover and cook 10 minutes longer or until fish flakes easily when tested with a fork. Yields 6–8 servings.

Coastal Flavors (Oregon)

Chilled Zucchini Bisque

2 (10½-ounce) cans chicken
   broth, condensed or
   homemade
1 cup water
2 cups thinly sliced zucchini
¼ cup chopped onion
3 tablespoons rice
1 tablespoon curry powder
½ teaspoon ground ginger
½ teaspoon dry mustard
Salt and pepper to taste
1½ cups milk
Yogurt (optional)
Green onion, chopped

In 3-quart saucepan, combine broth, water, zucchini, onion, rice, curry powder, ginger, and mustard. Cover and simmer 20 minutes. Pour small amounts into blender and whirl until smooth. Season to taste. Allow to stand 6 hours or overnight.

   Just before serving, add milk. May add a dollop of yogurt, if desired. Add a few green onions for color. Serve cold. Makes 6 servings.

Cook Book (California)

Seafood Bisque

This is the best seafood bisque ever!

2 sticks butter (no substitute)
⅓ cup finely chopped celery
⅓ cup finely chopped onion
½ bay leaf
Pinch of Italian seasoning
½ pinch tarragon
4 drops Tabasco

3 tablespoons clam juice
⅓ cup flour
2 tablespoons sherry
1 quart half-and-half
1 pound seafood chunks (crab, shrimp, scallops, white fish)
1½ teaspoons salt

Melt butter in skillet; add celery, onion, and bay leaf. Sauté until tender. Add Italian seasoning, tarragon, Tabasco, clam juice, and flour. Stir to make a roux (remove bay leaf). Remove from heat; add sherry and set aside.

In top of double boiler, heat the half-and-half. Stir in roux and heat (stirring) until thickened, 7–10 minutes. Add mixed seafood (raw ones before cooked or covered ones). Heat until seafood is cooked through, 10 minutes. Add extra clam juice if it gets too thick. Salt to taste.

Manna by the Sea (Oregon)

Puget Sound Oyster Bisque

The distinctive taste of oysters is a favorite of many Whidbey Island residents. This bisque makes the perfect starter to any entrée. It is equally suitable as a meal in itself when accompanied by a warm loaf of freshly baked bread.

¼ cup flour
¼ cup water
2 teaspoons salt
4 teaspoons Worcestershire
3 (10-ounce) jars shucked oysters

6 cups half-and-half
3 tablespoons margarine
Snipped parsley for garnish

In a large saucepan, whisk together flour, ¼ cup water, salt, and Worcestershire. Add oysters and their liquid. Depending on the size of the oysters, you may want to cut them into bite-size pieces. Cook over medium heat for 10 minutes, stirring constantly. The centers will be firm and the edge of oysters will curl a bit when cooked. Add half-and-half and margarine and heat to boiling. Let the bisque stand at least 15 minutes to blend flavors. Garnish with snipped parsley, if so desired. Makes 6 servings.

Simply Whidbey (Washington)

Crab and Rice Chowder

1 small onion, chopped
½ pound mushrooms,
  thinly sliced
2 tablespoons oil
2 cups coarsely chopped
  broccoli
1 small red pepper, chopped
½ teaspoon thyme leaves

2 cups chicken broth
2 cups milk
1 (17-ounce) can cream-style
  corn
⅓ pound crabmeat
3 cups cooked rice
Salt and pepper

Sauté onion and mushrooms in oil till limp. Add broccoli, bell pepper, and thyme. Simmer till broccoli is tender, about 4 minutes. Stir in chicken broth, milk, and corn. Cook, uncovered, about 10 minutes or until hot. Stir in crabmeat and rice. Simmer, uncovered, until hot, about 2 minutes. Ladle soup into bowls. Add salt and pepper to taste. Serves 5–6.

Cooking Treasures of the Central Coast (California)

Mahi Chowder

4 slices bacon, diced
1 cup diced onion
6 cups water, divided
1 bay leaf, wrinkled
3 potatoes, diced

2 pounds mahi, cubed
2 cups powdered milk, dry
Salt
White pepper

Fry bacon and onion in the bottom of your soup pot until the onion is browned. Add 4 cups water, the bay leaf, and potatoes. Bring water up to boiling and let it simmer until the potatoes are tender. Add mahi. Mix dry milk with remaining water and add it to the pot. When the mahi is tender, add salt and white pepper to taste, and serve. You may want to serve this with a crispy green salad and crusty brown bread.

Kau Kau Kitchen (Hawaii)

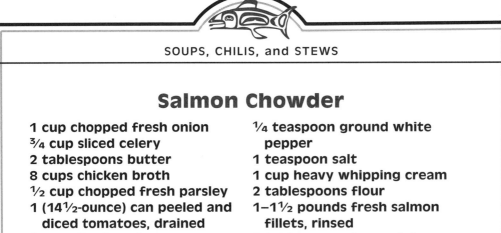

Salmon Chowder

1 cup chopped fresh onion
¾ cup sliced celery
2 tablespoons butter
8 cups chicken broth
½ cup chopped fresh parsley
1 (14½-ounce) can peeled and
   diced tomatoes, drained
2 cups fresh or frozen corn
2 cups peeled and diced russet
   potatoes
1 teaspoon dried thyme

¼ teaspoon ground white
   pepper
1 teaspoon salt
1 cup heavy whipping cream
2 tablespoons flour
1–1½ pounds fresh salmon
   fillets, rinsed
2 tablespoons lemon juice
Chopped fresh parsley for
   garnish

In a large stockpot over medium-high heat, sauté onion and celery in butter until limp—about 5 minutes. Add chicken broth, chopped parsley, tomatoes, corn, potatoes, thyme, pepper, and salt. Bring soup back to a boil, then reduce heat and simmer, uncovered, for 30 minutes. In a small bowl, whisk together cream and flour—then stir into soup. Cut salmon fillets into 1-inch cubes, making sure to remove all bones. Add salmon and lemon juice to soup and simmer for 15–20 minutes, stirring occasionally. Serve hot, garnished with chopped parsley. Makes 4½ quarts.

Glorious Soups and Breads! (Oregon)

Oregon Coast Clam Chowder

4 slices bacon, diced
1 tablespoon pan drippings
1½ cups chopped onion
¼ cup flour
¼ cup grated carrot
¼ cup chopped celery

3 cups peeled, diced potatoes
1 teaspoon salt
⅛ teaspoon pepper
2 (8-ounce) cans chopped clams,
   drained (reserve liquid)
1 cup evaporated milk

In large saucepan, cook diced bacon until lightly browned; drain, reserving 1 tablespoon. In reserved drippings, sauté onions until translucent. Stir in flour; add bacon, carrot, celery, potatoes, and seasonings. To reserved clam liquid, add enough water to make 3 cups. Stir into vegetable mixture, bring to boil. Reduce heat and boil gently, uncovered, 20 minutes, stirring occasionally. Add clams; cook 5 minutes longer. Stir in milk; reheat. Makes 7½ cups.

Oregon Cook Book (Oregon)

Chunky Meat Stew

A meat lover's favorite dish.

5 slices bacon
½ pound Italian sausage, sliced
1½ pounds beef stew meat, diced
1 cup chopped onion
1 green bell pepper, chopped
1 garlic clove, minced
2 pickled jalapeño peppers, rinsed, seeded, and chopped

1½ tablespoons chili powder
½ teaspoon crushed red pepper
½ teaspoon salt
¼ teaspoon oregano
2½ cups water
1 (12-ounce) can tomato paste
1 (15½-ounce) can pinto beans

Cook bacon until crisp. Drain and crumble. Brown sausage. Reserve 2 tablespoons drippings. Brown beef, onion, green pepper, and garlic. Add bacon, sausage, jalapeños, chili powder, red pepper, salt, and oregano. Stir in water and tomato paste. Bring to a boil. Simmer 1½ hours. Stir in beans. Simmer 30 minutes. Serves 8.

Recipe by John McLaren, Coach, Seattle Mariners
Mariners Mix'n and Fix'n Grand Slam Style (Washington)

In Alaska, along the Denali Highway between Mount McKinley and the Talkeetna Mountain range stands Igloo City Resort, where you can gaze at the amazing view, buy gifts and T-shirts, buy a drink, get fuel for your car, and refuel your helicopter.

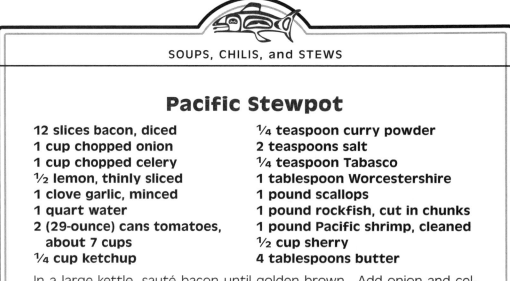

Pacific Stewpot

12 slices bacon, diced
1 cup chopped onion
1 cup chopped celery
½ lemon, thinly sliced
1 clove garlic, minced
1 quart water
2 (29-ounce) cans tomatoes, about 7 cups
¼ cup ketchup

¼ teaspoon curry powder
2 teaspoons salt
¼ teaspoon Tabasco
1 tablespoon Worcestershire
1 pound scallops
1 pound rockfish, cut in chunks
1 pound Pacific shrimp, cleaned
½ cup sherry
4 tablespoons butter

In a large kettle, sauté bacon until golden brown. Add onion and celery; cook for 5 minutes. Add lemon slices, garlic, water, tomatoes, ketchup, curry powder, salt, Tabasco, and Worcestershire; cook slowly for 30 minutes. If scallops are large, cut in half. Add scallops, fish, and shrimp along with the wine and butter. Cook 10 minutes, or until fish flakes when tested with a fork. Serve with thick slices of garlic bread.

Clam Dishes and Rock Fishes (Oregon)

Garden Chili

A crusty cornbread makes an ideal accompaniment.

3 cloves garlic, minced
2 cups chopped onions
2 cups sliced fresh mushrooms
2 cups sliced fresh sweet peppers (red, yellow or green or a combination)
2 tablespoons olive oil
4 cups peeled and chopped fresh tomatoes
3 tablespoons chili powder

1 teaspoon ground cumin
1 tablespoon crushed dried oregano
½ teaspoon salt
4 cups sliced raw zucchini
4 cups unsalted cooked black beans (well-rinsed canned beans may be used)
2 cups water

In heavy skillet or Dutch oven, sauté garlic, onions, mushrooms, and peppers in olive oil about 10 minutes or until tender. Add tomatoes, chili powder, cumin, oregano, and salt. Bring to gentle boil. Reduce heat and simmer about 25 minutes. Add zucchini and continue simmering 5 minutes longer. Stir in cooked beans and water; heat through. Adjust seasonings to taste. Yields 11 (1-cup) servings.

Note: To peel tomatoes easily, cover with boiling water; let stand 2–5 minutes. Drain and rinse under cold water. Skins should slip off easily.

Taste California (California)

Ray's Turkey Chili

An amazing chili made without beef or beans!

3 tablespoons vegetable or
   olive oil
1 red onion, chopped
1 yellow onion, chopped
2 leeks, chopped
6 garlic cloves, chopped
2 tablespoons flour
4–6 tablespoons chili powder
1 tablespoon oregano
1 tablespoon salt
2 tablespoons cumin powder
1–2 teaspoons cayenne pepper

Bottle of cold beer
3 pounds cooked, chopped
   turkey breast
2 (14½-ounce) cans stewed
   tomatoes (with juice)
1 (14-ounce) can tomato sauce
1 tablespoon peanut butter
6–8 tablespoons beer (or
   water), divided
Chopped onion for garnish
Shredded Cheddar cheese for
   garnish

Heat oil in a large soup pot and add onions, leeks, and garlic, stirring until cooked. Mix together, flour, chili powder, oregano, salt, cumin, and cayenne pepper. Add just enough beer (1–2 tablespoons) to form a thin paste. Stir paste into cooked vegetables. Add and stir well chopped turkey, tomatoes with juice, tomato sauce, and peanut butter. Stir often and simmer on low heat 2–5 hours. Add beer or water to thin, but not too much. Serves 8–10. Garnish with chopped onion and Cheddar cheese. Serve with tortilla chips or corn bread.

The Colophon Cafe Best Recipes (Washington)

Picante Chili

1 large onion, chopped
2 tablespoons oil or butter
1 pound steak, cut into cubes
1 pound ground beef
1 (8-ounce) can tomato sauce
1 (28-ounce) can tomatoes
1 tablespoon chili powder
2 tablespoons chopped
  cilantro or parsley
1 cup hot picante sauce, or
  to taste

1 clove garlic, minced
½ teaspoon salt
½ teaspoon oregano
1 ounce Mexican chocolate,
  grated (or substitute baking
  chocolate with 1 teaspoon
  sugar and ½ teaspoon
  cinnamon)
1–1½ cups grated Cheddar or
  Monterey Jack cheese
  (optional)

Brown onion in oil or butter in large skillet until soft. Transfer to crockpot. Brown cubed steak and ground beef, a little at a time, in same skillet. Transfer to crockpot.

Combine remaining ingredients and simmer until chocolate melts. Add to crockpot and mix well. Cook for 7–10 hours on low setting. Yields 6–8 servings. Serve with cornbread and a green or fruit salad.

Note: Transports well in the crockpot and will stay hot for several hours.

Only in California (California)

SALADS

Created by pounding taro root, poi is a staple in the Hawaiian diet and a traditional lū'au food. Poi, usually eaten with your fingers, is named based on the number of fingers needed to eat it: three-finger, two-finger, or the thickest, one-finger poi.

Spinach Salad with Basil Dressing

For feta cheese lovers everywhere!

SALAD:

1 bunch spinach, torn into pieces

1 small avocado, cubed

4 ounces (½ cup) feta cheese, crumbled

½ small red onion, thinly sliced

½ cup coarsely chopped walnuts or pecans

In a large bowl, combine spinach, avocado, feta, onion, and nuts.

BASIL DRESSING:

2 large garlic cloves, minced

¼ cup fresh basil leaves (packed) or 2 tablespoons dried

¼ cup red wine vinegar

2 teaspoons granulated sugar

½ cup olive oil

½ teaspoon freshly-ground black pepper

In food processor or blender, add garlic and pulse 4–5 times. Add basil, pulse to combine, then add vinegar and sugar. With processor running, drizzle in olive oil until emulsified. Season with pepper. Pour Dressing over Salad and toss well. Serve immediately. Yields 6–8 servings.

Note: A mixture of spinach and red leaf lettuce adds festive color. Consider jicama root as an addition also.

From Portland's Palate (Oregon)

WWW.UMTPRI.ORG

The Columbia River is the largest river in the Pacific Northwest. The river forms most of the border between Oregon and Washington. The Columbia and its tributaries are home to numerous spawning fish. These fish—especially the various species of salmon—have been a vital part of the river's ecology and the local economies for thousands of years. The Columbia River Basin is the most hydroelectrically developed river system in the world with more than 400 dams.

Spinach Salad with Bacon and Apples

2 large bunches spinach
6 strips bacon
⅓ cup sliced almonds
⅓ cup olive or salad oil
3 tablespoons tarragon
  vinegar or white wine
  vinegar
⅛ teaspoon salt
1 teaspoon sugar
½ teaspoon dry mustard
Dash pepper
1 large red-skinned apple
3 tablespoons sliced green
  onion

Remove and discard tough spinach stems; wash leaves, drain well, and chill for at least 2 hours.

In frying pan over medium heat, cook bacon until crisp; drain (reserving 1 tablespoon drippings), crumble, and set aside. Place almonds in remaining bacon drippings and sauté until lightly browned (3 or 4 minutes); lift from pan and set aside. Combine oil, vinegar, salt, sugar, mustard, and pepper; blend well. Core and dice apple. Break spinach into bite-sized pieces and place in a large bowl; add onion, apple, and almonds. Pour dressing over salad, top with reserved bacon, and toss gently. Makes 6–8 servings.

Extraordinary Cuisine for Sea & Shore (Washington)

Citrus Salad

This unusual salad is great with Mexican food. The addition of fruit gives this salad an interesting and refreshing taste.

1 grapefruit, peeled
1 orange, peeled
1½ quarts lettuce
1 small red onion, sliced thin
2 tablespoons cider vinegar
1 tablespoon lime juice
1 tablespoon salad oil
1 tablespoon water
¼ teaspoon pepper
¼ teaspoon cumin
⅛ teaspoon salt (optional)

Cut fruit in bite-size pieces. Toss with lettuce and onion. Mix remaining ingredients for dressing. Drizzle over salad and toss just before serving. Yields 8 cups.

Quick & Healthy Volume II (ScaleDown) (Oregon)

Blue Cheese–Pear Salad with Hazelnuts

DRESSING:

1½ tablespoons vegetable oil

2 tablespoons hazelnut oil (available at specialty shops)

2 tablespoons hazelnut liqueur

1 tablespoon white wine vinegar

1½ teaspoons lemon juice

¼ teaspoon Dijon mustard

Salt to taste

Pepper to taste

In a jar combine all ingredients and shake well to blend. Chill.

SALAD:

6 cups mixed greens, such as romaine, spinach, or leaf lettuce, torn into bite-size pieces

¼ cup (2 ounces) crumbled blue cheese

2 green onions, thinly sliced (optional)

2 pears

3 tablespoons hazelnuts, toasted, skin removed, and chopped

Prepare greens and add the blue cheese and green onion, if desired. Immediately before serving, core and dice pears, leaving skin on. Add to greens mixture along with Dressing. Sprinkle hazelnuts on top. Serves 6–8.

Collection Extraordinaire (Oregon)

The United States imported most of its hazelnuts from Italy, Spain, France, and Turkey until the 1940s. They are now grown in Oregon and Washington. Oregon is the only state that has an official state nut—the hazelnut. Almost all of the hazelnuts grown in the United States are from the rich soil of the Willamette Valley in Oregon. These hazelnuts, also known as filberts, are considered to be the best in the world.

Roasted Hazelnut Salad

The warm smell of roasting hazelnuts will remind you of the cozy atmosphere in your grandmother's kitchen. Serve with salmon or steelhead.

SALAD:

½ cup Oregon hazelnuts, roasted

1 head romaine lettuce, torn into bite-size pieces

1 avocado, peeled and cubed

2 tomatoes, seeded and cubed

½ cup alfalfa sprouts

⅓ cup sliced green onions

½ cup shredded mozzarella cheese

To roast hazelnuts, place on a cookie sheet in a 275° oven for 20–30 minutes, until skins crack. To remove skins, rub warm nuts between your hands or in a towel. (Or microwave 3–4 minutes on full power.) Chop nuts, saving a few whole nuts for garnish.

In a large salad bowl toss romaine, avocado, tomatoes, nuts, sprouts, onions, and cheese.

DRESSING:

2 tablespoons white wine vinegar

1–2 tablespoons Dijon mustard

⅓ cup olive oil

Freshly ground pepper to taste

In a small bowl, whisk together vinegar and mustard. Gradually drizzle in olive oil. Whisk; add pepper. Chill and pour over Salad just before serving. Garnish with whole roasted hazelnuts. Yields 10 servings.

Rogue River Rendezvous (Oregon)

California Caesar Salad

Sun-dried tomatoes marinated in olive oil give a contemporary twist to the classic Caesar salad.

GARLIC CROUTONS:

**3 teaspoons of oil from
 sun-dried tomatoes**

2 garlic cloves, chopped

3 cups (½-inch) bread cubes

In a skillet over medium heat, warm 3 tablespoons of oil from tomatoes, and garlic. Add bread cubes; toss to coat. Transfer in a single layer to a baking sheet. Bake in a preheated 325° oven, tossing occasionally, until crisp and golden, about 12–15 minutes. Cool.

DRESSING:

2 garlic cloves

**1 (2-ounce) can anchovies,
 drained**

½ cup olive oil

**¼ cup freshly squeezed
 lemon juice**

**½ teaspoon Dijon-style
 mustard**

½ teaspoon Worcestershire

**Coarsely ground black pepper
 to taste**

**1 head romaine lettuce, washed
 and dried**

Garlic Croutons

**½ cup drained marinated
 sun-dried tomatoes, oil
 reserved**

**¼ freshly grated Parmesan
 cheese**

Purée garlic and anchovies in a blender or food processor. Add oil, lemon juice, mustard, and Worcestershire; blend thoroughly. Season with pepper. Gently tear lettuce into a salad bowl. Top with Garlic Croutons, tomatoes, and cheese. Drizzle with Dressing. Toss and serve immediately. Makes 4–6 servings.

A Little San Francisco Cookbook (California)

The Best Avocado Caesar Salad

No eggs needed in this one. We like it with heavy garlic, so use less if you don't want to taste it all day. Also, many people put the dressing in the bowl first and then add the lettuce. That's fine if you want most of the dressing to stay in the bowl. We prefer to drizzle over the top, then toss.

DRESSING:

⅓ cup olive oil

6 garlic cloves, pressed or minced

3 teaspoons lemon juice

1 teaspoon Worcestershire

Freshly ground pepper to taste

Mix all Dressing ingredients in cruet with lid and shake until blended. May be done hours ahead and held in refrigerator.

SALAD:

2 large heads of green leaf or romaine lettuce

1 cup shredded Parmesan cheese

2 or 3 peeled, sliced ripe avocados

Croutons (optional)

Wash lettuce thoroughly, dry, and tear into bite-size bits. Place in a large bowl. Drizzle Dressing over lettuce. Toss with Parmesan. Garnish with avocado and croutons. Serve with French bread.

The Colophon Cafe Best Vegetarian Recipes (Washington)

Classic Avocado Salad

½ head Boston lettuce

½ head romaine

½ head chicory

½ pint cherry tomatoes, halved

2 avocados, peeled and sliced

3 slices bacon, cooked and crumbled

3 ounces Roquefort or Bleu cheese, crumbled

Into large salad bowl, tear greens in bite-sized pieces. Add tomatoes and avocados. Sprinkle with bacon and cheese. Toss lightly with Herb Dressing.

HERB DRESSING:

1 cup vegetable oil

6 tablespoons wine vinegar

¼ cup lemon juice

1 teaspoon salt

1 teaspoon sugar

½ teaspoon basil leaves

2 cloves garlic, crushed

Dash pepper

Combine all ingredients and chill, covered. Makes 1½ cups.

California Country Cook Book (California)

Salad Coquille

1 head lettuce, bite-size
1 bunch leafy lettuce, bite-size
1 cup mandarin oranges, drained
1 red onion, sliced in thin rings
¼ cup toasted slivered almonds

Layer lettuce, oranges, and onion in bowl. Toss with Dressing. Sprinkle with toasted almonds.

DRESSING:
2½ tablespoons wine vinegar
½ tablespoon lemon juice
½ teaspoon dry mustard
2½ tablespoons honey
⅓ cup sugar
½ teaspoon grated onion
½ cup salad oil

Heat all ingredients, except oil, until sugar dissolves. Add oil. Chill before serving. Toss well.

What's Cooking?? (Oregon)

WIKIPEDIA.COM

The Three Sisters are three volcanic peaks of the Cascade Range in Oregon, each of which exceeds 10,000 feet in elevation. They are the third, fourth, and fifth highest peaks in the state of Oregon (after Mt. Hood and Mt. Jefferson). The Sisters were named Faith, Hope, and Charity by early settlers.

Cobb Salad

The best Cobb Salad is made with freshly prepared ingredients, carefully seasoned. This wonderful combination of flavors and textures was invented by Bob Cobb at Hollywood's Brown Derby Restaurant in 1936.

DRESSING:

¾ cup olive oil

3 tablespoons red wine vinegar

½ teaspoon salt

¼ teaspoon freshly ground black pepper

To make Dressing, combine oil, vinegar, salt and pepper in tightly capped jar and shake vigorously until blended; set aside.

SALAD:

2 hard-boiled eggs, peeled and chopped

2 tablespoons chopped fresh parsley or chives

Salt and pepper

2 large red, ripe tomatoes, peeled, seeded and diced

2 cups finely diced cooked chicken breast

4 cups finely chopped iceberg lettuce

2 cups chopped chicory or curly endive

1 cup watercress sprigs

½ cup crumbled bleu cheese

1 avocado, peeled and diced

6 slices bacon, cooked crisp and crumbled

In small bowl, toss eggs with parsley or chives, a sprinkling of salt and pepper, and 2 tablespoons Dressing. In another bowl, toss tomatoes with 2 tablespoons Dressing, and season with salt and pepper. In another bowl, season chicken with salt and pepper and toss with 2 tablespoons Dressing. In large bowl, toss together lettuce, chicory, and watercress sprigs. Pour on remaining Dressing and toss to combine; season with salt and pepper to taste.

Spread greens in a shallow mound on large platter or salad bowl. Arrange eggs, tomato, chicken, cheese, avocado, and bacon nicely on top. Take to the table and toss just before serving. Serves 6–8.

A Little California Cookbook (California)

24 Hour Salad

1 head lettuce
5 hard-boiled eggs, sliced
Salt and pepper
½ teaspoon sugar
1 pound bacon, fried crisp

1 (10-ounce) package frozen
  peas
½ medium onion
1½ cups mayonnaise
½ pound Swiss cheese, grated

Cover bottom of 9x13-inch dish with 1 inch chopped lettuce; then cover with egg slices. Sprinkle with salt and pepper and a little sugar. Break up fried bacon and spread over eggs. Next, spread frozen peas (not cooked) over bacon. Thinly slice onion over peas. Stir mayonnaise and spread over onions. Spread grated Swiss cheese over all. Cover and let stand in refrigerator 24 hours.

Taste of Fillmore (California)

Fresh Cucumber Salad

Will keep up to 2 months.

7 cups thinly sliced unpeeled
  cucumbers
1 cup sliced onions
1 cup sliced green peppers
1 tablespoon salt

1 cup vinegar
2 cups sugar
1 teaspoon celery seed
1 teaspoon mustard seed

Mix first 4 ingredients and let stand for 1 hour. Mix next 4 ingredients in saucepan and bring to a boil. Cool liquid mixture; pour over cucumber mixture. Store in refrigerator. Yields approximately 3 pints.

Durham's Favorite Recipes (California)

Baja Salad

Great for a festive luncheon on the patio.

1 (16-ounce) package dried
   black beans, picked over,
   soaked overnight in cold
   water to cover, and drained
1 red bell pepper, diced
1 green bell pepper, diced
⅓ cup chopped green onions
1 (10-ounce) package frozen
   corn, thawed

⅓ cup chopped cilantro
8 chicken breast halves, skinned
   and grilled
1–2 avocados, sliced, garnish
1 cup salsa, garnish
½ cup sour cream, garnish
Chopped cilantro, garnish

In large saucepan, combine black beans and enough cold water to cover by 2 inches. Bring water to boil and simmer 45 minutes to 1 hour, or until tender, but not too soft. Drain black beans and mix with vegetables in large mixing bowl. Toss with Cumin-Lime Dressing. Place vegetables with dressing on large round platter. Cut chicken into strips and arrange on top with sliced avocado. Drizzle salsa on top. Put extra salsa, sour cream, and cilantro in bowls.

CUMIN-LIME DRESSING:
½ cup lime or lemon juice
1 tablespoon Dijon mustard
2 tablespoons ground cumin
1 teaspoon minced garlic

1 teaspoon pepper
½ teaspoon salt
¾ cup olive oil
¾ cup vegetable oil

Mix together dressing ingredients and let stand for 1 hour or more.

Note: This can also be made with grilled shrimp instead of chicken.

California Sizzles (California)

Northwest Seafood Salad

SESAME DRESSING:

⅓ **cup white vinegar**	**2 tablespoons sesame oil**
¼ **cup vegetable oil**	**2 tablespoons sherry**
3 tablespoons soy sauce	**1 tablespoon sugar**
2 tablespoons dry mustard	⅓ **cup water**

Combine all ingredients in a jar. Shake well to mix; set aside.

SALAD:

2 dozen large shrimp, shelled and deveined	**2 cucumbers, peeled and sliced**
1½ pounds scallops	**4 celery stalks, sliced**
½ **pound snow peas**	**1 lemon, quartered for garnish**

Cook shrimp in boiling water for 2 minutes or until they are pink. Drain well and transfer to a small bowl. Cool slightly. When they are cool, spoon 3 tablespoons dressing over shrimp and refrigerate until serving.

Cook scallops in boiling water until white and opaque. Drain well and chill. Place snow peas in a colander and pour boiling water over them. Drain well. Transfer snow peas to a salad bowl and add cucumbers and celery. Toss slightly and chill.

To assemble, add scallops and shrimp to the salad bowl. Pour Sesame Dressing over all and toss to coat. Garnish each serving of this colorful main dish salad with a lemon quarter. Let it be the focus of a summer party. Makes 4 servings.

Simply Whidbey (Washington)

Crab Louis

This classic salad originated in San Francisco, and every wharfside restaurant features its own version. Tiny shelled shrimp, called bay shrimp in San Francisco, can be substituted for crab.

LOUIS DRESSING:

½ cup mayonnaise
½ cup sour cream
3–4 tablespoons tomato-based chili sauce
1 tablespoon fresh lemon juice

Few drops hot pepper sauce
¼ cup finely diced green bell pepper
¼ cup finely sliced green onions

Combine ingredients in a small bowl; blend well. Cover and refrigerate at least 1 hour to let flavors blend.

1 head iceberg lettuce
¾ to 1 pound cooked crabmeat, shredded
Louis Dressing
2 medium tomatoes, cut in wedges

2 hard-cooked eggs, cut in wedges
Capers
Black olives

Rinse, core, and drain lettuce. Place 1 large lettuce leaf on each of 4 plates. Shred remaining lettuce to make 6 cups. (Refrigerate any remaining lettuce for another use.) Place shredded lettuce on lettuce leaves. Arrange crabmeat evenly over it. Spoon about half of dressing over crabmeat. Garnish each plate with tomato wedges, egg wedges, capers, and olives. Serve remaining dressing separately. Makes 4 servings.

A Little San Francisco Cookbook (California)

Baked King Crab Salad

2 tablespoons chopped onion
1 cup chopped celery
1 green pepper, chopped
2 cups crabmeat
¾ cup mayonnaise
½ teaspoon salt

Pepper to taste
1 teaspoon Worcestershire
½ cup buttered bread crumbs
   or small croutons
Lemon slices for garnish
Lettuce for garnish

Combine all ingredients, except crumbs and garnish. Place in 2-quart casserole and top with crumbs or small croutons. Bake at 350° for 20 minutes. Serve with lemon slices on a bed of lettuce.

Alaska's Cooking Volume II (Alaska)

Back Country Wild Rice Smoked Salmon Salad

½ cup wild rice
1 cup brown rice
3 cups plus 2 tablespoons
   water
1 teaspoon salt
1 yellow bell pepper, chopped

1 red pepper, chopped
1 pound smoked Chinook
   salmon, cubed
½ cup chopped walnuts
Lettuce leaves

DRESSING:
2 tablespoons red wine vinegar
½ teaspoon salt
¼ teaspoon black pepper
¼ teaspoon marjoram

1 teaspoon soy sauce
½ teaspoon grated lemon peel
4 green onions, chopped
1 large clove garlic, minced

Rinse the rice under running water. Bring the salted water to boil in medium saucepan. Add rice and stir. Reduce heat to low, cover and simmer until the rice is plump and tender, 35–45 minutes. If any liquid remains, drain it off. Cool slightly in a large bowl. Stir together the Dressing ingredients and toss the Dressing together with the rice. Chill. Add peppers, salmon, and walnuts and serve in lettuce cups. Serves 4–6 people.

Alaska Cooking: Featuring Skagway (Alaska)

Salmon Seashell Salad

3 cups seashell pasta, cooked,
    drained, and cooled
1 (8-ounce) can salmon,
    drained and dark pieces
    removed
½ cup chopped onion

½ cup chopped celery
¼ cup chopped dill pickle
¼ cup sliced black olives
2 tablespoons chopped fresh
    parsley or 1 tablespoon dry

Place shells in large mixing bowl, toss with salmon, onion, celery, pickle, olives, and parsley.

DRESSING:
1 cup mayonnaise
½ cup sour cream
½ cup buttermilk or milk

½ teaspoon garlic salt
1 teaspoon lemon juice
¼ teaspoon cayenne

Mix until well blended and pour over salad ingredients. You may have to add more milk or mayonnaise if too dry.

Grannie Annie's Cookin' Fish from Cold Alaskan Waters (Alaska)

Curried Turkey and Grapes

2¼ cups cooked turkey,
    cut in ½-inch cubes
1 cup thinly sliced celery
1 cup red seedless grapes
1 (8-ounce) can pineapple
    chunks,drained
1 cup chopped cashews or
    almonds
1½ teaspoons lemon juice
½ cup mayonnaise

½ teaspoon curry powder
½ teaspoon dry mustard
4 red lettuce leaves
4 cups small pieces of salad
    greens
4 tablespoons chopped cashews
    or almonds
4 small bunches grapes for
    garnish

Combine turkey, celery, grapes, pineapple, and nuts. In another bowl, combine lemon juice, mayonnaise, curry, and dry mustard. Combine the two mixtures and mix well. Line 4 plates with red lettuce leaves and divide salad greens evenly. Mound the turkey mixture evenly on each of the 4 plates. Sprinkle with chopped nuts and garnish with bunches of grapes. Serves 4.

Savor the Flavor of Oregon (Oregon)

Arugula, Prosciutto and Pear Salad

**¼ pound prosciutto, thinly
  sliced**

1½ cups arugula
1 pear, thinly sliced

Arrange prosciutto around outside edges of plate. Dress arugula and pear slices in center with Vinaigrette Dressing. Serves 4.

VINAIGRETTE DRESSING:

½ cup sherry vinegar
¼ cup honey
**2 tablespoons chopped
  rosemary**

4 tablespoons minced shallots
3 cups olive oil
Salt and pepper to taste

In a medium-sized saucepan, combine vinegar, honey, rosemary, and shallots until warm. Remove from heat and let cool. Whisk in olive oil and season with salt and pepper.

San Francisco's Cooking Secrets (California)

Hawaiian Horseradish Salad

Delicious and easy to prepare, this Waldorf-like salad is a nice blend of Hawaiian and traditional Passover flavors.

3 celery stalks
2 large apples, peeled
**1 (8-ounce) can crushed
  pineapple in its own juice,
  drained**
1 cup walnuts

½ cup mayonnaise
2 tablespoons lemon juice
2 tablespoons sugar
**2 tablespoons white
  horseradish**

Dice celery and grate apples. Mix all ingredients. Chill and serve in a glass bowl or on lettuce leaves. Serves 6.

*The When You Live in Hawaii You Get Very Creative
During Passover Cookbook (Hawaii)*

Broccoli-Peanut Salad

SALAD:
1 bunch broccoli
8 strips bacon, crisped and
  crumbled

1 cup chopped celery
¾ cup raisins
¼ cup peanuts

Break broccoli into small flowerets. Mix broccoli, bacon, and celery. Add raisins and peanuts.

DRESSING:
1 cup mayonnaise
2 tablespoons vinegar

¼ cup sugar

Mix Dressing ingredients thoroughly. Combine with Salad. Refrigerate. This salad keeps nicely for several days. You may want to adjust the amount of Dressing.

Treasured Recipes (Oregon)

Green Bean Tossed Salad

Buck and Judy Lovett of Mountain Spring Farms in Myrtle Creek saw a need for a farmers' market in their area, so they started the Douglas County Farmers' Market in 1994 in addition to their community supported agriculture (CSA) project based on their farm.

DRESSING:
2 cloves garlic, minced
½ cup chopped and packed
  fresh basil
2 tablespoons white wine
  vinegar

1 tablespoon grated Parmesan
  cheese
Salt and pepper to taste

Mix Dressing ingredients together and set aside.

SALAD:
1½ pounds fresh green beans,
  blanched
8 sun-dried tomatoes, sliced
  with some of the oil

½ cup pine nuts, toasted
  (toast on cookie sheet at
  300° for 5 minutes)

Mix Salad ingredients and toss with Dressing. Serve on chilled plates.

Oregon Farmers' Markets Cookbook and Guide (Oregon)

Chattaroy Gardens Marinated Vegetables

1 can tomato soup
½ cup oil
1 cup sugar
¾ cup vinegar
1 teaspoon prepared mustard
1 tablespoon Worcestershire

1 head cauliflower
2 cups sliced carrots
2 green peppers
1 medium white onion
1 can cut green beans, drained

Mix tomato soup, oil, sugar, vinegar, prepared mustard, and Worcestershire. Cut cauliflower into flowerets. Boil lightly. Boil sliced carrots lightly. Cut green peppers into rings or bite size. Slice and separate onion into rings. Drain green beans. Mix vegetables together. Mix marinade well and pour over vegetables. Let set for 2 days.

Our Best Home Cooking (Washington)

Greek Potato Salad
(Patatosalata)

2 pounds small potatoes
1 bunch green onions,
  chopped
2 garlic cloves, chopped
2 tablespoons chopped fresh
  parsley

1 tablespoon chopped fresh dill
½ cup olive oil
2 tablespoons white vinegar
Salt and pepper to taste

Boil potatoes in their skins in a stockpot until tender. Cool. Remove skins and cut potatoes into small cubes. Add onions, garlic, parsley, dill, oil, vinegar, salt and pepper. Toss gently. Serve at room temperature.

Flavor it Greek! (Oregon)

Christine's Coleslaw

1 head cabbage, finely
   shredded
¼ cup finely diced carrots
2 tablespoons finely diced
   onion
½ cup granulated sugar
1 teaspoon salt

½ cup Miracle Whip salad
   dressing
½ cup sour cream
3 tablespoons distilled white
   vinegar
2 tablespoons vegetable oil

In a large bowl, toss together cabbage, carrots, onion, sugar, and salt and set aside. In a small bowl, combine salad dressing, sour cream, vinegar, and oil; mix well. Toss the dressing with the cabbage mixture. Chill at least 1 hour before serving.

Dilley Family Favorites (Oregon)

Picnic Coleslaw

6 cups shredded cabbage
2 cups shredded carrots
8 bacon strips, cooked and
   crumbled
12 green onions with tops,
   thinly sliced

½ cup cider vinegar
⅓ cup vegetable oil
⅓ cup sugar
1 teaspoon salt

Combine cabbage, carrots, bacon, and onions. In jar with tight fitting lid, mix vinegar, oil, sugar, and salt. Shake well. Just before serving, pour dressing over cabbage mixture and toss. Makes 12–16 servings.

Recipes from Our Friends (Washington)

LaConner Slough Salad

This is a definite pleaser for pasta lovers. In combination with sun-dried tomatoes, Greek olives and feta cheese, this salad is mouthwatering. Fourth of July celebrations aren't complete without this crowd-pleaser.

**16 ounces rotini pasta,
    uncooked**
**10 ounces Greek olives, pitted
    and chopped; reserve brine**
**8½ ounces sun-dried
    tomatoes in oil, drained
    and chopped; reserve oil**

1 large red onion, chopped
8 ounces feta cheese, crumbled
**3 cups large shrimp, fresh
    cooked and chilled**

DRESSING:

3 tablespoons red wine vinegar
1¼–1½ cups mayonnaise
**2 tablespoons chopped fresh
    basil leaves**
**2 tablespoons chopped fresh
    oregano**

**2 tablespoons chopped fresh
    parsley**
2 cloves garlic, minced
Salt and pepper to taste

Cook pasta according to package directions and cool. In a large bowl, combine olives, tomatoes, and onion. Add pasta and mix together. In a separate bowl, whisk together Dressing ingredients. Mix into salad. Before serving, add feta cheese and shrimp and toss. May substitute chicken for shrimp, if desired. Serves 10–12.

Note: This salad is best if made the day before serving.

LaConner Palates (Washington)

Dell Neely's Pineapple Pickles

6 cups fresh pineapple chunks
2 cups white sugar
1 cup cider vinegar

12 whole cloves
**6 (2-inch) pieces cinnamon
sticks**

Put all ingredients into saucepan, bring to a boil, turn heat to medium, and continue cooking until pineapple turns a clear golden yellow. Pour fruit and syrup into hot, sterilized glass jars and seal. Let jars "ripen" about 2 weeks so fruit will absorb spices.

Paradise Preserves (Hawaii)

Spam Pasta Salad

**1 (12-ounce) bag pasta
(veggie spirals are nice)**
¼ medium onion, minced
1 cup diced Spam
**1 (6-ounce) jar artichoke
hearts, including juice**
**1 cup chopped cucumber or
zucchini**

**⅓ cup Italian dressing
(such as zesty Italian)**
½ teaspoon salt
¼ teaspoon pepper
¼ teaspoon oregano
**Sliced tomatoes, sliced hard-
boiled eggs, olives, etc., for
garnish**

Cook pasta according to package directions. Do not overcook. Rinse with cold water and drain well.

Place all other ingredients in a bowl and mix together. Add drained pasta and toss together. Chill. Decorate top with sliced tomatoes, sliced hard-boiled eggs, olives, etc.

Hawai'i's Spam Cookbook (Hawaii)

Hawaiians consume some 4.3 million cans of Spam a year. In fact, Spam is so popular there, it is sometimes dubbed "The Hawaiian Steak." Spam was introduced to the islands during U.S. military occupation in World War II. Surpluses of Spam from the soldiers' supplies made their way into native diets. One popular Spam dish in Hawaii is Spam musubi, in which cooked Spam is combined with rice and nori seaweed.

Wild Rice Salad

A wonderful picnic or potluck dish!

1 cup wild rice, rinsed
8 cups chicken broth, divided
1 cup white, red, or brown rice
1 cup chopped apricots
¾ cup yellow raisins
⅓–½ cup sun-dried tomatoes
   (in oil, drained on paper)
3 cloves garlic, squeezed (less
   if desired)

1 cup julienne smoked turkey
1 small jar artichokes, drained
   and halved
6 green onions, diced (including
   green tops) or 1 small red
   onion, chopped
¾ cup chopped toasted pecans
   for garnish

Cook wild rice in 4 cups chicken broth until tender. Drain and cool. Cook other rice separately in remaining 4 cups broth. Drain and cool. When both are cool, mix and fluff with fork. Toss together all but onions and pecans; chill until ready to serve. When ready to serve, add onions, toss with Dressing, and garnish with toasted pecans. Can be prepared the night before, but do not mix in onions or dressing until the next day. Serves 8–10.

DRESSING:

1 small lemon, squeezed
2–3 tablespoons Japanese
   vinegar

1–2 tablespoons pure olive oil
Fresh ground pepper

Combine lemon juice, vinegar, olive oil, and pepper. Set aside until ready to toss with Salad.

Variations: Add baby shrimp; walla walla onions; currants instead of raisins; mandarin oranges; fresh chopped tomatoes; fresh chopped green (or red) pepper; chopped filberts instead of pecans—use your imagination.

Rainy Day Treats and Sunny Temptations (Oregon)

VEGETABLES

Considered to be one of the nation's most photographed lighthouses, Heceta Head's light first shone in 1894. Still in use and seen 21 miles from land, it is rated as the strongest light on the Oregon coast.

Esta's Onion Patties

I don't want to say that these will cause riots, but I have seen unsightly human behavior when "just cooked" onion patties were placed within arms' reach.

¾ cup flour
2 teaspoons baking powder
2 tablespoons sugar
½ teaspoon salt
1 tablespoon cornmeal

½ cup powdered milk
Cold water
2½ cups chopped onions
Cooking oil

Mix together the first 6 ingredients. Stir in enough cold water to form thick batter. Stir in onions and drop by the teaspoon into hot deep oil. Flatten patties slightly as you turn them. Fry to a golden brown. Drain on paper towels.

Recipes from the Paris of the Pacific—Sitka, Alaska (Alaska)

Parmesan Steamed Onions

Best when made with Walla Walla sweet onions.

¼ cup margarine
5 medium onions, sliced
  ¼ inch thick
¼ teaspoon salt
¼ teaspoon pepper

¼ teaspoon sugar
¼ cup cooking sherry or white
  wine vinegar
1 tablespoon Parmesan cheese

Place margarine into wok or fry pan; heat to 225° until margarine melts. Separate onions into rings. Add onions, salt, pepper, and sugar; stir. Cover and simmer for 20 minutes. Stir every 5 minutes. Add cooking sherry or wine vinegar and cheese. Increase heat to 300°. Stir gently and cook for 3 minutes. Reduce heat to warm for serving. Yields 4–6 servings.

Sharing Our Best (Washington)

Only onions grown in the Walla Walla Valley of southeast Washington and northeast Oregon can be called Walla Walla Sweet Onions, as protected by a Federal marketing order designating Walla Walla Sweet Onions as a unique variety and establishing a specific growing area for the crop.

Roasting Walla Walla Sweets & Potatoes

3 large Walla Walla sweet onions
3–4 medium russet potatoes

2 tablespoons vegetable oil
⅛ teaspoon black pepper

Halve each onion lengthwise through the top and root, then skin, peeling away any slippery membrane. Dig into center of each half with a metal spoon, and scoop out flesh, leaving a ½-inch-thick shell. Chop enough of the inner flesh to measure 2 cups and set aside. Scrub potatoes and cut enough of the potatoes into ¼- to ½-inch dices to make 4 cups. Heat oil in large skillet, adding chopped onion, potatoes, salt and pepper. Sauté over medium-high heat, stirring occasionally, about 5 minutes until onion begins to soften.

Arrange 6 scooped-out halves in large greased baking dish. Spoon about ½ cup of potato mixture into the onion shells, then arrange remaining potato mixture all around them in a layer no deeper than 1 inch. Bake in 375° oven for 1 hour, until potatoes are thoroughly cooked and deeply browned. Serves 6.

Washington Cook Book (Washington)

Cheesed Potatoes in Foil

3 large baking potatoes, pared
Salt
Cracked or coarsely ground pepper
4–5 slices bacon, crisp-cooked

1 large onion, sliced
8 ounces sharp processed American cheese, cubed
½ cup butter or margarine

Slice potatoes into a big piece of heavy aluminum foil and sprinkle with salt and pepper. Crumble bacon over. Add onion and cheese. Slice butter over all. Mix on foil; bring edges up—leaving space for expansion of steam—and seal well with double fold. Place package on grill and cook over coals about 1 hour or till done; turn several times. (Or cook on grill with barbecue hood down, about 45 minutes, or cook in 350° oven 1 hour.) Makes 4–6 servings.

Tasty Temptations (California)

Golden Potatoes

8 red potatoes
¼ cup butter
1 cup shredded sharp cheese
1 can cream of chicken soup

2 cups sour cream
⅓ cup chopped onion
1 teaspoon salt

Boil potatoes in jackets; chill unpeeled. Peel and shred potatoes. In saucepan, melt butter and cheese, using low heat. Add soup, sour cream, onion, and salt; stir. Pour mixture over potatoes and gently stir to blend. Pour into greased baking dish. Bake 45 minutes at 350°. Serves 6–8.

Durham's Favorite Recipes (California)

Scalloped Potatoes

4 pounds potatoes, sliced
2 tablespoons minced onion
1 green pepper, chopped
2 cans cream of celery soup
1 (8-ounce) package cream cheese

1½ cups half-and-half
1 teaspoon salt
½ teaspoon pepper
½ pound bacon, cooked crisp, crumbled

Stir together potatoes, onion, and green pepper. Heat soup, cream cheese, half-and-half, salt and pepper. Mix with potato mixture and place all in a greased casserole. Bake at 350° for 1½ hours. About 15 minutes before removing from oven, sprinkle bacon bits over top and return to oven.

Our Favorite Recipes (Oregon)

Potatoes Romanoff

1½ cups shredded Cheddar cheese, divided
1 bunch green onions, chopped fine
1 pint sour cream
1½ teaspoons salt
½ teaspoon pepper
6 large potatoes, baked, cooled, and shredded
Paprika

Mix well 1 cup cheese, onions, sour cream, and seasonings. Add potatoes. Place in greased casserole and top with remaining cheese. Sprinkle with paprika. Can be covered and refrigerated overnight. Bake, uncovered, at 350° for 30–40 minutes.

Nautical Niceaty's from Spokane Yacht Club (Washington)

Coconut Baked Sweet Potatoes

10 medium-size sweet potatoes
⅓ cup butter
¾ cup brown sugar
½ cup flaked coconut

One day before serving, cook the sweet potatoes in boiling water until almost tender (approximately 20 minutes). Drain, cool, peel and cut them in half lengthwise. Arrange the potatoes in a greased 9x13-inch baking dish.

In a small saucepan over medium heat melt the butter, brown sugar and ¼ cup water. Pour this over the cooked potatoes. Cover the potatoes and allow them to stand overnight. On the day of serving, pour Glaze over the potatoes. Bake in a 350° oven to heat thoroughly. Sprinkle coconut over the potatoes before serving. Serves 12.

GLAZE:
¼ cup butter
½ cup brown sugar
¼ cup heavy cream

Preheat oven to 350°. Combine butter, brown sugar, and cream in a small saucepan. Melt over medium heat until smooth.

Simply Whidbey (Washington)

Perfect Baked Sweet Potatoes

4 medium sweet potatoes   **Safflower oil**

Preheat oven to 400°. Wash and scrub potatoes; dry thoroughly. Coat potatoes lightly with oil. Prick surface with fork. Bake until tender, about 40–60 minutes.

Note: Rubbing potatoes with oil before baking makes them so creamy, they do not need additional butter. Makes 4 servings.

Favorite Island Cookery Book V (Hawaii)

Steamed Artichokes
with Garlic Mayonnaise

4 large artichokes   **1 bay leaf**
½ lemon (juice only)   **2 garlic cloves**

Cut artichokes ½ inch from top cone and clip leaf tips. Squeeze juice from lemon over artichokes. Steam in 1 inch of boiling water, with bay leaf and garlic cloves, for 30 minutes. Remove and drain by holding artichoke upside down and squeezing. Place on serving dish and fan leaves out around the plate. Serve hot or cold with Pisto's Garlic Mayonnaise. Serves 4.

PISTO'S GARLIC MAYONNAISE:
2 eggs*   **2 garlic cloves**
Salt and pepper to taste   **½ teaspoon tomato paste**
1 teaspoon lemon juice   **Pinch of saffron**
1 teaspoon red wine vinegar   **½ cup light olive oil**
½ teaspoon dry mustard

Place all ingredients except oil in a food processor. Process for 8 seconds. With machine running, slowly drizzle oil into mixture. Blend until thick. Chill for 1 hour. Spoon mayonnaise into center of each artichoke. Makes 1 cup.

*For those people concerned about raw eggs, pasteurized liquid eggs or pasteurized liquid egg whites can usually be successfully substituted.

Monterey's Cookin' Pisto Style (California)

Saki Sesame Broccoli

2 cups water
1 large bunch broccoli (stems
   cut away)
½ teaspoon garlic granules
½ teaspoon sesame seeds
3 tablespoons saki

2 tablespoons soy sauce
1 tablespoon vinegar
   (preferably apple cider)
1 tablespoon olive oil
3 tablespoons sugar
½ teaspoon sesame seeds

In large saucepan, boil water. Discard stem shoots from broccoli, leaving a small spear. Place speared flowerets in boiling water for 2–3 minutes. Sprinkle garlic granules and salt and pepper over cooking broccoli. Remove broccoli from saucepan with slotted spoon to medium-size bowl, and set aside.

In a small pan, combine saki, soy sauce, vinegar, olive oil, sugar, and sesame seeds. Heat over medium to low heat while blending all ingredients. Stir constantly about 5–10 minutes until liquids are clear and glazed. Pour over broccoli and serve. Serves 4–6.

Cooking with Booze (California)

Snow Peas Kahala Style

12–14 water chestnuts, sliced
   ¼-inch thick
1 cup thinly sliced, fresh
   mushrooms
1 cup diced onion
2 tablespoons peanut oil
¾ pound fresh snow peas, or
   3 (6-ounce) packages frozen
   Chinese snow peas

1 teaspoon salt
1 tablespoon soy sauce
1 tablespoon water
½ teaspoon garlic salt

In a wok or large skillet with a tight fitting cover, sauté water chestnuts, mushrooms, and onion in peanut oil for 5 minutes or until onion is tender. Add snow peas, salt, soy sauce, and water. Mix well. Sprinkle with garlic salt. Cover tightly and simmer 5 minutes or until snow peas are tender but still crisp. Serves 4–6.

A Taste of Aloha (Hawaii)

Crisp Zucchini Pancakes

3 medium-size zucchini,
trimmed and shredded
(about 1 pound)
¾ teaspoon salt, divided
½ cup chopped onion
1 tablespoon unsalted butter

2 eggs, slightly beaten
¼ cup unsifted all-purpose
flour
⅛ teaspoon pepper
Vegetable oil (for frying)

Place zucchini in colander after shredding. Sprinkle with ½ teaspoon salt. Set aside for 30 minutes. Squeeze as much liquid as possible from zucchini with your hands. Reserve.

Sauté onions in hot butter in a medium-size skillet over medium-high heat until softened, 3 minutes. Transfer reserved zucchini and onion to a large bowl. Stir in eggs, flour, remaining ¼ teaspoon salt and pepper. Pour oil into clean skillet to a depth of ⅛ inch, and heat. Drop slightly rounded tablespoonfuls of batter into hot oil. Flatten to 3-inch diameter with back of spoon. Cook, turning once, 1 minute on each side, or until golden. Remove pancakes with a slotted spoon. Drain on paper towel. Keep hot until all pancakes are cooked. Serve immediately. Makes 14 pancakes.

...Fire Burn & Cauldron Bubble (California)

RAINBIRD.COM

The Tournament of Roses Parade is Pasadena's most colorful attraction. It began in 1890 when the Valley Hunt Club hosted a picnic on New Year's Day. They wished to showcase California's mild winter weather with scores of flowers on display, covering the horse-drawn carriages. Over the next few founding years, marching bands and motorized floats were added. The first associated football game was played on Jan. 1, 1902. Originally titled the "Tournament East-West football game," it is considered to be the first Rose Bowl.

Zucchini Fritters

½ pound zucchini, coarsely
  grated
2 tablespoons grated onion
1 teaspoon minced fresh basil,
  or ¼ teaspoon dried
¼ teaspoon salt
Pepper

1 tablespoon flour
1 egg, well beaten
2 teaspoons olive oil
Grated Cheddar or mozzarella
  cheese (optional)

Put grated zucchini and onion in mixing bowl and add basil, salt and pepper to taste. Add flour and toss. Stir in egg. Put oil in a 10-inch nonstick skillet and place over medium heat until oil ripples, then reduce heat to low. Drop zucchini batter by heaping tablespoons into pan to make 3 fritters at a time. Cook until golden brown on both sides, 5–6 minutes total. Serve hot and sprinkle with cheese, if desired.

Dilley Family Favorites (Oregon)

Spinach Frittata

This basic frittata recipe lends itself to endless variations.

2 (10-ounce) packages frozen
  chopped spinach
3 eggs
3 ounces (3/4 cup) grated
  Parmesan cheese

3 tablespoons oil
3 tablespoons matzo meal or
  bread crumbs
8 ounces small curd cottage
  cheese (optional)

Place spinach in large mixing bowl and let stand until thawed. Do not drain. Blend in all other ingredients. Pour into a greased 9-inch square pan. Bake at 350° about 1 hour or until golden brown. Allow to cool 10 minutes and cut into serving portions. Serves 8.

California Kosher (California)

Kirk's Feta Compli

What we had to go through to get this recipe—you shouldn't know from it. So, enjoy.

CRUST:

1 stick margarine
1¼ cups matzo meal
1 tablespoon sugar

1 egg
¾ cup finely chopped almonds
    or walnuts

Cut margarine into matzo meal until it is in pieces the size of peas. Add sugar. Beat egg and blend into mixture with a fork; add nuts. Form into a ball. Flatten into greased, 10-inch deep-dish pie pan, building up sides. Prick with a fork. Bake in preheated 400° oven for 7 minutes. Cool thoroughly before filling.

FILLING:

2 large bunches of spinach
3 tablespoons oil
1 onion, chopped
1 cup grated Swiss cheese
2 eggs
1¼ cups light cream

½ teaspoon salt
¼ teaspoon pepper
⅛ teaspoon nutmeg
¼ cup soft cream cheese
6 ounces feta cheese, grated or
    crumbled

Wash and stem spinach; steam until wilted. Squeeze out excess water; chop. Heat oil; sauté onion until golden. Remove from heat, mix with spinach and add Swiss cheese.

In a blender or with a whisk, mix eggs, cream, and seasonings with cream cheese.

Spread spinach and onion mixture in Crust. Top with feta cheese. Pour cream cheese mixture on top, making sure it soaks through to the Crust. Bake in preheated 350° oven for 40–45 minutes. If Crust edges begin to burn, cover them with foil. Good hot or at room temperature. Serves 8.

The When You Live in Hawaii You Get Very Creative
During Passover Cookbook (Hawaii)

Sukiyaki

6–8 shiitake mushrooms
  (half-dollar size), slivered
2 cups water, divided
1 medium round onion or
  green onions, slivered
1 teaspoon sesame oil
Pinch sea salt
¼ cup low-sodium soy sauce
2–4 tablespoons maple syrup
1½ cups bamboo shoots

1 (3-ounce) package cellophane
  noodles, soaked in 2 cups
  boiling water
2–3 carrots, sliced into
  matchsticks
4 cups watercress
2–3 cups mung bean sprouts
4 cups won bok cabbage
½ block tofu (about 6 ounces)

Rinse the shiitake mushrooms and soak in 1 cup of water. Save the water for sukiyaki stock.

Sauté slivered onions and slivered mushrooms in remaining 1 cup water and sesame oil. Sprinkle some sea salt to prevent sticking. Add mushroom water and season to taste with low-sodium soy sauce and maple syrup. Add bamboo shoots to mixture, bring to a boil, and simmer at a low boil. Add soaked and drained cellophane noodles to mixture. Sprinkle julienned carrots. Layer watercress, bean sprouts, won bok, and tofu. Cover and allow layers of vegetables to be steamed. Makes 6–8 portions.

Eat More, Weigh Less Cookbook (Hawaii)

Aloha, pronounced *ah-LO-ha*, is a Hawaiian greeting but means so much more than hello and goodbye. Aloha is the way people treat each other, a way of life, and a state of mind. Known as the Aloha State, Hawaii is a string of 137 islands encompassing a land area of 6,422.6 square miles in the Pacific Ocean about 2,400 miles from the west coast of the continental United States. Stretching from northwest to southeast, the eight major islands are: Ni'ihau (Nee-ee-how), Kaua'i (ka-Wah-ee), O'ahu (Oh-Wa-who), Moloka'i (mo-lo-Kah-ee), Lana'i (la-Nah-ee), Kaho'olawe (kaw-ho-oh-la-vay), Maui (Mow-ee, rhymes with Now-ee), and Hawai'i (ha-Wa-ee or ha-Va-ee).

Savory Carrots with Hazelnuts

4 large carrots, peeled
¼ cup (½ stick) butter or
   margarine
2 tablespoons honey
¼ teaspoon nutmeg
½ teaspoon salt

¼ teaspoon pepper
3 tablespoons finely chopped
   fresh parsley
1 tablespoon apple juice
¼ cup toasted hazelnuts
¼ teaspoon garlic powder

Steam carrots until tender-crisp. Remove to a plate and let cool enough to handle. Grate the carrots into a bowl and set aside. Melt the butter in a saucepan over medium-low heat. Stir in honey, nutmeg, salt, pepper, parsley, apple juice, hazelnuts, and garlic powder. Add grated carrots and sauté until just heated through. Yields 6 servings.

Cooking from the Coast to the Cascades (Oregon)

Frontier Hazelnut Vegetable Pie

1 cup chopped fresh broccoli*
1 cup sliced fresh cauliflower*
2 cups chopped fresh spinach*
1 small onion, diced
½ green pepper, diced
1 cup grated Cheddar cheese
1 cup coarsely chopped,
   roasted hazelnuts

1½ cups milk
1 cup baking mix (Bisquick)
4 eggs
1 teaspoon garlic salt
½ teaspoon pepper

Pre-cook broccoli and cauliflower until almost tender (about 5 minutes). Drain well. Mix broccoli, cauliflower, spinach, onion, green pepper, and cheese and put into a well-greased 10-inch pie plate. Top with hazelnuts. Beat together the milk, Bisquick, eggs, garlic salt, and pepper; pour over hazelnuts and vegetables. Bake at 400° for 35-40 minutes; let pie stand 5 minutes before cutting and serving.

*Ten ounce packages of frozen chopped broccoli, cauliflower, and spinach may be substituted for fresh. Thaw and drain well. Do NOT pre-cook.

Cooking with Love (Oregon)

Herb Roasted Vegetables

Vary this recipe by substituting whatever vegetables you have on hand!

1 red bell pepper, seeded, and cut into triangles

1 yellow bell pepper, seeded, and cut into triangles

2 medium-sized sweet onions, peeled and cut into 1-inch wedges

5 medium red potatoes, cut into 1-inch pieces

2 small zucchini and yellow squash, halved lengthwise and cut into 1-inch slices

½ cup grated Parmesan cheese (optional)

MARINADE:

2 tablespoons each: chopped fresh rosemary, thyme and parsley, or 1 tablespoon each dried

4–6 cloves garlic, minced

2 tablespoons olive oil

1 tablespoon balsamic vinegar

Place vegetables in a 9x13-inch roasting pan. Combine Marinade ingredients and toss with vegetables. Let stand for up to 2 hours and then bake, uncovered, at 400° for 30 minutes, stirring 3–4 times. Toss with Parmesan, if desired, and serve immediately. Serves 6–8.

Gold'n Delicious (Washington)

GARY TYLER

Giant vegetables are common in Alaska thanks to the extremely long days in summer—a summer's day in Alaska can last as long as 20 hours. Records at the State Fair as of 2007: Broccoli 39.50 pounds; Cabbage 105.60 pounds; Celery 63.30 pounds; Pumpkin 1,019.00 pounds; Squash 569.00 pounds; Sunflower (tallest) 16.75 feet. Editor Gwen McKee and husband Barney are amazed by the giant vegetables at the Alaska State Fair.

Stuffed Acorn Squash

1 acorn squash
Brown rice
1 small onion
1 cup sliced carrot
1 cup sliced celery
1 cup diced green pepper

¼ cup raisins
Curry powder
1 tablespoon cornstarch
½ cup water
Shredded coconut

Slice acorn squash in half and cook in microwave (about 6–8 minutes on high, covered). Cook a serving of brown rice, enough for 2. Stir-fry chopped onion, carrot, celery, and pepper. Add approximately ¼ cup raisins and curry powder to taste. Stir in cornstarch mixed with water. Mix rice and stir-fry together; fill hollows in squash. Serve excess filling on side.

Harvest Feast (Washington)

Tasty Whipped Squash

5 pounds Hubbard or
    butternut squash
2 tablespoons margarine
2 tablespoons brown sugar
⅓ cup golden raisins
½ teaspoon salt
¼ teaspoon nutmeg

⅛ teaspoon pepper
1 tablespoon margarine
1 tablespoon brown sugar
1 tablespoon light corn syrup
2 tablespoons pecans, finely
    chopped

Cut squash in halves lengthwise and remove seeds. Place cut-side-down in shallow baking pan; add ½ inch water. Cover and bake at 400° for 40–50 minutes or until tender. Drain, scoop out pulp, and discard shell.

Combine squash pulp, margarine, and brown sugar in a large bowl; beat with electric mixer until smooth. Spoon squash mixture into large saucepan; cook over medium heat 5 minutes, stirring often. Spoon squash into serving dish and keep warm. Combine remaining ingredients in a small saucepan; cook over medium heat until sugar dissolves, stirring constantly. Pour over squash. Serves 6–8.

Alaska Connections Cookbook III (Alaska)

Eggplant Parmesan

This is my specialty to cook. I make it all of the time. Sometimes I refrigerate the finished dish overnight and make a sandwich. It's delicious.

5 eggs
5 tablespoons water
2 or 3 large eggplants
Vegetable oil
Salt to taste
1 large jar spaghetti sauce
1 cup fresh Parmesan cheese

Beat eggs with water. Peel eggplant and slice about ¼ inch thick. Dip each eggplant slice in egg wash. Then fry in frying pan with vegetable oil until it is golden brown. May salt lightly. Place eggplant on paper towels to drain grease. When done with each slice, make casserole.

In a 9x13-inch casserole dish, pour a small amount of spaghetti sauce on bottom. Layer eggplant. Pour a little more sauce and lightly dust with cheese. Repeat layers until dish is full. Cover top with sauce and cheese. Bake in oven at 350° for 30 minutes. Serves 4–6.

Recipe by Rick Rizzs, Announcer, Seattle Mariners
Mariners Mix'n and Fix'n Grand Slam Style (Washington)

Baked Beans

1 pound hamburger
1 pound bacon
3 (16-ounce) cans pork and beans
1 (16-ounce) can lima beans, drained and rinsed
1 (16-ounce) can kidney beans, drained and rinsed
3 large onions, chopped
1 cup ketchup
½ cup white sugar
¾ cup brown sugar
2 tablespoons vinegar
1 teaspoon dry mustard

Brown hamburger and bacon; drain. Combine all ingredients in large baking dish and bake at 350° for 1 hour, or put into 5-quart crockpot and cook on high for 6 hours.

Sagebrush Surprises Cookbook (Oregon)

Fresh Corn Pudding

Fresh corn is the key to this simple pudding.

12 medium-size ears fresh
corn, shucked

About ⅔ cup milk or cream
as needed for curdled
cream consistency

Salt and freshly ground pepper
to taste

1–2 tablespoons sugar
(optional)

3–5 tablespoons butter

Preheat oven to 375°. Using a corn scraper (available in some super-markets and kitchenware stores) or a grater, scrape juice from kernels into a buttered baking dish. Add enough milk or cream to make the corn look like thick curdled cream (more is needed for old corn and winter corn). Add salt, pepper, and optional sugar (if corn is not fresh from the garden). Dot with butter. Bake 45 minutes to 1 hour, or until pudding is firm. Serves 4.

The Art Lover's Cookbook: A Feast for the Eye (California)

Sesame Asparagus

Tired of the butter, cheese, or hollandaise sauce usually served with asparagus? Try this for a change. It's tasty, and the combination of sesame seeds and bread crumbs will add valuable protein to your menu.

1 pound asparagus

3 tablespoons oil or butter

2 tablespoons sesame seeds

½ cup bread crumbs

Salt and pepper to taste

Cut off the bottom part of the asparagus stalks as necessary to remove any tough fiber. Slice them in 2-inch lengths and sauté in oil or butter until almost tender. Toast the sesame seeds by stirring them in a frying pan over fairly high heat. Then add a little oil or butter and the bread crumbs, and stir together until well blended. Pour this mixture over the hot asparagus, season with salt and pepper, and stir gently until the asparagus is well coated with the seeds and bread crumbs. Serve immediately. Serves 4.

Note: This does wonders for broccoli and cauliflower, too!

The 99¢ a Meal Cookbook (Washington)

Sweet and Sour Red Cabbage

At the west end of the Columbia Gorge situated on a high hill is Winters Farms, a family farm first begun in the 1940s by Howard and Ruth Winters. The Winters family grows an assortment of popular and unique berries along with many vegetables including green and wax beans, pickling and slicing cucumbers, sweet onions, beets, English peas, and sweet corn. Summer and winter squash, tomatoes, red and green cabbage and many herbs top the list. In addition to growing for the Beaverton and Portland Farmers' Markets, their wholesale customers and brokers remain an important part of their business. Their red cabbage is frequently requested at the market and so is this recipe.

4 cups red cabbage
1 tart apple
4 tablespoons butter
1 heaping tablespoon brown sugar
1 cup minced onions

6 tablespoons red wine vinegar
1 cup beef or chicken broth or water
1 teaspoon salt
½ cup red currant jelly

Wash, dry, and shred cabbage. Chop apple. Melt butter in a large frying pan and stir in brown sugar. Add apple and onions, cover, and cook over low heat for 4–5 minutes or until wilted. Stir in cabbage and vinegar, cover, and braise for 10 minutes.

Pour in broth or water and salt; cook, covered, over low heat for 2 hours (or bake in a preheated 300° oven for 2½ hours). Stir in jelly before serving. Depending on the freshness of the cabbage, cooking time can be reduced. Start checking texture after 1 hour of cooking. Makes 6 cups.

Oregon Farmers' Markets Cookbook and Guide (Oregon)

Oregon is the nation's leading producer of Christmas trees, growing more than eight million firs for holiday decorating.

Apple Cranberry Relish

1 can whole cranberry sauce
1 can frozen orange juice
1 large apple, chopped
½ cup chopped walnuts

1 tablespoon cinnamon
1 tablespoon ground cloves
1 cup grape wine

Combine all ingredients. Chill. Eat and enjoy. Serves 8–12.

Apples Etc. Cookbook (California)

Hot Fruit Casserole

1 (16-ounce) can pear halves
1 (16-ounce) can peach halves
1 (16-ounce) can apricot halves
1 (16-ounce) can sliced
   pineapple
1 (14-ounce) jar spiced apple
   rings

2 tablespoons flour
½ cup firmly packed brown
   sugar
¾ cup butter or margarine
1 cup dry sherry

Drain all fruits and cut pineapple slices in half. In a large 18x28-inch baking dish, arrange fruits in alternating layers, with apple rings on top.

Combine flour, sugar, butter, and sherry in top of a double boiler over simmering water and cook, stirring until mixture is thickened and smooth, about 10 minutes. Pour mixture over fruit, cover with plastic wrap, and let stand overnight in refrigerator.

Preheat oven to 350°. Place casserole in oven and bake until bubbly hot and slightly glazed on top, 20–30 minutes. Makes 12–14 servings.

Then 'til Now (Oregon)

PASTA, RICE, ETC.

The 605-foot-high, steel-and-glass Space Needle in Seattle was built for the 1962 World's Fair and still attracts over 1.3 million visitors a year. The revolving restaurant SkyCity™, atop the Space Needle, makes one complete revolution every 48 minutes. The Space Needle was designated a historic landmark on April 19, 1999.

Fettuccine with Walnuts and California Avocado

Prize winner at the California Avocado Festival.

2 tablespoons olive oil
½ cup diced sun-dried tomatoes
¼ cup sherry wine vinegar
½ cup chopped fresh basil
2 tablespoons chopped green onions
¼ cup diced green bell pepper

2 tablespoons chopped walnuts
1 California avocado, diced, divided
1¼ pounds dried fettuccine noodles (if not available, substitute any dried pasta)
Salt and pepper to taste

In a large bowl combine olive oil, sun-dried tomatoes, vinegar, basil, green onions, bell pepper, walnuts, and ½ the avocado. Toss ingredients well so they are evenly coated with oil and vinegar.

Cook pasta in boiling water for 3 minutes or until al dente. Drain pasta and pour into salad bowl with other ingredients while pasta is still hot. Toss all ingredients and serve immediately using remaining California avocado as garnish on top of pasta. Yields 6 servings.

Celebrating California (California)

Avocados were scarce in the United States until the 1920s when a mailman in southern California named Rudolph Haas figured out how to best grow them. Today, the most popular avocados in the U.S. are the "Haas" variety that come from California.

Halibut Fettuccine

1 (16-ounce) package
 fettuccine
1 pound halibut chunks
¼ cup butter or margarine
1 clove garlic, minced
¼ cup chopped green onions

1 cup whipping cream
½ cup dry vermouth
1 cup grated Parmesan cheese
½ cup chopped fresh parsley
¼ teaspoon pepper

Cook fettuccine to desired doneness according to package directions; drain and rinse with hot water. Rinse and drain halibut chunks, making sure they are cut into small uniform pieces.

In a large saucepan, melt butter or margarine; add garlic, onions, and halibut. Sauté over medium heat for 3–4 minutes, stirring constantly. Add whipping cream and vermouth; cook until thoroughly heated, about 1 minute. Immediately stir in cooked fettuccine; toss to coat with sauce. Cook over medium heat for 3–5 minutes, or until mixture thickens slightly, stirring constantly. Remove from heat. Stir in cheese, parsley, and pepper; toss to coat. Serve immediately.

Just for the Halibut (Alaska)

Crab Fettuccine

4 tablespoons butter
2 garlic cloves, minced
4 tablespoons flour
½ cup sherry or dry white
 wine
2 cups half-and-half

½ pound mushrooms, sliced
Butter for sautéing
⅓ cup Parmesan cheese
Salt and pepper
1 pound crabmeat
Cooked fettuccine

Melt 4 tablespoons butter in large skillet; add garlic and sauté until soft. Add flour and cook briefly. Gradually add sherry and half-and-half. Cook until sauce is smooth and thick; set aside. Sauté mushrooms in generous amount of butter. Add mushrooms and any juice to cream sauce. Stir in Parmesan cheese and add salt and pepper to taste. Gently fold in crabmeat. Heat through. Serve over freshly cooked fettuccine (your own or store bought). Serves 6.

A Taste of Oregon (Oregon)

Smoked Salmon Fettuccine

This eye-pleasing pasta dish uses smoked or cooked salmon in a tomato-cream sauce seasoned with basil and garlic.

1 (16-ounce) package
   fettuccine
5 tablespoons extra-virgin
   olive oil, divided
3 tablespoons pesto sauce
3 cloves garlic, minced
1 cup sliced mushrooms
4 Roma tomatoes, seeded and
   chopped

½ cup dry white wine
2 cups heavy cream
2 cups smoked salmon
1½ teaspoons dry basil or ¼
   cup chopped fresh basil
⅓ cup chopped fresh parsley
Salt and freshly ground pepper
   to taste
Parmesan cheese for garnish

In a large pot, cook pasta al dente, according to package directions. Drain and return to pot. Add 3 tablespoons oil and pesto sauce; toss to coat. Cover to keep warm.

Over medium heat in a large frying pan, heat remaining 2 tablespoons oil and sauté garlic about 1 minute; add mushrooms and cook about 5 minutes or until golden brown. Stir in tomatoes and wine and cook 2–3 minutes. Add cream and gently simmer to reduce, about 10 minutes. Do not boil.

Add salmon, basil, and parsley to sauce and heat through to blend flavors, about 5 minutes. Just before serving, salt and pepper to taste. Turn pasta onto individual heated plates and top with salmon sauce, garnish with cheese. Serve with additional Parmesan. Makes 6 servings.

San Juan Classics II Cookbook (Washington)

Thai Chicken Fettuccine

An entrée for a warm summer day. Serve with fruit and roll for a complete meal.

1 cup picante sauce
¼ cup peanut butter
2 tablespoons honey
¼ cup orange juice
1 teaspoon soy sauce
½ teaspoon ground ginger
12 ounces dry fettuccine,
  cooked and well drained
2 cups cooked chicken breast,
  cut in chunks (3 breasts)

Iceberg lettuce or savory
  cabbage leaves for garnish
¼ cup chopped cilantro
¼ cup chopped unsalted
  peanuts
¼ cup thinly sliced red bell
  pepper

Combine picante sauce, peanut butter, honey, orange juice, soy sauce, and ginger in small saucepan. Cook and stir over low heat until blended and smooth. Reserve ¼ cup picante sauce mixture; toss remaining mixture with hot cooked fettuccine. Mix reserved picante sauce mixture with cooked chicken pieces. Line large platter with lettuce leaves, if desired. Arrange fettuccine mixture over lettuce; top with chicken mixture. Sprinkle with cilantro, peanuts, and red bell pepper. Cool to room temperature before serving, or serve chilled. Serves 6.

Tastefully Oregon (Oregon)

Microwave Chicken Alfredo

8 ounces fettuccine noodles,
  uncooked
6 boneless chicken breast
  fillets
½ teaspoon garlic powder
4 tablespoons margarine
¼ cup finely chopped onion
2 cups sliced fresh mushrooms

3 tablespoons flour
1½ cups chicken broth
1½ cups half-and-half
¼ teaspoon nutmeg
¼ cup Parmesan cheese
¼ teaspoon salt
¼ teaspoon pepper
½ cup mozzarella cheese

Boil noodles for 10 minutes; drain. Sprinkle chicken breasts with garlic and cook 10–12 minutes on high in microwave. Slice into cubes after cooled. In baking dish, cook margarine, onions, and mushrooms for 3–4 minutes on high. Add flour and cook 1 more minute. Add remaining ingredients (except mozzarella cheese) and cook on high 10–12 minutes, or until sauce is boiling and thick. Stir in noodles and chicken. Cover with cheese. Serves 4.

Liberty Lake Community Cookbook (Washington)

Angel Hair Pasta with Tomatoes and Basil

This is a perfect side dish with baked salmon and makes a wonderful light entrée. If you reheat this dish, first add a little wine or water.

8 ounces angel hair pasta
1 teaspoon olive oil
2 cloves garlic, minced
½ cup dry white wine
2 tablespoons freshly
  squeezed lemon juice
2 cups chopped Roma
  tomatoes

½ cup chopped fresh basil, or
  2 tablespoons dried basil
  leaves
½ teaspoon (or less) Lite Salt
¼ teaspoon pepper
¼ cup grated Parmesan
  cheese

Cook pasta in unsalted water according to package directions. Meanwhile, heat olive oil and sauté garlic until golden brown. Add wine and cook 2 minutes. Stir in lemon juice and tomatoes. When pasta is done, drain and put into serving bowl. Add tomato mixture, basil, Lite Salt, and pepper. Toss. Sprinkle with Parmesan cheese just before serving. Makes 4 servings (1½ cups each).

The New American Diet Cookbook (Oregon)

Sun-Dried Tomatoes & Artichoke Pasta

1 (12- to 16-ounce) package
  mostacolli pasta
2 tablespoons olive oil
1 medium onion, chopped
2–4 cloves garlic, chopped
1 can artichoke hearts in
  water, drained

1 (8-ounce) jar sun-dried
  tomatoes in oil
½ cup bread crumbs
½ cup fresh parsley, chopped
  or ¼ cup dried
1 cup pasta water
Parmesan cheese

Cook pasta. While pasta is cooking, heat oil in large skillet; add onion and garlic. Cook until onion is soft; add artichokes, sun-dried tomatoes, bread crumbs, and parsley; heat through. Add 2 ladles of water pasta is cooking in, to artichoke mixture. Drain pasta and add to artichoke mixture. Transfer to serving dish; sprinkle with Parmesan cheese. Serves 10.

Tasty Temptations (California)

Pasta Capri—A Domenico's Original

Perhaps the most copied dish in Monterey!

½ pound linguini pasta
1 ounce olive oil
6 green onions
2 medium shallots
1 ripe tomato
6 ounces butter
12 ounces bay shrimp,
  cooked and peeled

½ cup black and green olives,
  pitted and chopped
½ cup sliced black olives
Freshly cracked black pepper
¼ cup dry white wine
Lemon and parsley for garnish

Cook pasta according to package instructions, in lightly salted, boiling water. Drain and toss lightly with olive oil. Chop onions and shallots coarsely. Dice tomato. Preheat a large, oiled sauté pan over high heat. Add butter, shrimp, tomato, and onions and sauté for 1 minute. Add shallots, olives, and black pepper and sauté for 1 minute. Add wine, reduce heat and simmer until creamy. Add more wine or pasta water if it becomes too dry. Place drained pasta in bowl and pour sauce on top of pasta. Garnish with sliced lemon and parsley. Serves 2.

Monterey's Cookin' Pisto Style (California)

The Hollywood Sign is a famous landmark in the Hollywood Hills area of Los Angeles, California, spelling out the name of the area in 50-feet-high white letters. The sign originally read "HOLLYWOODLAND," and its purpose was to advertise a new housing development. The sign was officially dedicated on July 13, 1923. It was not intended to be permanent, but garnered increasing recognition after its initial purpose had been fulfilled, and so it remained. The "land" came off in 1949, and the sign was completely restored in 1978.

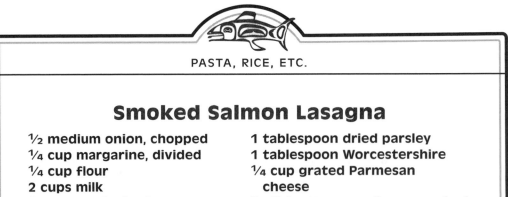

Smoked Salmon Lasagna

½ medium onion, chopped
¼ cup margarine, divided
¼ cup flour
2 cups milk
2 cups smoked salmon, crumbled
¼ teaspoon pepper, or to taste
1 pint cottage cheese

1 tablespoon dried parsley
1 tablespoon Worcestershire
¼ cup grated Parmesan cheese
9–12 lasagna noodles, uncooked (yes, uncooked)
½–¾ pound grated mozzarella cheese

Sauté the onion in ½ the margarine. Cook until onions are soft. Add remaining margarine, then blend in the flour and gradually add milk to make a sauce. Add smoked salmon and pepper. In a bowl, stir together cottage cheese, parsley, Worcestershire, and Parmesan cheese.

In a greased, 9x13x2-inch casserole dish, layer creamed fish mixture, cottage cheese mixture, uncooked lasagna. Then add mozzarella cheese. Repeat, ending with creamed fish mixture. Bake in a 350° oven for 45 minutes covered, and an additional 15 minutes uncovered.

Panhandle Pat's Fifty Years (Alaska)

Vegetable Lasagna

A low-fat pasta recipe with all the goodness of fresh farm produce for robust flavor.

2 teaspoons oil
3 cups chopped unpeeled eggplant
¾ cup chopped onion
1 teaspoon minced garlic
1 (28-ounce) can crushed tomatoes
½ teaspoon sugar
¼ teaspoon basil
1 pound carrots, peeled and shredded

1 (10-ounce) package thawed frozen spinach
15 ounces ricotta cheese
1 cup shredded part-skim mozzarella cheese
1 egg, well beaten
Dash each of salt and nutmeg
1 package lasagna noodles, cooked
Parmesan cheese

Heat oil in skillet over low heat. Stir in eggplant, onion, and garlic; sauté for 5 minutes. Stir in crushed tomatoes, sugar, and basil. Add a dash of salt to taste. Cover and simmer for 20 minutes or till eggplant is tender.

Meanwhile, boil 2 quarts water and cook carrots 3–5 minutes. Drain well and add spinach, ricotta cheese, mozzarella cheese, beaten egg, dash of salt and nutmeg. Add eggplant mixture and stir to combine—this is your sauce.

In a greased 9x13-inch baking dish, make layers of cooked noodles, then sauce, then repeat, ending with a last layer of sauce. Sprinkle Parmesan cheese on top. Bake at 350° for 30 minutes or till heated through. Serves 8–10.

Washington Farmers' Markets Cookbook and Guide (Washington)

Macaroni and Cheese

Everyone loves my macaroni and cheese. It is creamy and easy to make. A terrific potluck casserole. Very rich and yummy!

1 (7-ounce) package elbow
  macaroni
6 tablespoons butter, divided
3 tablespoons flour
2½ cups milk (can use part
  canned milk)
1 (8-ounce) package cream
  cheese

3 cups grated Cheddar cheese,
  divided
½ teaspoon salt
½ teaspoon pepper
1 cup dry bread crumbs

Cook macaroni until tender, as directed on package. Melt 4 tablespoons butter in saucepan. Stir in flour until smooth. Gradually add milk. Bring to a boil, stirring constantly. Add cream cheese, 2 cups Cheddar cheese, salt and pepper. Stir over low heat until cheeses are melted and mixture is smooth. Drain and rinse macaroni and mix cheese mixture into macaroni. Transfer to a greased casserole dish or 9x13-inch pan. Sprinkle remaining 1 cup Cheddar cheese on top. Melt remaining 2 tablespoons butter and add bread crumbs. Spread on top of cheese. Bake uncovered at 400° for 20–25 minutes or until golden brown.

Bounteous Blessings (Washington)

Sundried Tomato Pesto

Great as a pizza topping, on crackers with cream cheese, tossed into salads, or baked into bread dough. Try it in soups and stews, or even stir into pasta.

2 cups sun-dried tomatoes,
  packed in oil; drain and
  reserve oil
¾ cup oil, preferably olive oil
½ cup fresh rosemary
½ cup fresh parsley

½ cup fresh oregano
3–5 cloves garlic
½ cup pine nuts or walnuts
  (optional)
¾ cup shredded Parmesan
  cheese

Process all the above ingredients except for cheese in food processor until smooth. Add cheese, mix well, and refrigerate up to 2 days. Can also be frozen.

Washington Farmers' Markets Cookbook and Guide (Washington)

California Rice

A delicious rice dish, equally good with poultry or pork.

1 cup short-grain brown rice
2 cups chicken stock
1 cup Riesling or Chenin Blanc, divided
1 teaspoon salt
3 tablespoons butter, divided
¾ cup slivered dried apricots
¾ cup quartered pitted prunes
1 cup chopped celery
1 cup chopped onions
2 teaspoons crumbled dried sweet basil
½ teaspoon crumbled thyme
¾ cup coarsely chopped walnuts, lightly toasted
¼ cup chopped parsley

In a 3-quart saucepan with a tight-fitting lid, combine rice, chicken stock, ½ cup of the wine, salt, and 1 tablespoon butter. Bring to a boil. Lower heat until liquid is just simmering. Cover and simmer about 1 hour without removing lid. When liquid has evaporated, remove from heat and allow to steam, covered, for 10–15 minutes. Fluff rice with fork.

Meanwhile, place apricots in small pot. Top with prunes and remaining ½ cup of wine, and bring to a boil. Remove from heat and set aside to cool. Melt remaining 2 tablespoons butter in skillet. Add celery, onions, basil and thyme. Sauté over medium heat for 5 minutes. Add to rice, along with cooled fruits, walnuts and parsley. Toss well to combine. Spoon into buttered baking dish, cover, and heat in 325° oven for 30 minutes before serving. Serves 8.

California Wine Country Herbs and Spices Cookbook (California)

Margarita Pizza

¼ cup frozen orange juice
   concentrate, thawed
¼ cup tequila
¼ cup fresh lime juice
2 cloves garlic, crushed
1 teaspoon dried oregano
⅛ teaspoon ground red
   pepper
Salt and black pepper to taste

2 cups cubed chicken breasts
1 tablespoon olive oil
1 unbaked homemade or
   commercial pizza crust
1 cup shredded mozzarella
   cheese
Extra virgin olive oil
Orange Salsa

Combine orange juice concentrate, tequila, lime juice, garlic, oregano, red pepper, salt and black pepper in a bowl and mix well. Add chicken and mix to coat. Marinate, covered, in refrigerator for 4 hours to overnight. Drain chicken and discard marinade. Sauté chicken in 1 tablespoon olive oil on medium heat until cooked through. Spread over pizza crust and sprinkle with cheese. Drizzle desired amount of extra virgin olive oil over top. Bake according to pizza crust requirements. Garnish with chopped fresh cilantro and lime wedges. Serve with Orange Salsa.

ORANGE SALSA:

1 whole orange
6 tablespoons finely chopped
   red onion
4 tablespoons chopped fresh
   cilantro

2 tablespoons fresh lime juice
2 tablespoons olive oil
½ teaspoon dried oregano
Salt to taste

Peel and seed orange and chop into ½-inch pieces. Combine orange, red onion, cilantro, lime juice, olive oil, oregano, and salt in a small bowl and mix well. Refrigerate, covered, 2 hours or longer. Use as additional garnish or topping for pizza. Yields 6 servings.

La Jolla Cooks Again (California)

Oregon Crab Quiche

This simple quiche is so elegant; good at any time, but try it for a special luncheon. It's also a splendid way to stretch and share a small amount of expensive crabmeat.

1 cup (4 ounces) shredded natural Swiss cheese
1 (9-inch) pastry shell, unbaked
½ pound fresh Dungeness crabmeat, flaked, or 1 (7½-ounce) can crabmeat, drained and flaked
2 fresh green onions (including tops), sliced

3 eggs, beaten
1 cup light cream or half-and-half
½ teaspoon salt
½ teaspoon grated lemon peel
¼ teaspoon dry mustard
Dash of mace
¼ cup sliced almonds

Sprinkle cheese evenly over bottom of pastry shell. Spread crabmeat over cheese; sprinkle green onions over crabmeat.

Combine beaten eggs, cream, and seasonings; pour over all. Sprinkle top with sliced almonds. Bake at 325° for about 45 minutes or until set (when knife blade inserted in center comes out clean). Remove from oven and let stand for 10 minutes before cutting and serving.

Begged, Borrowed and Stöllen Recipes (Oregon)

LIGHTHOUSEGETAWAY.COM

The Yaquina Head Lighthouse is Oregon's tallest lighthouse. The 93-foot tower is located on a narrow point of land jutting due west into the Pacific Ocean north of Newport, at Yaquina Head Outstanding Natural Area. Winds and rain have buffeted this lighthouse since its construction in 1873.

Broccoli Salmon Quiche

1 (9-inch) pie crust
2 cups fresh broccoli, cut in
   florets
1 (16-ounce) can salmon
   (or leftover cooked salmon,
   if available)

1 cup shredded Swiss cheese
¼ cup chopped, fresh chives
5 eggs, beaten
1 cup heavy whipping cream
¼ teaspoon cayenne pepper
1 teaspoon dried dill weed

Preheat oven to 350°. Prepare bottom of 9-inch deep pie dish by spraying with nonstick cooking spray. Line with pie pastry. Cover bottom of dish with broccoli florets, chunks of salmon, and sprinkle with cheese and chives. Set aside. In medium bowl, beat eggs, whipping cream, cayenne, and dill until thoroughly combined. Bake in preheated oven for 1 hour, or until crust and eggs are lightly browned, and quiche is puffy in center. Yields 6 servings.

Alaska's Gourmet Breakfasts (Alaska)

Pesto Quiche

Traditional egg pie with an Italian touch.

1 (9-inch) unbaked pie shell
2 cups shredded mozzarella,
   divided
¾ cups ready-made pesto

½ cup sun-dried tomatoes
4 eggs
1½ cups milk

In unbaked pie shell, layer 1 cup mozzarella, pesto, sun-dried tomatoes and then remaining cheese. Blend together eggs and milk. Pour batter over top of tomato/cheese mixture. Bake at 400° for 10 minutes, or until crust is lightly browned. Reduce temperature to 300° and bake until quiche is set and knife comes out clean.

The Colophon Cafe Best Recipes (Washington)

MEATS

Mount McKinley, the highest mountain in North America at 20,320 feet, provides a stunning background for a large bull moose in Denali National Park. Denali, the "High One," is the name the native Athabascan people gave the massive, snow-covered peak that crowns the 400-mile-long Alaska Range.

Polynesian Style Brisket

Polynesian flavors seem to blend perfectly in this brisket recipe. This is a wonderful dinner for company, as it cooks without any fuss in the oven. It may even be made a day ahead. This method of cooking with a foil cover keeps all the flavorful juices captured inside the pan. Just be sure to carefully tuck the foil around the pan so you retain a sealed cover without any breaks. You might want to double the recipe and have an extra brisket for a picnic. It is also marvelous cold.

1 (4- to 5-pound) beef brisket
1 cup soy sauce
½ cup dry sherry
½ cup brown sugar
1 cup orange, lemon, or
 pineapple juice
2 cloves garlic, peeled and
 minced

Salt and pepper to taste
2 tablespoons freshly grated
 ginger (or 1 tablespoon
 dried)
1 cup fresh or canned
 pineapple, diced (for garnish)

Place brisket in a bowl or shallow pan. Mix together remaining ingredients, except garnish, and pour over the brisket. Make sure all parts of the meat are covered. Refrigerate at least 4 hours, or preferably overnight.

Place brisket in a baking pan with marinade. Cover tightly with a double layer of foil. Bake at 325° for 3½ hours. Check during baking to make sure there is enough liquid; if not, add extra soy sauce or fruit juice, being sure to replace the foil tightly.

To serve, remove meat from juices. Slice and serve with warmed pan juices and pineapple on top. This will serve 4–5. In Honolulu, rice is usually served with the brisket.

Honolulu Hawaii Cooking (Hawaii)

In 1978, Hawaiian was made an official language of the state of Hawaii. In 1990, the United States government established a policy recognizing the right of Hawaii to preserve, use, and support its indigenous language. Hawai'i is the only state to officially recognize a native language.

Beef Brisket

Garlic powder
1 (4- to 5-pound) beef brisket
Onion, sliced
1 bottle Heinz Chili Sauce
½ cup cider vinegar
8 tablespoons brown sugar
2 cups water

Sprinkle garlic powder on brisket. Mix remaining ingredients together and pour over roast. Bake at 350° for 3 hours. One hour before roast is done, put in refrigerator for about an hour, then slice. Return slices to pan with juices and cook additional hour.

Crime Stoppers: A Community Cookbook (Washington)

Killer Flank Steak

This is a deliciously different soy-based marinade.

1 (2-pound) flank steak,
  trimmed of fat
¼ cup soy sauce
¼ cup olive oil
½ tablespoon dried Italian
  seasoning
1 tablespoon lemon juice
2 cloves garlic, minced

Place steak in a covered container or ziploc bag. Combine remaining ingredients and pour over steak. Marinate at least 20 minutes at room temperature or up to 24 hours in the refrigerator, turning occasionally.

   Grill over medium coals for 6 minutes. Turn and grill for an additional 6–8 minutes or until cooked to desired doneness. Slice thinly on the diagonal. Serves 4.

Gold'n Delicious (Washington)

Steak Sandwich with Avocado Salsa and Roasted Peppers

¼ cup plus 1 tablespoon
  olive oil
2 large garlic cloves, minced
2 teaspoons dried oregano
2 teaspoons ground cumin
1 (2-pound) flank steak
Salt and pepper
2 firm but ripe avocados,
  pitted, peeled and chopped

1 (16-ounce) container thick
  chunky salsa, well drained
1 (10- to 12-inch) round loaf
  sourdough bread
1 (7-ounce jar) roasted red bell
  peppers, drained, thinly sliced
7 ounces thinly sliced Monterey
  Jack or provolone cheese

Prepare barbecue (medium-high heat) or preheat broiler. Combine ¼ cup olive oil, garlic, oregano and cumin in a small bowl. Rub mixture over both sides of steak. Sprinkle steak with salt and pepper. Grill or broil to desired doneness, about 5 minutes per side for medium-rare. Transfer steak to work surface. Cool. Cut steak across grain into thin strips.

Toss chopped avocados with salsa in medium bowl. Season salsa with salt and pepper.

Using a serrated knife, split bread loaf in half lengthwise. Scoop out bread from center of each half, leaving 1-inch thick layer of bread and crust intact. Brush cut surface with remaining 1 tablespoon olive oil. Arrange steak slices in hollow of bottom half of bread. Arrange bell peppers over steak. Arrange cheese over peppers. Spoon avocado salsa over cheese. Top with second half of bread. Wrap sandwich in foil and refrigerate at least 4 hours and up to 8 hours. Cut sandwiches into wedges and serve. Serves 6–8.

Symphony of Flavors (California)

Walla Walla Steak Sandwich
with Horseradish Sauce

2 pounds flank steak

MARINADE:

¾ cup beer	½ teaspoon black pepper
¼ cup olive oil	2 cloves garlic, minced
1 teaspoon salt	¼ teaspoon crushed red pepper

Trim steak of fat and score both sides. Place in a covered container or ziploc bag. Combine Marinade ingredients and add to steak. Refrigerate for 4–24 hours, turning occasionally.

ONIONS:

3 tablespoons butter	6 cups Walla Walla sweet onions,
¾ teaspoon paprika	sliced into ¼-inch rings

Melt butter in large skillet over medium-low heat. Add paprika and onions and sauté until onions are tender, 20–25 minutes. Keep warm until ready to serve.

HORSERADISH SAUCE:

1 cup sour cream	¼ teaspoon salt
2 tablespoons horseradish	⅛ teaspoon paprika
1 tablespoon parsley	

Combine sauce ingredients in a small saucepan and cook over low heat until thoroughly heated, about 7 minutes. Keep warm until ready to serve.

Remove steak from Marinade and grill or broil about 5 minutes per side or until steak reaches desired degree of doneness. Slice steak thinly on the diagonal and keep warm until ready to serve.

ROLLS:

¼ cup butter, softened	6 French rolls, split
1 tablespoon Italian herb seasoning	

Combine butter and Italian seasoning and spread on rolls. Toast rolls briefly under broiler. To serve, place steak on rolls, then top with Onions and Horseradish Sauce. Serves 6.

Note: If you can't find Walla Walla sweets, substitute Vidalia or Maui onions. Be sure to sauté them slowly over low heat to bring out their natural sweetness.

Gold'n Delicious (Washington)

Round Steak Pasties

1 cup shortening
3 cups flour
1 teaspoon salt
½ teaspoon baking powder
About ⅔ cup cold water
1–1½ pounds round steak, cubed
2 cups diced potatoes
2 cups diced carrots
½ cup chopped celery
½ cup chopped onion
Salt and pepper to taste
6 tablespoons water
6 teaspoons butter

Cut shortening into dry ingredients. Add water. Mix. Divide dough into 6 (8-inch) circles (roll). Combine round steak with diced potatoes, carrots, celery, and onion; season to taste. Divide meat and vegetable mixture over the 6 circles. Brush edges of pastry circles with water. Fold into semicircles and seal edges. Cut ½-inch slits on top. Place on cookie sheet. Pour about 1 tablespoon of water into each pastie through slit. Also add about 1 teaspoon butter. Bake about 1 hour; bake at 450° for first 10 minutes, reduce heat to 350° to finish. Serve with gravy or ketchup.

Favorite Recipes from Our Best Cooks (Washington)

Round Steak Sauerbraten

1½ pounds round steak
1 tablespoon oil
1 package brown gravy mix
2 cups water
1 onion, sliced
1 tablespoon brown sugar
1 tablespoon wine vinegar
1 teaspoon Worcestershire
¼ teaspoon ground ginger
1 bay leaf
½ teaspoon salt
¼ teaspoon pepper

Cut meat into 1-inch pieces each, about ½ inch thick. Brown in hot oil, then remove from pan. Add gravy mix and water, and bring to a boil, stirring constantly. Add onion, brown sugar, vinegar, Worcestershire, and seasonings. Add meat and mix well. Turn into 1½-quart casserole. Cover and bake 1½ hours at 350°. Remove bay leaf and serve with noodles. Serves 6–8.

Note: Can be made the day before and just heated up.

Manna by the Sea (Oregon)

California Tri-Tip

Tri-tip is California's own cut of beef and it's become a popular one. Tri-tip is the popular name for the triangle tip, part of the bottom sirloin. Barbecued whole is a popular way to serve tri-tip, which is smaller than most roasts we're accustomed to seeing in markets.

2 (2-pound) whole beef tri-tips
1¼ cups beef broth
⅔ cup lime juice
½ cup olive oil
2 tablespoons dried cumin

2 tablespoons dried coriander
5 garlic cloves, minced
Vegetable oil
Salt and freshly ground pepper

Remove all fat from tri-tips. Make marinade by whisking broth with lime juice, olive oil, cumin, coriander and garlic until well blended. Place tri-tips in glass baking dish. Pour marinade over beef and cover. Refrigerate at least 6 hours, no longer than 24.

Remove tri-tips from marinade. Barbecue over medium-hot coals, turning occasionally, about 1 hour for medium-rare or until desired doneness. Use a meat thermometer or instant-read thermometer to be certain meat is cooked the way you want it. Brush meat with oil frequently while barbecuing. To serve, cut across the grain into thin slices; season with salt and pepper. Yields 12 servings.

Jan Townsend Going Home (California)

The Golden Gate Bridge is a suspension bridge spanning the Golden Gate, the opening of the San Francisco Bay onto the Pacific Ocean. The bridge was the longest suspension bridge span in the world when it was completed in 1937, and has become an internationally recognized symbol of San Francisco and California. Often shrouded in a thick fog, the Golden Gate Bridge sways 27 feet to withstand winds of up to 100 miles per hour. Its two great cables contain enough strands of steel wire (about 80,000 miles) to encircle the equator three times, and the concrete poured into its piers and anchorages would pave a five-foot sidewalk from New York to San Francisco.

Beef in Walnut Sauce

A crockpot recipe.

4 pounds rump roast, cubed	1 whole cinnamon stick
Seasoned flour	8 whole cloves
Olive oil (about 3 tablespoons)	8 whole allspice
½ cup water	1 cup ground walnuts
1 (8-ounce) can tomato sauce	1 tablespoon lemon juice
4–6 cloves garlic, minced	Sliced sourdough French bread,
⅓ cup cider vinegar	toasted

Dredge meat in seasoned flour. Shake off excess. Heat oil in large frying pan. Brown meat well. Transfer to crockpot. Pour water into frying pan to loosen drippings. Add to crockpot with tomato sauce, garlic and vinegar. Place cinnamon stick, cloves and allspice in a tea ball of cheesecloth. Add to pot. Cover. Cook on LOW (200°) for 8–10 hours. Add walnuts and lemon juice. Serve over toasted French bread slices. Serves 8–10.

Treasured Recipes (California)

Barbecued Beef Cubes

1 pound beef cubes	1 (10-ounce) can tomato soup
2½ tablespoons flour	½ cup water
Dash of pepper	1 tablespoon vinegar
¼ cup chopped onion	½ teaspoon Worcestershire
1½ teaspoons brown sugar	Dash of Tabasco
½ teaspoon chili powder	3 cups cooked rice
½ teaspoon dry mustard	

Dredge beef cubes in flour seasoned with pepper. Brown meat in large skillet; add onion. Combine brown sugar, chili powder, dry mustard, tomato soup, water, vinegar, Worcestershire, and Tabasco. Pour over meat mixture. Bring to a boil. Cover. Cook over low heat or in a 350° oven for 1½ hours or until tender. Stir occasionally during cooking time. Serve over cooked rice. Makes 3–4 servings.

Look What's Cooking (Oregon)

Hawaiian Teriyaki Burger

This is definitely a local favorite.

1½ pounds ground beef
1 small onion, chopped
1 egg
¼ cup shoyu (soy sauce)
¼ cup sugar

2 cloves garlic, minced
½ teaspoon minced fresh ginger
2 stalks green onions, chopped
1 tablespoon sesame oil

Combine all ingredients; mix well. Form into patties. Fry, grill, or broil.

Hawai'i's Best Local Dishes (Hawaii)

Stuffed Burgers

1½ pounds lean ground beef

Divide beef into 8 parts and shape into patties (do not squeeze all the juice from the beef).

FILLING:
1 (2¼-ounce) can chopped black olives
1 green pepper, chopped
1 cup grated Cheddar cheese
1 small bunch green onions, chopped (including tops)

2 tablespoons mayonnaise
Hamburger buns and condiments

In a bowl mix together all ingredients except buns and condiments. Place a generous portion of filling on top of 4 single patties. Cover each with the remaining 4 patties, pressing the edges of each to secure the filling. Grill, barbeque, or broil the burgers to desired doneness.

Serve each Stuffed Burger on large hamburger buns with assorted condiments. Serves 4.

Simply Whidbey (Washington)

Make-Ahead Barbecued Meatballs

These are so handy to have in the freezer for unexpected company or a quick meal anytime.

MEATBALLS:

3 pounds ground beef
1 cup quick oats
1 cup cracker crumbs
½ cup chopped onion
1 (12-ounce) can evaporated milk

2 eggs
2 teaspoons chili powder
½ teaspoon garlic powder
2 teaspoons (or less) salt
½ teaspoon pepper

Combine all ingredients (mixture will be soft) and shape into walnut-size balls. Arrange in a single layer on wax paper-lined cookie sheets. Freeze until solid and store frozen Meatballs in freezer bags. Makes 80 Meatballs.

BARBECUE SAUCE:

2 cups ketchup
½ teaspoon liquid smoke
¼ cup chopped onion

1 cup brown sugar
½ teaspoon garlic powder

Combine all ingredients and stir until sugar dissolves. To serve, place 20–30 Meatballs in a 9x13-inch pan and pour Sauce over Meatballs. Bake at 350° for 1 hour.

Note: These are very versatile and may be added to spaghetti sauce and simmered until done, or cooked with a mushroom soup sauce in the oven and served with mashed potatoes.

Then 'til Now (Oregon)

ADVENTUREPIX.COM

Crater Lake, Oregon, is the nation's clearest, deepest lake at 1,932 feet. Its "crystal-blue-ness" is phenomenal on sunny days and extraordinary in winter when the rim is covered with snow. Lake Tahoe, located along the border between California and Nevada, is America's second-deepest lake at 1,645 feet.

Nana's Meatballs

These are the best meatballs I've ever had. My mother-in-law always makes them for me when I'm home or when she visits.

½ pound ground Italian
  sausage (mild)
¼ pound ground veal
¼ pound ground pork
1 pound lean ground beef
2 eggs, beaten
¼ cup chopped parsley
½ cup Parmesan cheese
1 cup Italian seasoned bread
  crumbs
Garlic salt and oregano to taste
2 (15½-ounce) jars spaghetti
  sauce
1 pound pasta, cooked

Mix all ingredients together (with your hands) except pasta. Shape into baseball-sized balls. Put in a large pot and cover with 2 jars of your favorite spaghetti sauce. Bring to a boil and quickly reduce heat to low and simmer for about 4 hours. Check to make sure meatballs aren't sticking to the bottom of the pot. Cook your favorite pasta. Drain and put on a dish. Arrange meatballs around the pasta and pour sauce on top. Sprinkle with some Parmesan cheese. Makes 12 large meatballs.

Recipe by Jamie Moyer, Pitcher, Seattle Mariners
Home Plates (Washington)

Sweet-Sour Meat Loaf

1 (15-ounce) can tomato sauce
½ cup brown sugar
¼ cup vinegar
1 teaspoon prepared mustard
2 pounds ground beef
1 pound pork or veal (or all
  ground beef)
2 eggs, slightly beaten
2 small onions, chopped
½ cup fine soft bread crumbs
1 tablespoon salt
½ teaspoon pepper

Mix the first 4 ingredients until thoroughly blended. Set aside. Combine remaining ingredients in large mixing bowl. Mix 1 cup of sauce into meat mixture. Bake at 350° for 1 hour (maybe a little longer). Baste after 30 minutes with ¼ cup sauce. Heat remaining sauce and pour over meat loaf at serving time.

A Taste of Tillamook (Oregon)

Lasagna in a Bun

8 sub or hoagie buns or round
  French bread
1 pound ground beef
1 large onion, chopped
1 cup spaghetti sauce
1 tablespoon garlic powder
1 tablespoon dried Italian
  seasoning

1 cup ricotta cheese
¼ cup grated Parmesan cheese
1 cup (4 ounces) shredded
  Cheddar, divided
1 cup (4 ounces) shredded
  mozzarella, divided

Cut thin layer off top of buns or bread. Hollow out centers, leaving ¼-inch-thick shells. Discard tops and centers. Brown ground beef and onion; drain. Add spaghetti sauce, garlic powder and Italian seasoning. Cook 4 or 5 minutes.

Combine ricotta, Parmesan, ½ Cheddar and ½ mozzarella cheese. Spoon meat mixture into buns. Top with cheese mixture. Place on baking sheet. Cover loosely with foil and bake at 350° for 25 minutes. Uncover; sprinkle with remaining cheeses. Bake 2 or 3 minutes more. Makes 8 servings.

New Covenant Kitchens (California)

The Pacific Ocean is the deepest of the world's five oceans with an average depth 13,215 feet. It is also the largest, covering approximately one-third of the earth's surface—more surface area than all the continents combined. It is commonly divided at the Equator into the North Pacific and the South Pacific. Several different species of whale live in the Pacific Ocean, including the bowhead whale, pacific gray whale, humpback whale, and orcas (killer whales), as well as many species of dolphins.

Lazy Loco Moco

1 tablespoon oil
1 pound ground beef
1 clove garlic, minced
3 tablespoons shoyu
  (soy sauce)
2 stalks green onions,
  chopped

1 cup hot water
2 tablespoons cornstarch
2 tablespoons cold water
4 eggs
3 cups hot cooked rice

In a large skillet, heat oil and brown beef with the garlic. Add shoyu, green onions, and hot water. Let mixture come to a boil and cook 2–3 minutes. Mix cornstarch with cold water and add to the beef mixture. Cook until sauce thickens. Reduce heat to simmer.

Using a large spoon, make 4 holes in the beef mixture and break an egg into each hole. Cover and cook until eggs are cooked the way you like them. Serve the beef-egg mixture over hot rice. Serves 4.

Aunty Pua's Keiki Cookbook (Hawaii)

Easy Enchilada Pie

1 pound lean ground beef
1 small onion, chopped
1 (8-ounce) can tomato sauce
1 (1¼-ounce) package taco
  seasoning mix
1 (10¾-ounce) can condensed
  cream of chicken soup

½ cup milk (can use skim milk)
12 (6-inch) corn tortillas
8 ounces shredded Cheddar
  cheese (2 cups)

In a large skillet, brown ground beef and chopped onion. Drain off fat. Stir in tomato sauce and taco seasoning. Bring mixture to a boil. Reduce heat and simmer, uncovered, 5 minutes. Remove skillet from heat.

Stir together soup and milk. Spoon ½ soup mixture into a 9x13x2-inch baking dish. Cut tortillas in half. Use 12 halves to place over soup in dish. Spoon meat mixture over tortillas. Top with remaining tortillas and soup, then with cheese. Bake in a 350° oven for 30 minutes or until heated through. Serves 6–8.

Nuggets, Nibbles and Nostalgia (California)

Slow-Cooked Pork with Wine Sauce

2 pounds boneless pork
  (shoulder or butt)
½ tablespoon sugar
½ cup light soy sauce
¼ cup water
½ teaspoon black pepper
¼ cup dry sherry
½ teaspoon freshly grated
  ginger
2 green onions, chopped
2 cloves garlic, crushed

Mix all ingredients except pork. Place pork in ovenproof casserole dish (large enough to hold meat so it is covered by sauce). Pour sauce over pork; cover and bake at 275° for 6 hours.

San Ramon's Secret Recipes (California)

Oven Kalua Pig

2 tablespoons Hawaiian salt
¼ cup soy sauce
1 teaspoon Worcestershire
2 cloves garlic, crushed
1 (½-inch) slice ginger, crushed
1 tablespoon liquid smoke
1 (4- to 5-pound) pork butt
Ti or banana leaves

Mix together salt, soy sauce, Worcestershire, garlic, ginger, and liquid smoke. Place pork on several ti or banana leaves. Rub with seasonings and let stand one hour. Fold leaves over to wrap the pork. Wrap the leaf-enclosed pork in foil. Place in a baking pan and bake in a 325° oven for 4–5 hours. Unwrap pork, cool, and shred meat. Serves 8–10.

Ethnic Foods of Hawai'i (Hawaii)

Korean Ribs

¾ cup shoyu (soy sauce)
2 tablespoons water
4 tablespoons sherry
½ teaspoon sesame oil
3 tablespoons brown sugar
2 teaspoons minced garlic
¼ teaspoon ginger
2 tablespoons minced green onion
1 tablespoon sesame seeds
3 pounds short ribs

Combine all ingredients except short ribs, mixing well. Add ribs to marinade and allow to marinate for several hours. Broil ribs, basting frequently.

Tailgate Party Cookbook (Hawaii)

Barbecued Short Ribs

5 pounds meaty short ribs, cut in 2-inch pieces
Salt and pepper to taste
Flour
2 medium onions, sliced
2 teaspoons vinegar
2 tablespoons Worcestershire
1 tablespoon salt
1 teaspoon paprika
1 teaspoon chili powder
¾ cup tomato catsup
½ teaspoon cayenne pepper
½ teaspoon black pepper (optional)
¾ cup water

Sprinkle short ribs with salt and pepper to taste; dredge in flour. Place in a roaster and cover with onions. Combine remaining ingredients; mix well and pour over short ribs. Cover and bake at 350° for 3 hours, basting occasionally, and turning meat over once or twice during baking. Remove cover during last 15 minutes of baking. Serves 6–8.

Note: This can be cooked a day or two ahead and refrigerated. Remove and discard solidified grease before reheating to serve.

The Tastes and Tales of Moiliili (Hawaii)

Tropic Sun Spareribs

3–4 pounds spareribs or
  country-style ribs
3 large cloves garlic, pressed
Salt and pepper
1 large onion, sliced
¼ cup water

1 (20-ounce) can crushed
  pineapple, undrained
1 (12-ounce) bottle chili sauce
½ cup brown sugar, packed
1 teaspoon ground ginger
½ teaspoon dry mustard

Rub ribs with garlic. Sprinkle with salt and pepper. Arrange onion in large baking pan. Place ribs on top. Add ¼ cup water to pan. Cover with foil. Bake in a 350° oven for 1½ hours. Combine remaining ingredients. Spoon over ribs. Bake, uncovered, 1 hour longer. Serves 4.

...Fire Burn & Cauldron Bubble (California)

Pork Chops à la Rogue

An appropriate main course for an elegant dinner.

8 pork chops
½ teaspoon oil
Salt and pepper
6 fresh pears, peeled, halved
  and cored
3 tablespoons orange juice
¼ cup firmly packed brown
  sugar

¼ teaspoon cinnamon
⅓ cup dry sherry
1½ tablespoons butter or
  margarine
1 teaspoon cornstarch
1 tablespoon water

Preheat oven to 350°. In a skillet, over medium heat, brown pork chops in oil. Place pork chops in shallow pan; sprinkle with salt and pepper. Place pears rounded-side-down on and around pork chops. Pour orange juice over all; sprinkle with brown sugar and cinnamon. Pour sherry over all. Divide butter and place in hollows of pears. Cover and bake 20 minutes. Continue baking uncovered for an additional 20 minutes.

    Remove from oven and place pears and pork chops in a warm serving dish. Dissolve cornstarch in water, add to juices in pan, and cook until mixture thickens. Pour over chops and pears. Yields 6–8 servings.

Rogue River Rendezvous (Oregon)

Margaret's Sesame Pork Chops

6 pork chops
¼ cup soy sauce
1 tablespoon ketchup
¼ teaspoon ground ginger
⅛ teaspoon pepper

½ cup water
3 tablespoons honey
1 small onion, finely chopped
1 tablespoon sesame seeds,
   toasted

Brown chops in a small amount of fat. Place in a 9x13-inch pan. (Do not salt.) Combine soy sauce, ketchup, ginger, pepper, water, honey, and chopped onion. Pour over chops and sprinkle with sesame seeds. Cover and bake 1 hour at 325°.

Christian Bakers Cookbook (Oregon)

Spiced Pork Chops

A make-ahead recipe.

¼ cup flour
½ teaspoon dry mustard
¼ teaspoon pepper
⅛ teaspoon ground allspice
4 pork chops, cut 1 inch thick

2 tablespoons oil
1½ cups apple juice
2 tablespoons brown sugar
½ teaspoon cinnamon
2 apples, peeled and sliced

Combine flour, dry mustard, pepper, and allspice. Dredge pork chops in mixture, reserving remaining flour mixture. In skillet, brown chops in oil; remove and keep warm. To drippings add apple juice, brown sugar, and remaining flour mixture. Cook and stir until bubbly. Return pork chops to skillet, and sprinkle with cinnamon. Pour juice mixture over all. Cover and simmer for about 60 minutes until pork is no longer pink. Add apples during the last 20 minutes of cooking. Cool and place in Ziploc bag to freeze.

Thaw. Arrange in baking dish sprayed with nonstick spray. Bake covered at 350° until fully heated and bubbly. Serves 4.

Note: Ham slices can be a yummy replacement for the pork chops.

What's for Dinner? (Oregon)

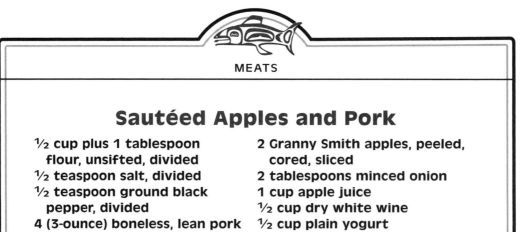

Sautéed Apples and Pork

½ cup plus 1 tablespoon
  flour, unsifted, divided
½ teaspoon salt, divided
½ teaspoon ground black
  pepper, divided
4 (3-ounce) boneless, lean pork
  steaks
3 tablespoons butter or
  margarine, divided
2 tablespoons vegetable oil

2 Granny Smith apples, peeled,
  cored, sliced
2 tablespoons minced onion
1 cup apple juice
½ cup dry white wine
½ cup plain yogurt
2 tablespoons Dijon mustard
¼ teaspoon dried thyme
  leaves

In pie plate or shallow dish, combine ½ cup flour, ¼ teaspoon salt, and ¼ teaspoon pepper; mix well. Dredge pork steaks in flour mixture to coat lightly. In large skillet, heat 2 tablespoons butter and the oil over medium heat; add pork and cook until brown on both sides and juices run clear. Remove pork to heated platter and reserve.

Add remaining butter to skillet, sauté apples and onions until both are tender. Remove to platter with pork. Add apple juice and wine to skillet; simmer 5 minutes. Combine yogurt, mustard, thyme, and remaining flour, salt and pepper; stir into juice mixture. Simmer 5 minutes, stirring until smooth. Spoon sauce over pork steaks and apples and serve. Serves 4.

Recipe by Washington Apple Commission, Wenatchee
Washington Cook Book (Washington)

U.S. NATIONAL OCEANIC AND
ATMOSPHERIC ADMINISTRATION

Cape Flattery on Washington's Olympic Peninsula is the northwestern most point in the contiguous United States. Neah Bay, Washington, is the closest town to the cape.

Veal Marsala

6 veal cutlets, medium-thick
    slices of range-fed veal
2 cups seasoned bread crumbs
2 tablespoons extra virgin
    olive oil

2 tablespoons unsalted butter
Salt and pepper to taste
1 lemon, cut in wedges
4 sprigs Italian flat-leaf parsley

Prepare veal by sprinkling with water. Then cover each cutlet with plastic wrap and pound lightly. Unwrap and rub each cutlet with a drop or two of olive oil. Dredge cutlets in bread crumbs, pressing hard so they adhere to the meat.

Heat a skillet, and add olive oil, butter, salt and pepper. Place coated veal chops three at a time in skillet. Cook veal chops for 4–6 minutes on each side over medium-high heat. Clean skillet after each batch to avoid charred bread crumbs.

Serve veal chops on plate with Mushroom Marsala Sauce drizzled over top and along sides. Garnish with lemon and sprigs of flat-leaf parsley or fresh basil.

MUSHROOM MARSALA SAUCE:

1 cup wild mushrooms (2 or 3
    varieties if possible), sliced
¼ cup water
3 cloves garlic, chopped
6 green onions, sliced (white
    part only)

2 tablespoons extra virgin
    olive oil
2 tablespoons chopped Italian
    flat-leaf parsley
½ cup Marsala wine

In a large skillet, heat water, mushrooms, garlic, and onions over low heat and sauté a few minutes. Add olive oil and stir. Add parsley and wine; then stir until slightly reduced (approximately 4–5 minutes). Serves 6.

Cooking with Mushrooms (California)

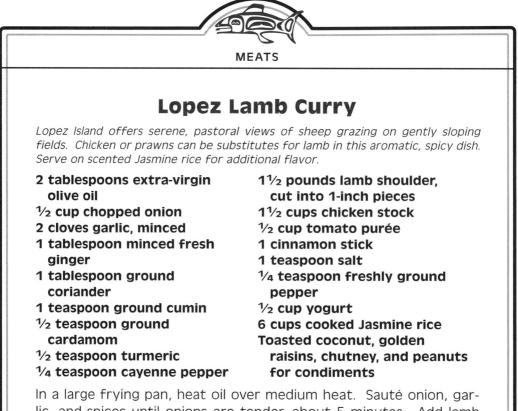

Lopez Lamb Curry

Lopez Island offers serene, pastoral views of sheep grazing on gently sloping fields. Chicken or prawns can be substitutes for lamb in this aromatic, spicy dish. Serve on scented Jasmine rice for additional flavor.

2 tablespoons extra-virgin olive oil
½ cup chopped onion
2 cloves garlic, minced
1 tablespoon minced fresh ginger
1 tablespoon ground coriander
1 teaspoon ground cumin
½ teaspoon ground cardamom
½ teaspoon turmeric
¼ teaspoon cayenne pepper

1½ pounds lamb shoulder, cut into 1-inch pieces
1½ cups chicken stock
½ cup tomato purée
1 cinnamon stick
1 teaspoon salt
¼ teaspoon freshly ground pepper
½ cup yogurt
6 cups cooked Jasmine rice
Toasted coconut, golden raisins, chutney, and peanuts for condiments

In a large frying pan, heat oil over medium heat. Sauté onion, garlic, and spices until onions are tender, about 5 minutes. Add lamb and sauté until lightly browned on all sides, about 10–15 minutes. Add remaining ingredients, except yogurt, rice, and condiments. Cover pan with lid ajar and simmer curry for 30–40 minutes. While curry is cooking, prepare rice.

Discard cinnamon stick. Just before serving, remove pan from heat and stir in yogurt. Serve curry over rice and offer bowls of condiments at the table. Serves 4.

San Juan Classics II Cookbook (Washington)

Lamb Loin with Pesto Mint Sauce

Lamb loin (1 loin serves
  2 people)
Hot, sweet mustard
4 thin slices bacon or pancetta
Fresh mint or fresh rosemary,
  chopped (optional)
1 cup pesto, your own or jarred
  bought

2 tablespoons Cross &
  Blackwell's mint sauce
2 tablespoons chopped fresh
  mint
1 tablespoon chopped fresh
  rosemary, or 1 teaspoon dried
  rosemary

Spread lamb loin generously with mustard. Wrap with bacon or pancetta. Sprinkle with herbs. Preheat oven to 350°. Grill or pan-fry lamb on all sides. Place on cookie sheet or roasting pan and put in oven to finish cooking off. If you like your lamb rare, this should take about 5–10 minutes. Cook longer for more well-done lamb. Remove from oven and let meat rest 10 minutes before slicing.

   To make sauce, combine pesto with mint sauce. Add fresh mint and rosemary. Combine well. Serve with sliced lamb. Serves 2.

Sounds Tasty! (California)

Succulent Moose Roast

1 (3- to 6-pound) moose roast
Bacon fat
Flour
Salt to taste
Pepper to taste

Ginger to taste
1 onion, diced
Water
3–4 potatoes, quartered

Thaw roast, if frozen. Coat a broiling pan with bacon fat, then flour the bottom. Rub the roast with bacon fat, salt, pepper, and ginger. Place the roast in pan; cover with onion and add a bottom-full of water. Add quartered potatoes around roast. Bake covered at 350° for 2 hours and 25 minutes, or until done.

Moose in the Pot Cookbook (Alaska)

Alaskaladas

An Alaskan version of enchiladas.

1–2 pounds ground mooseburger, or 3 chicken breasts, cubed in small pieces
½ onion, chopped
1 tablespoon minced garlic
2 cans cream of mushroom soup
1 can stewed diced tomatoes
½ cup sour cream
1 (8-ounce) can chopped green chiles (do not drain)
1 cup cubed Mexican Velveeta
1 teaspoon garlic salt (or more)
½ teaspoon black pepper
1 teaspoon ground cumin
6–8 corn tortillas, divided
Mozzarella cheese
Additional garlic salt
Additional black pepper
Paprika

Brown meat (moose or chicken), onion, and garlic in saucepan. In a large bowl, place soup, tomatoes, sour cream, green chiles, and Velveeta. When meat is almost cooked through, stir in garlic salt, black pepper, and cumin. Add meat mixture to soup mixture and stir until well blended. Taste for more salt.

Soften tortillas in small amount of hot vegetable oil in cast-iron skillet. Drain on paper towels and place 3½–4 in oblong casserole dish. Spoon ½ the mixture onto the tortillas. Place the rest of the tortillas over mixture and spoon remaining mixture on top. Top with shredded mozzarella cheese. Sprinkle top with garlic salt, pepper, and paprika. Bake for 45 minutes to 1 hour, until bubbly and brown on top. Let set 15 minutes before serving with a nice green salad and a tall glass of cold limeade . . . lime sherbet for dessert or key lime pie.

Grannie Annie's Cookin' at the Homestead (Alaska)

Grilled Moose Steak

**4 boneless moose steaks, cut
  1½ inches thick
¼ cup vegetable oil
½ teaspoon salt
½ teaspoon pepper**

**1 teaspoon Worcestershire
1 teaspoon chili powder
1 tablespoon dry mustard
2 tablespoons beef broth**

Brush steak with oil. Sprinkle with salt and pepper. Combine remaining ingredients to make a thin paste. Place steaks on grill 4 inches above source of heat. Brush with paste and grill 4–5 minutes. Turn steaks with tongs to prevent piercing and brush with remaining paste. Grill to desired doneness. Serves 4.

Moose & Caribou Recipes of Alaska (Alaska)

Caribou Pot Roast
with Sour Cream Sauce

**Caribou shoulder roast
1 onion, sliced
2 carrots, sliced
1 small turnip, diced
2 stalks celery, sliced
¼ cup oil
Salt and pepper**

**Thyme, pinch
1 bay leaf
4 juniper berries
1 lemon, sliced thin
1 cup red wine
1 cup beef broth
½ cup sour cream**

In large pan, brown meat and vegetables in hot oil. Add spices, berries, lemon, wine, and broth. Cover and simmer over low flame for 2 hours. Remove meat. Strain sauce back into pan, pressing vegetables through sieve. Add sour cream to sauce and blend. Return meat to pan and simmer until tender.

Moose & Caribou Recipes of Alaska (Alaska)

Bear Tenderloins
with Blackberry Sauce

Be sure not to overcook wild game because of the low-fat content of the meat.

2 pounds bear meat tenderloin
½ cup butter
1 cup seedless blackberry jam

1 can beef broth, or 2 beef
bouillon cubes in 1½ cups
hot water

In an ovenproof pan, brown tenderloin in butter on all sides (4–5 minutes). Transfer to 450° oven and bake, turning once, until a meat thermometer inserted in thickest part registers 150° (12–15 minutes). Cut to test; meat should no longer be pink in center of thickest part. Transfer meat to a warm platter and keep warm. Add jam and broth to drippings in pan; bring to a boil. Cook, stirring until reduced to about ⅔ cup (about 8 minutes). Slice meat, stirring any juices into sauce. Spoon sauce over meat to serve. Serves 6.

License to Cook Alaska Style (Alaska)

Braised Venison

3 pounds venison
3 slices salt pork
Salt, pepper, and flour
¼ cup fat
¼ cup hot water

½ teaspoon vinegar
½ cup chopped celery
1 carrot, diced
1 tart apple, chopped
½ tablespoon lemon juice

Use the less tender cuts of venison for this method. Lard venison with salt pork and rub with salt, pepper, and flour. Sauté in hot fat until well browned, turning frequently. Add hot water with vinegar. Cover and cook until tender, about 2–2½ hours, adding more water as it evaporates. One-half hour before meat is done, add remaining ingredients. Cook until vegetables are tender. Serve with a tart jelly.

The Original Great Alaska Cookbook (Alaska)

POULTRY

Inyo County, California, is home to the highest point in the contiguous 48 states, Mt. Whitney (14,495 feet) of the Sierra Nevada Range. Inyo County is also home to the lowest spot in the western hemisphere, Badwater (282 feet below sea level) located in Death Valley. These two points are less than 80 miles apart.

Cranberry Chicken

1 (8-ounce) bottle Catalina
  French Dressing
1 package powdered onion
  soup mix

1 can whole cranberries
6–8 chicken breasts

Mix together the dressing, soup mix, and cranberries. Arrange chicken pieces in a 9x13-inch casserole and pour sauce mix over chicken. Bake for 1 hour at 350°.

Dilley Family Favorites (Oregon)

Chicken/Mushroom Stroganoff

2 chicken breasts, skinned
  and boned
1 cup diced carrots
½ cup chopped onions
2 garlic cloves, minced
2 cups mushrooms
1 tablespoon water
½ cup nonfat cottage cheese

2 tablespoons nonfat sour
  cream
2 tablespoons Dijon mustard
1 tablespoon soy sauce (low
  sodium)
3 cups eggless noodles, cooked
  in water

Wrap chicken, carrots, onions, and garlic in aluminum foil. Place in oven and bake at 375° for 30 minutes. While chicken is cooking, sauté mushrooms in large skillet, using 1 tablespoon of water. Place cottage cheese, sour cream, and mustard in blender and blend until smooth. Cut cooked chicken into strips, and place in large bowl. Add vegetables, cottage cheese mixture, and soy sauce; mix well. Serve over noodles. Makes 4 servings.

From My Heart For Yours (Washington)

Chicken Satay with Peanut Sauce

2 whole fryer breasts, skinned
  and boned
¼ cup soy sauce
¼ cup dry white wine

1 tablespoon honey
1 tablespoon grated fresh
  gingerroot
Peanut Dipping Sauce

Flatten chicken breasts and slice into strips about 1 inch wide. Thread on skewers and place in shallow pan. Combine soy sauce, wine, honey, and ginger; pour over chicken and marinate 30 minutes, turning occasionally to coat. Drain; broil or grill until chicken is cooked and juices run clear when cut. Serve warm with Peanut Dipping Sauce. Makes 4–6 servings.

PEANUT DIPPING SAUCE:
½ cup peanut butter
¼ cup unsweetened coconut
  milk
2 tablespoons soy sauce
1 tablespoon honey

2 tablespoons minced fresh
  cilantro
1 clove garlic, minced
⅛ teaspoon hot pepper sauce

Combine all ingredients until well blended. Makes about ¾ cup.

The Chicken Cookbook (Washington)

Golden Marinade Chicken on Sticks

½ cup soy sauce
½ cup gin (or sherry)
¼ cup honey
½ teaspoon black pepper
1 teaspoon grated gingerroot

1 clove garlic, grated
About a pound of boneless
  chicken
1 can large button mushrooms
Barbecue bamboo sticks

Combine first 6 ingredients and set aside. Cut chicken into small pieces that would hold on sticks, then marinate in sauce for at least half an hour. Place chicken pieces on sticks (that have been soaked in water) with mushrooms in between. Broil.

Cook 'em Up Kaua'i (Hawaii)

Amaretto Chicken

**4 large chicken breasts, boned
  and skinned
Italian-seasoned bread crumbs
Butter or margarine
1 cup orange juice**

**½ cup amaretto liqueur
2 teaspoons cornstarch
2 teaspoons brown sugar
Parsley
Orange, thinly sliced**

Pound and cut chicken into 2x3-inch pieces. Shake in bread crumbs and brown in butter or margarine. Place in a 9x13-inch baking dish. Mix other ingredients together (except parsley and orange) and pour over chicken. Bake uncovered at 350° for about 45 minutes. Garnish with parsley and thinly sliced orange. Serves 4–6.

Extraordinary Cuisine for Sea & Shore (Washington)

Hibachi-Style Teriyaki Chicken

**1 cup soy sauce
1 cup chicken stock
½ cup brown sugar
1 cup mirin or sake**

**2 tablespoons grated onion
2 cloves garlic, minced
2 pounds chicken pieces**

Put soy sauce, chicken stock, and brown sugar in a saucepan. Dissolve sugar over low heat. Add mirin or sake, onion, and garlic. Cook and stir 5 minutes over low heat. Cool sauce. Pour over chicken and refrigerate 5 hours or overnight. Turn occasionally.

   Cook over coals, brushing on marinade while you cook. Or cook in oven at 350° for about 45 minutes in sauce. Turn chicken once.

A Taste of Sitka, Alaska (Alaska)

Alaska is so big it has its own time zone, Alaska Standard Time, which is one hour behind Pacific Standard Time. The Aleutian Islands west of Umak Island and the Hawaiian Islands are on Hawaii-Aleutian Time, which is an hour behind Alaskan time.

Sonora Style Chicken

3 slices bacon, diced
1 large onion, coarsely
  chopped
3 cloves garlic, minced
1 (28-ounce) can tomatoes,
  drained and coarsely
  chopped

⅔ cup picante sauce
¼ cup sliced green olives
1 (3-pound) fryer chicken, cut
  up, skinned and visible fat
  removed
¼ cup coarsely chopped
  cilantro

Cook bacon in 10-inch skillet until crisp. Remove with slotted spoon to paper towel; reserve. Pour off all but 1 tablespoon of drippings. Cook onion and garlic in drippings until tender, about 4 minutes. Add tomatoes, picante sauce, and olives; bring to boil. Add chicken; spoon sauce over chicken. Reduce heat; cover and simmer until chicken is tender, about 30 minutes. Remove chicken to serving platter; cook sauce over high heat until thickened to desired consistency. Spoon sauce over chicken; sprinkle with bacon and cilantro. Makes 4 servings.

Cookin' with CASA (California)

Baked Guava Chicken

12 small chicken breasts, or
  5 pounds chicken parts
1 (10-ounce) jar guava jelly
1 tablespoon cornstarch
1 cup water
½ cup lemon juice

1½ teaspoons Worcestershire
¼ cup shoyu (soy sauce)
1 teaspoon allspice
½ teaspoon Hawaiian salt
½ teaspoon white pepper

Place chicken in baking pan. Mix all other ingredients in a saucepan and simmer for 5 minutes. Pour over chicken. Bake in preheated 350° oven for 40 minutes to 1 hour. Baste frequently. Add water if necessary.

We, the Women of Hawaii Cookbook (Hawaii)

Chicken Piccata

**4 boneless, skinless split
  chicken breasts**
1 cup flour
1 teaspoon garlic powder
½ teaspoon salt
¼ teaspoon white pepper

4 teaspoons oil
1 tablespoon butter
1 tablespoon chopped basil
1 tablespoon lemon juice
2 teaspoons white wine

Flatten chicken breasts between 2 sheets of plastic wrap. Coat chicken with flour, garlic powder, salt, and pepper. Sauté each breast in 1 teaspoon oil in nonstick skillet. Keep warm in 200° oven. In same skillet, melt 1 tablespoon butter; add basil. When butter bubbles, splash with lemon juice and wine. Pour over warm chicken breasts. Serve with rice or pasta and a good salad.

Recipes to Remember (Washington)

Chicken Quick Meal

This is a good recipe to use when you are too tired to cook or need to have a good meal to cook for a person living alone, a family, or for company. This recipe is low calorie, low cholesterol, low salt, and low sugar, yet, it's delicious.

PER PERSON:
2 pieces skinless chicken
1 medium potato, peeled
2 carrots, cut in chunks

Salt and pepper
1 medium onion, sliced

Place chicken, potato, and carrots in ungreased casserole dish; add salt and pepper. Arrange onion slices over top. Add no water. Cover. Put in oven at 375°; set the timer for 1 hour; forget it. In 1 hour it's ready to eat!

Note: Chicken can be used still frozen from the refrigerator or fresh; makes no difference as to time or taste. Stick with these recommended vegetables. No other combination seems to work.

Coastal Flavors (Oregon)

Chicken Lūʻau

2 cups coconut milk
2 pounds chicken
2 tablespoons oil
2 cloves garlic, crushed

1½ teaspoons salt, divided
2½ cups water, divided
2 pounds taro leaves (lūʻau)

Prepare fresh coconut milk or use canned coconut milk. Cut chicken into bite-sized pieces. In saucepan, heat oil; add crushed garlic. Add chicken and brown. Sprinkle with 1 teaspoon salt and add 1 cup water. Cover and simmer until chicken is tender.

Wash taro leaves; remove tough stems. Place leaves in a pan with 1½ cups water and ½ teaspoon salt. Simmer, partially covered, for one hour. Drain and squeeze water out. Drain chicken; combine with lūʻau leaves. Add coconut milk and bring to a boil. Serve immediately. Serves 4–6.

Note: Fresh spinach may be substituted if lūʻau is not available.

Ethnic Foods of Hawaiʻi (Hawaii)

Always held at sunset, usually near the beach where the sun sets beautifully over the ocean, a Hawaiian lūʻau typically lasts several hours. While you are enjoying the feast, talented performers entertain and educate you about Hawaiian culture with colorful and dramatic dances in traditional costumes. The hula is the most popular dance, where girls in grass skirts perform graceful movements to the strums of the ukulele. Usually the audience gets an opportunity to learn the dance as well.

Typical Lūʻau Food

- Kalua Pig
- Laulau (Chicken, pork, or fish wrapped in ti leaves and steamed)
- Poi (Pounded taro root)
- Lomi Salmon (Cold diced salmon with diced tomatoes, onions, and green onions)
- Chicken Long Rice (Opaque noodles)
- Chicken Lūʻau (Baked in taro leaves)
- Mahimahi (fish)
- Yams or Sweet Potatoes
- Tropical Fruit (Pineapples, mangoes, papayas)
- Sweet Potato or Poi Rolls
- Haupia (Coconut-flavored dessert; a stiff pudding)
- Mai Tais or other tropical drinks and punches

PHOTO BY GWEN McKEE

Chicken Casserole Amandine

8 chicken thighs
½ cup honey
½ cup prepared mustard
1 tablespoon chopped onion
1 tablespoon lemon juice
½ teaspoon curry powder
½ cup slivered almonds

Place chicken thighs, single layer, in baking dish. Combine remaining ingredients (except almonds) and pour over meat. Cook, covered, 30 minutes at 300°. Remove cover, sprinkle slivered almonds over the top, and bake another 10 minutes, uncovered. Serves 4–6.

Durham's Favorite Recipes (California)

Zesty Chicken Italiano

2 tablespoons butter or
  margarine
1 pound boneless chicken
  breast, cut into 1-inch pieces
1 clove garlic, minced
1½ cups thinly sliced zucchini
1½ cups sliced fresh
  mushrooms
1 (15-ounce) can tomato sauce
1 (14½-ounce) can tomatoes,
  undrained and quartered
½ teaspoon dried oregano
½ teaspoon lemon pepper
Salt and pepper to taste
8 ounces vermicelli (or other
  pasta)
Grated Parmesan cheese

In a large skillet, melt butter and sauté chicken pieces until lightly browned. Add garlic, zucchini, and mushrooms, and sauté 2 minutes. Stir in remaining ingredients except pasta and Parmesan cheese. Simmer, uncovered, 10 minutes to blend flavor and thicken sauce. Meanwhile, cook pasta according to directions on package; drain. Serve sauce over hot cooked pasta and sprinkle with Parmesan cheese.

What's Cooking in Sisters (Oregon)

Chicken Bundles

¾ cup chopped green onions
¾ cup mayonnaise
3 tablespoons lemon juice
3 cloves garlic, minced, divided
¾ teaspoon dry tarragon
⅔ cup margarine, melted

12 sheets phyllo
6 chicken breast halves, boned
   and skinned
Salt and pepper to taste
2 tablespoons grated Parmesan
   cheese

Mix together onions, mayonnaise, lemon juice, 2 cloves garlic, and tarragon. Set aside. Combine remaining garlic and butter. For each bundle, place 2 sheets of phyllo on a board and brush with garlic butter. Spread one side of chicken breast with about 1½ tablespoons of mayonnaise mixture. Turn over onto corner of phyllo sheets and top with 1½ tablespoons more of mixture.

Wrap breast in phyllo as follows: Flip corner of phyllo over chicken. Roll once. Fold side over top and roll again. Fold opposite over, then roll up. Folds like an envelope. Place bundles slightly apart on an ungreased baking sheet. Brush with remaining garlic butter. Sprinkle with cheese. Bake at 375° for 20–25 minutes or until golden. Serves 6.

Note: May be frozen—but thaw completely, covered, before baking.

The Steinbeck House Cookbook (*California*)

Founded in 1776 by Franciscan Padres, Mission San Juan Capistrano in Orange County, California, is best known for its swallows, which return every year to their nests in the old stone church, the largest and most ornate of any of the missions. The church shattered and collapsed in a tremendous earthquake in 1812 and much of the mission is in ruins, but efforts are underway for restoration.

Savory Chicken Squares

This is a great luncheon dish.

1 (3-ounce) package cream
   cheese, softened
2 tablespoons milk
2 tablespoons chopped onion
3 tablespoons margarine,
   melted
2 cups cooked cubed chicken

¼ teaspoon garlic salt
¼ teaspoon pepper
1 (8-ounce) tube refrigerated
   crescent rolls
Seasoned bread crumbs

Preheat oven to 350°. Blend cream cheese and milk until smooth. Sauté onion in margarine. Mix chicken, seasonings, onion, and cream cheese mixture together; stir well. Separate the dough into 4 rectangles, press perforation to seal. Spoon meat mixture on crescent dough, fold up corners, and seal. Brush tops with remaining melted margarine and sprinkle with seasoned bread crumbs. Bake on ungreased cookie sheet 20–25 minutes, or until golden.

Recipes from Our Friends (Washington)

Cheesy Chicken Casserole

2 cups milk
2 (8-ounce) packages cream
   cheese
1½ cups Parmesan cheese,
   divided
1 teaspoon salt

1 teaspoon garlic salt
2 (10-ounce) packages broccoli,
   cooked and drained
6 chicken breasts, poached and
   cubed
1 can onion rings

Over medium heat, blend milk, cream cheese, ¾ cup Parmesan cheese, salt, and garlic salt. In a greased 2-quart casserole, arrange broccoli in the bottom. Pour 1 cup of heated sauce over broccoli. Arrange chicken and onion rings on top. Cover with remaining sauce. Top with remaining Parmesan. Cook at 350° for 30 minutes.

Your Favorite Recipes (Washington)

Huli Huli Chicken

This aromatic chicken turned (huli huli) on the spit is a staple at beach picnics, roadside stands, and at fundraisers.

SAUCE:

¼ **cup catsup**
¼ **cup shoyu (soy sauce)**
½ **cup chicken broth**
⅓ **cup sherry**
½ **cup fresh lime juice**
¼ **cup frozen pineapple**
  juice concentrate

½ **cup brown sugar**
1 **tablespoon crushed fresh**
  ginger
1 **clove garlic, crushed**
1 **teaspoon Worcestershire**

Mix Sauce ingredients in bowl.

3 **chicken fryers, halved**
  or quartered

Hawaiian sea salt and pepper
  to taste

Thread chicken onto rotisserie spit. Use clean 1½-inch paintbrush to coat Sauce over cleaned chicken pieces, then sprinkle with salt and pepper. Grill on rotisserie, turning and basting frequently with Sauce until done, 45–60 minutes.

For grilling, place on rack over coals, turning and basting for about 45 minutes. Or roast in 325° preheated oven, basting frequently, for 90 minutes. Serves 6.

Kona on My Plate (Hawaii)

The origin of the ukulele can be traced to immigrant Manual Nunes who arrived in Hawaii from Madeira in 1879 to work in the sugar cane fields. He is responsible for transforming the Portuguese *braguinha* into the Hawaiian ukulele. Nunes established one of the first ukulele manufacturing companies and remained in business for over 40 years. The ukulele remains Hawaii's most popular musical instrument.

Fabulous Chicken Cacciatore

1¾ ounces dried porcine
  mushrooms (no substitute)
1 cup water
3 whole chicken breasts, split
  in half
½ cup olive oil
3 beef bouillon cubes
1 medium onion, chopped
4–6 cloves garlic, crushed
2 teaspoons sweet basil (dried
  or fresh)

½ teaspoon salt
Pinch pepper
1 (6-ounce) can tomato paste
1 bay leaf
1 (16-ounce) can stewed
  tomatoes
1 cup rosé wine (no substitute)
2 green peppers, sliced

Preheat oven to 350°. Soak mushrooms in water for 15 minutes, reserving liquid. Brown chicken in olive oil; remove chicken, leaving oil in pan. Add bouillon cubes, onion, and garlic; sauté. Stir in basil, salt, pepper, and tomato paste. Then add mushroom liquid, bay leaf, stewed tomatoes, wine, and mushrooms. Place chicken in shallow baking dish. Cover with sauce. Bake covered for 30 minutes. Place pepper rings on top; continue baking another 40 minutes or until done. Serve with Polenta.

POLENTA:
1½ quarts water
2 teaspoons salt
1½ cups yellow polenta
  cornmeal

1 tablespoon Parmesan
  cheese

Bring water to a boil in 4-quart kettle. Add salt. Pour cornmeal into boiling water slowly, stirring constantly to keep from lumping. Reduce heat and cover. Cook over very low heat for another 20–30 minutes. You can now place mush in shallow baking dish and sprinkle with Parmesan cheese. Cut in squares and serve with cacciatore or any other Italian stew. Serves 6.

Cooking on the Fault Line—Corralitos Style (California)

The United States is the fourth largest wine-producing country in the world after France, Italy, and Spain. California leads the way, followed by Washington and Oregon. North America is home to several native species of grape, but it was the introduction of the European *Vitis v inifera* by European settlers that led to the growth of the wine making industry.

Chicken and Spinach Enchiladas

2 eggs, beaten
1 cup minced, cooked chicken
1 cup chopped, cooked, drained spinach
¼ cup heavy cream
1 clove garlic, minced
2 tablespoons hot salsa
1 cup grated Monterey Jack cheese
⅓ cup freshly grated Parmesan cheese
1 (4-ounce) can green chiles
1 (7-ounce) can mild or green chile salsa, divided
6 flour tortillas
1 tomato, diced
1 cup grated Cheddar cheese
Garnish: chopped green onion, picante sauce, sour cream

Preheat broiler. Combine first 9 ingredients in a bowl and mix well. Add 2 tablespoons green chile salsa and transfer the mixture to a saucepan. Warm over medium heat until cheeses are melted and well blended. Fill each tortilla with ⅙ of the chicken-salsa mixture. Divide the tomato evenly between the tortillas and fold tortillas to close. Place side-by-side in a buttered baking dish. Sprinkle the top with Cheddar cheese and pour remaining salsa on top. Place the enchiladas on lowest level of broiler and broil for 5–10 minutes, or until cheese on top is melted and bubbly. Don't allow tortillas to become crisp. Serve immediately; garnish with green onion, picante sauce, and sour cream.

Heavenly Temptations (Oregon)

Sour Cream Chicken Enchiladas

2 cans cream of chicken soup
8–16 ounces sour cream
2 cans chopped green chiles, drained
1 small onion, chopped
¾ pound grated Jack cheese
1 chicken, cooked and boned, cubed
12–15 flour tortillas
½ cup grated Cheddar cheese

In a large bowl combine soup, sour cream, chiles, onion, and grated Jack cheese. Reserve ⅓ of this mixture. To other ⅔ add chicken pieces. Soften tortillas in microwave (1 minute). Fill tortillas, roll up and place in 9x13-inch pan. Spread remaining ⅓ mixture over top and sprinkle with Cheddar cheese. Bake at 350° until bubbly, 30–60 minutes. May be covered. Freezes well.

Cookin' with CASA (California)

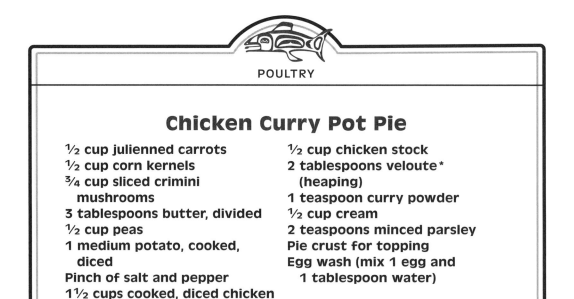

Chicken Curry Pot Pie

½ cup julienned carrots
½ cup corn kernels
¾ cup sliced crimini
  mushrooms
3 tablespoons butter, divided
½ cup peas
1 medium potato, cooked,
  diced
Pinch of salt and pepper
1½ cups cooked, diced chicken

½ cup chicken stock
2 tablespoons veloute*
  (heaping)
1 teaspoon curry powder
½ cup cream
2 teaspoons minced parsley
Pie crust for topping
Egg wash (mix 1 egg and
  1 tablespoon water)

Sauté carrots, corn, and mushrooms in 2 tablespoons butter for 3 minutes. Add peas and potatoes, cooking for 1 minute more. Season with salt and pepper. Add chicken and deglaze with stock. Whisk in veloute and let simmer. Add curry powder, cream, and parsley. Reduce by one-third. Finish with remaining 1 tablespoon butter.

Pour into a soufflé dish and top with your favorite pie crust. Egg-wash and bake in preheated 350° oven until golden, approximately 25 minutes. Serves 4.

*Veloute is a rich white sauce made from meat stock thickened with flour and butter.

San Francisco's Cooking Secrets (*California*)

WWW.PLANETWARE.COM

Yosemite National Park in California offers many breath-taking views. Bridalveil Falls is the height of a 62-story building and one of the most prominent waterfalls in the Yosemite Valley, seen yearly by millions of visitors. Three-tiered Yosemite Falls drops 2,425 feet, making it the highest in all North America. El Capitan is the largest single granite rock in the world, standing 3,000 feet from base to summit.

Gobbler Cobbler

PASTRY:

1½ cups flour
⅛ teaspoon salt
½ cup shortening

¼ cup milk
⅓ cup shredded Cheddar
   cheese

Combine flour and salt; cut in shortening. Add milk; blend in cheese and mix lightly. Roll out on floured board, place Pastry in 9-inch pie pan and prick with a fork. Bake at 425° for 12–15 minutes or until lightly browned.

FILLING:

2 cups chopped cooked turkey
1 cup pineapple chunks,
   drained
1 cup chopped walnuts
¼ cup chopped celery
¼ cup chopped onion

1 (8-ounce) carton sour cream
⅔ cup mayonnaise
3 tablespoons shredded
   Cheddar cheese
Sliced black olives

Combine turkey, pineapple, nuts, celery, and onion and mix well. In a separate bowl mix sour cream and mayonnaise. Add just enough sour cream mixture to the turkey mixture to moisten it. Pour turkey mixture into the pie shell, top with remaining sour cream mixture. Garnish with cheese and olives and bake 20 minutes at 350°. Makes 6 large servings.

Recipes and Remembering (Oregon)

Glazed Turkey Meatballs

1 pound ground turkey
½ cup shredded tart apples
¾ teaspoon salt
⅛ teaspoon garlic powder

2 teaspoons cooking oil
½ cup apple jelly
2 tablespoons spicy brown
   mustard

In a medium bowl, combine turkey, apple, salt, and garlic powder. Shape into 16 meatballs. Heat oil in large skillet over medium heat. Add meatballs, cook, and turn until brown (about 8 minutes). In small bowl, stir together jelly and mustard. Spoon over meatballs; simmer an additional 8–10 minutes, or until glazed. Turn meatballs several times. Sauce will thicken as it cools.

Christmas in Washington Cook Book (Washington)

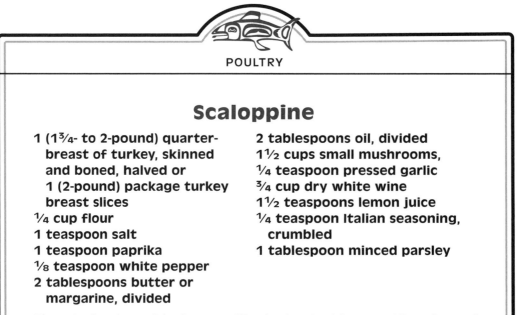

Scaloppine

1 (1¾- to 2-pound) quarter-
  breast of turkey, skinned
  and boned, halved or
  1 (2-pound) package turkey
  breast slices
¼ cup flour
1 teaspoon salt
1 teaspoon paprika
⅛ teaspoon white pepper
2 tablespoons butter or
  margarine, divided

2 tablespoons oil, divided
1½ cups small mushrooms,
¼ teaspoon pressed garlic
¾ cup dry white wine
1½ teaspoons lemon juice
¼ teaspoon Italian seasoning,
  crumbled
1 tablespoon minced parsley

Place turkey breast in freezer 45 minutes to 1 hour until surface of meat is thoroughly chilled and slightly firm. Cut meat crosswise in ¼-inch slices. Mix flour, salt, paprika, and white pepper together. Flour meat slices, shaking off excess. Heat 1 tablespoon each butter and oil in large skillet. Add layer of meat and brown lightly on both sides. As meat is browned, remove and keep warm. Brown remaining turkey, adding remaining butter and oil as needed. When all meat is browned, add mushrooms and garlic to skillet and sauté lightly. Return browned turkey meat to skillet. Combine wine, lemon juice, Italian seasoning, and parsley. Pour over all and simmer rapidly 5–10 minutes or until liquid is reduced and turkey is tender. Makes 6 servings.

Taste of Fillmore (California)

Hood River Turkey

4 apples
4 onions
1 fresh (10-pound) turkey

1 cup water
1 cup soy sauce
1 cup white wine

Cut up apples and onions. Stuff turkey with apples and onions. Secure legs and wings. Put turkey in large pan. Mix water, soy sauce, and wine. Cook on low setting of gas grill with lid closed. Baste the turkey with the soy mixture every 20–30 minutes. If the turkey becomes too brown, cover it with aluminum foil. The entire cooking time will be 1½–2 hours depending upon the exact size of the turkey. Serves 4–6.

Savor the Flavor of Oregon (Oregon)

Pheasant Jubilee

2 pheasants, quartered
Flour, enough to dredge
½ cup margarine
1 onion, chopped
½ cup raisins
1 cup chili sauce

½ cup water
½ cup packed brown sugar
2 tablespoons Worcestershire
¼ teaspoon garlic powder
1 cup sherry

Dust pheasants with flour in plastic bag. Melt butter in fry pan; brown birds thoroughly. Place pheasant in casserole. In fry pan, combine remaining ingredients except sherry. Bring to a boil. Scrape bottom and sides of pan and pour over pheasants. Bake covered at 325° for 1 hour. Remove cover, add sherry, and bake 20 minutes longer. Serve with brown or wild rice and a good red wine. Makes 4–6 servings.

Our Burnt Offerings (Washington)

Oyster Mushroom and Roasted Hazelnut Stuffing

Roasted hazelnuts, oyster mushrooms, and the fresh herb flavor of rosemary and sage blend to wonderful perfection.

1½ loaves of bread, cut into half-inch cubes
1 pound hazelnuts, roasted and coarsely chopped
1 stick butter
3 medium onions, chopped
1 pound oyster mushrooms, sliced (can also use shiitake)
5 celery stalks, chopped

½ pound prosciutto or other thin-sliced ham, chopped (optional)
4 tablespoons chopped fresh rosemary
3 tablespoons chopped fresh sage
3–4 cups chicken stock

Dry bread in advance, spread out on sheet pans and bake at 350° for 20 minutes; stir occasionally. Roast hazelnuts on a baking sheet at 350° for 12 minutes. Melt butter in large sauté pan over medium-high heat. Add onions and cook until golden brown. Add mushrooms and cook until they begin to release their juices, about 5 minutes. Add celery and cook a few minutes more. Remove from heat. Stir in prosciutto and mix with dry bread. Add fresh herbs and moisten with chicken stock. Use as you would any dressing or stuffing. Makes about 16 cups dressing.

Washington Farmers' Markets Cookbook and Guide (Washington)

SEAFOOD

The world-famous Polynesian Cultural Center in O'ahu showcases seven South Pacific island cultures in each of their villages. Events include a lū'au, Pageant of the Long Canoes, IMAX™ Theater, and "Horizons" evening show.

Deviled Dungeness Crab

Very good first course, since it can all be prepared ahead and refrigerated. Elegant and easy.

6 tablespoons butter, divided	**¾ pound fresh Dungeness**
2 tablespoons all-purpose flour	**crab (or any locally available fresh crab)**
1 cup light cream	**½ cup bread crumbs**
½ teaspoon Worcestershire	**4 lemon slices**
½ teaspoon grated onion	**½ teaspoon paprika**

Preheat oven to 425°. Melt 2 tablespoons butter in a saucepan until foamy. Add flour and cook 3 minutes. Slowly add light cream, Worcestershire, and onion, stirring until thoroughly blended and thickened. Remove from heat and stir in crabmeat until well mixed. Spoon mixture into 4 scallop shells and refrigerate until well chilled.

Remove filled shells from refrigerator and top with bread crumbs, dots of remaining butter, lemon slices and paprika. Bake for 15 minutes or until bread crumbs are browned and crab mixture is bubbly. Serve immediately. Serves 4.

Editors' Extra: If you don't have scallop shells, this works well in any shallow oven-proof dish.

San Francisco à la Carte (California)

WWW.CRABFESTIVAL.ORG

Dungeness crab is the world's standard for super-premium crab. It is unmatched for quality, texture and taste. Dungeness crabs are found only on the West Coast of the United States from central California to the Gulf of Alaska. It gets its name from the small fishing village of Dungeness on the Strait of Juan de Fuca in Washington state where the first commercial harvesting of the crab was done. The Dungeness Crab & Seafood Festival is held each year in Port Angeles, Washington, near Dungeness.

Dungeness Crab Cakes
with Red Pepper Sauce

We like these Crab Cakes with the Red Pepper Sauce, although they taste great by themselves.

RED PEPPER SAUCE:

2 cloves garlic
¾ cup roasted and peeled
  red peppers
2 teaspoons freshly squeezed
  lemon juice
¼ cup nonfat mayonnaise

Purée garlic, red peppers, lemon juice, and mayonnaise in food processor or blender until smooth. Place in covered container and chill in refrigerator.

CRAB CAKES:

3 teaspoons olive oil, divided
¼ cup minced green onions
3 tablespoons minced red
  bell pepper
1 tablespoon rice vinegar or
  other vinegar
¾ pound (2 cups) fresh
  crabmeat, or 1 (14¾-ounce)
  can salmon (2 cups), or
  1 (12-ounce) can tuna
3 tablespoons freshly
  squeezed lemon juice
½ cup dried bread crumbs,
  divided
2 egg whites, lightly beaten, or
  ¼ cup egg substitute, lightly
  beaten
1 teaspoon Dijon-style mustard
¼ cup chopped fresh parsley
⅛ teaspoon Tabasco
¼ teaspoon paprika
⅛ teaspoon pepper

Heat 1 teaspoon olive oil in a small nonstick skillet. Add green onions and bell pepper and sauté, stirring often, until green onions are wilted. Add vinegar and boil rapidly until it has evaporated. Set aside to cool.

Place crabmeat in a bowl and sprinkle with lemon juice. If using canned salmon, discard skin; mash bones well. If using tuna, mash well. Blend in cooled green onion-pepper mixture. Stir in ¼ cup bread crumbs, egg whites or egg substitute, mustard, parsley, Tabasco, paprika, and pepper. Cover and chill at least 2 hours.

When ready to cook, mold mixture into 8 cakes. Coat lightly on both sides with remaining ¼ cup bread crumbs. Do not coat salmon or tuna cakes. Heat remaining 2 teaspoons oil in a nonstick skillet. Add cakes, cover, and cook over medium heat 4 minutes or until nicely browned. Turn carefully and cook, uncovered, 4 minutes or until browned. Makes 8 Crab Cakes and 1 cup sauce.

The New American Diet Cookbook (Oregon)

Dungeness Crab Quesadilla

Make these for dinner served with salsa, green salad, and apple slices.

Spray cooking oil
½ cup finely chopped onion
½ cup finely chopped red bell
  pepper
¼ cup cream cheese
¼ cup diced jalapeño chiles
¼ cup mayonnaise
2 teaspoons lemon juice
1 teaspoon each, salt and
  pepper
1 pound Dungeness crabmeat
10 flour tortillas
1 cup diced tomatoes
1 cup shredded Monterey Jack
  cheese

Preheat oven to 350°. Coat skillet with oil. Sauté onion and bell peppers for 2 minutes. Add cream cheese and jalapeño chiles. Remove from heat and stir. Mix mayonnaise, lemon juice, salt and pepper into pan with onion/cheese mixture. Gently fold in crabmeat. Spread crab mixture on half of each tortilla. Sprinkle with tomatoes and cheese. Fold tortilla in half and press firmly to seal. Coat underside of tortilla with cooking spray and place on cookie sheet. Bake 6–8 minutes. Cut in wedges.

Note: You may substitute cooked, flaked halibut or salad shrimp.

Wild Alaska Seafood—Twice a Week (Alaska)

Tenakee Inlet Crab Cakes

2 tablespoons chopped onion
2 tablespoons butter
1 pound crabmeat, flaked
1 egg, beaten
½ teaspoon powdered
  mustard
½ teaspoon salt
½ teaspoon garlic powder
Dash of black pepper
Dash of cayenne pepper
½ cup cracker meal or
  crushed cornflakes
Parsley (approximately 2
  tablespoons)
Lemon wedges for garnish

Cook onion in butter until tender. Combine all ingredients, except crumbs and parsley. Shape into 6 cakes and roll in crumbs; place cakes in a heavy frying pan with ⅛ inch of oil, hot but not smoking. Fry at moderate heat. Brown on one side, then turn carefully to brown other side, approximately 6 minutes. Drain. Garnish with lemon wedges. Serves 6.

Tasty Treats from Tenakee Springs, Alaska (Alaska)

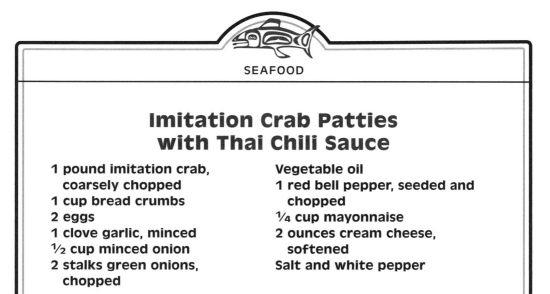

Imitation Crab Patties
with Thai Chili Sauce

1 pound imitation crab,
    coarsely chopped
1 cup bread crumbs
2 eggs
1 clove garlic, minced
½ cup minced onion
2 stalks green onions,
    chopped

Vegetable oil
1 red bell pepper, seeded and
    chopped
¼ cup mayonnaise
2 ounces cream cheese,
    softened
Salt and white pepper

In a mixing bowl, combine crab, bread crumbs, and eggs. Reserve. In a skillet over medium-high heat, sauté garlic and onions in oil. Add bell pepper and sauté until tender. Remove from heat and cool. Add with remaining ingredients to reserved crab mixture, blending well, seasoning with salt and pepper. Cover and refrigerate for one hour. Form crab mixture into patties and fry until golden brown. Drain on paper towels. Serve with Thai Chili Sauce. Serves 4.

THAI CHILI SAUCE:
1 cup sugar
½ cup water
½ cup rice wine vinegar
1 clove garlic, minced

1 teaspoon salt
1 tablespoon garlic chili paste
2 teaspoons chopped fresh
    cilantro

In a small saucepan, combine all ingredients; simmer until syrupy; cool. Stir in cilantro. Set aside. Makes 1½ cups.

Variation: Form mixture into 1-inch balls. Combine 1 egg and ¼ cup milk. Dip crab balls into egg wash. Wrap with shredded won ton pi, pressing firmly. Deep-fry until golden brown. Drain on paper towels; serve with your favorite sauce.

Dd's Table Talk (Hawaii)

Jake's Dungeness Crab Tortellini

1 tablespoon butter
6 mushrooms, sliced
1 tablespoon garlic
4 ounces heavy cream
Salt and pepper

8 ounces tortellini, cooked
4 ounces crabmeat
2 tablespoons Gorgonzola
  cheese

Heat butter in skillet until it starts to bubble. Sauté mushrooms in butter until they start to brown, approximately 2 minutes. Add garlic and stir; before garlic starts to brown, add cream and salt and pepper. Allow cream to start to reduce so that it begins to thicken. Add tortellini and toss together. Add crab and cheese and heat. Makes 1 serving.

Serving Up Oregon (Oregon)

Crab or Shrimp Stuffed Mushrooms

16 extra large mushrooms
½ cube of butter
1 pound crab or small salad
  shrimp

½ cup mayonnaise
2 shallots, minced and sautéed
1 teaspoon prepared mustard

Remove stem from mushrooms and sauté the caps, top-side-down, in butter for 1 minute. Place in ovenproof dish and set aside.

Mix crab or shrimp with mayonnaise, shallots, and mustard. Fill mushrooms with equal amounts of this mixture. Place in oven for 20 minutes at 300°. Remove from oven and cover lightly with Mornay Sauce. Garnish with fresh, chopped parsley.

MORNAY SAUCE:
3 tablespoons flour
2 tablespoons butter, melted
1½ cups hot milk
1½ cups shredded cheese
  (Cheddar, Swiss, Jack)

1 teaspoon salt
½ teaspoon white pepper

Add flour to melted butter in saucepan; cook a few minutes (do not brown). Add milk, stirring constantly until smooth and creamy. Add cheese; continue stirring. Mix in salt and pepper. Remove from heat and serve.

Multnomah Falls Lodge Cook Book (Oregon)

Fisherman's Wharf Garlic Prawns

4 garlic cloves, crushed
1 teaspoon salt
2 teaspoons coarsely crushed
  black peppercorns
2 teaspoons lemon juice
1 tablespoon brandy

1 pound shrimp (prawns), 16–20
  count, peeled, deveined,
  butterflied
3 tablespoons olive oil
½ cup heavy whipping cream
Fresh chopped parsley

Combine crushed garlic with salt; add crushed peppercorns, lemon juice, and brandy. Mix well. Place prawns in saucepan or in heavy-duty cast-iron skillet. Add garlic mixture and olive oil. Cover and cook quickly until prawns change color. Stir in cream. Serve hot and sizzling in small bowls garnished with chopped parsley. Serves 2.

Little Dave's Seafood Cookbook (California)

Garlic Shrimp

Here's one you can serve to company (plus it's quick and easy)!

8 cloves garlic, finely minced
1 tablespoon olive oil
1 cup dry white wine
4 whole cloves
2 fresh bay leaves
1½ pounds shrimp, peeled,
  deveined

1 teaspoon Dijon mustard
Salt and pepper to taste
½ teaspoon Worcestershire
2 cups cooked pasta
2 tablespoons chopped parsley

In a large skillet, brown garlic in oil. Add wine, cloves, and bay leaves. Cook slowly until wine reduces to ⅔ original volume. Add shrimp, mustard, salt, pepper, and Worcestershire to garlic/wine mixture. Cook for 3–4 minutes or just until shrimp are tender.

Fork pasta onto 4 individual plates. Transfer shrimp onto pasta and pour remaining garlic/wine sauce over shrimp. Garnish with chopped parsley. Yields 4 (1-cup) servings.

Taste California (California)

Shrimp Molokai

2 pounds raw shrimp	1 whole bay leaf
1 cup pineapple juice	Hot pepper sauce to taste
1 cup sherry	1 stick (¼ pound) butter,
3 tablespoons lemon juice	melted
1 clove garlic, crushed	Sesame seeds
6 peppercorns	

Shell and devein shrimp. Place in a bowl together with a mixture of all the ingredients except the butter and sesame seeds. Marinate for 2–3 hours.

Strain shrimp and brush with melted butter. Roll shrimp in sesame seeds and cook lightly in a buttered pan until they turn pink. Boil remaining marinade liquid for 10 minutes to reduce it, then strain and use as a dip for the shrimp.

Joys of Hawaiian Cooking (Hawaii)

Shrimp Shack's "Pan Fried Shrimp"

1 gallon water	½ cup margarine to cook and
¼ cup garlic powder	dip in
¹⁄₁₆ cup cayenne powder	5 tablespoons chopped fresh
4 pounds shell-on black tiger	garlic
shrimp	Rice

Bring water to a boil; add garlic powder and cayenne to water. Drop in shrimp; return to a boil; drain. In sauté pan, heat margarine and chopped garlic. Sauté shrimp till golden brown, serve with rice, garlic butter, and cocktail sauce.

Shrimp Shack (in Punalu'u, O'ahu) (Hawaii)

Sweet and Sour Shrimp

The colorful mix of fresh, golden pineapple and green beans makes this a tempting stir-fry.

1 cup teriyaki sauce
⅓ cup pineapple juice
1 tablespoon rice vinegar
¼ teaspoon hot sauce
¼ teaspoon cornstarch
2 teaspoons canola oil,
  divided
1 teaspoon peeled and
  minced fresh ginger
1 cup fresh pineapple chunks

2 tablespoons minced green
  onion
2 cups (1½-inch pieces) long
  beans or fresh, young green
  beans
1 pound fresh or frozen, peeled
  and deveined shrimp
Cooked rice
Toasted sesame seeds for
  garnish

Whisk together teriyaki sauce, pineapple juice, vinegar, and hot sauce. Mix into cornstarch and set aside.

In saucepan, heat 1 teaspoon oil, and sauté ginger. Add pineapple chunks and green onion and heat until pineapple begins to brown. Stir occasionally. Add teriyaki-pineapple mixture and long beans. Simmer for about 5 minutes.

In a separate heavy skillet or wok, heat remaining oil and sauté shrimp until they just turn pink. Add to sauce and remove from heat. Serve over a bed of rice, and garnish with toasted sesame seeds. Serves 4.

Hawai'i's Favorite Pineapple Recipes (Hawaii)

Alaska joined the Union on January 3, 1959, as the 49th state; the land was purchased from Russia in 1867 for $7.2 million, about 2 cents per acre. The *New York Tribune* called it "Seward's Folly" after Secretary of State Seward, criticising a purchase of this worthless, frozen territory. Other newspapers praised the acquisition. Today its oil revenues bring in more in one day than the entire cost of the purchase.

Hawaii, the 50th state, joined the United States on August 21, 1959; it had been annexed as a territory in 1898.

Grilled Shrimp
with Mango Dipping Sauce

Skewered, coconut-marinated shrimp with lots of taste nuances. Terrific.

1 (14-ounce) can unsweetened coconut milk	1 pound large shrimp, shelled with tail intact
1 tablespoon minced garlic	Wooden skewers, soaked overnight
3 Hawaiian chili peppers, minced	Salt and cracked pepper to taste
Zest of 1 lime, grated	¼ cup vegetable oil
½ teaspoon paprika	

In medium bowl, whisk together coconut milk, garlic, chili, zest, and paprika. Add shrimp and marinate overnight in refrigerator. Also soak wooden skewers overnight.

Heat grill. Drain shrimp and season with salt and pepper. Add vegetable oil and toss lightly until coated. Thread soaked skewers with 4 shrimp. Grill 1½ minutes on both sides or until shrimp are opaque. Serve with Mango Dipping Sauce. Makes 4–5 main-course servings.

MANGO DIPPING SAUCE:

1 cup red wine vinegar	½ red bell pepper, small dice
½ cup sugar	½ green bell pepper, small dice
½ mango, puréed	
1 lime, juiced	

In medium saucepan, bring vinegar and sugar to a boil, then lower heat to medium and cook until syrupy consistency. When cooled, combine in blender with mango purée and lime juice. Stir in diced peppers. Reserve.

Kona on My Plate (Hawaii)

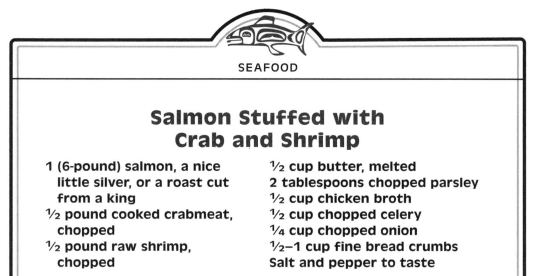

Salmon Stuffed with Crab and Shrimp

1 (6-pound) salmon, a nice little silver, or a roast cut from a king	½ cup butter, melted
	2 tablespoons chopped parsley
½ pound cooked crabmeat, chopped	½ cup chicken broth
	½ cup chopped celery
½ pound raw shrimp, chopped	¼ cup chopped onion
	½–1 cup fine bread crumbs
	Salt and pepper to taste

Remove scales, fins, head and tail. Using a very sharp filet knife, peel back the skin, beginning at the belly and working towards the backbone. Leave ⅛- to ¼-inch meat attached to the skin. Do to both sides, so that skin is completely released from the backbone. Set skin aside. Filet the meat from the backbone. Discard the bones and cut the fish into 1-inch cubes. Place the cubes in a large mixing bowl.

Mix remaining ingredients well with the salmon cubes. Add more stock, if too dry. Lay the reserved skin out flat. Mound the salmon mixture onto one half of the skin in an even thickness. Fold the other half of the skin over the filling. If you have used a small salmon rather than a roast, it will again look like a fish. Soak a piece of long cotton twine in a little cooking oil. Wrap around the fish in several places and tie. Cover lightly with foil. Bake at 325° for 1 hour or more until done. Remove wrap before serving. Serves 8–10.

Methodist Pie (Alaska)

The king crab, as its name might imply, is the largest of all the commercially important crab species and is always in demand. An adult king crab might reach lengths of up to six feet. King crabs are generally found in cold seas. In Alaska, there are three commercial king crab species: Blue king crabs, Golden king crabs, and Red king crabs, which are the most sought-after. Since statehood in 1959, nearly 2 billion pounds of king crab have been harvested off Alaskan coasts.

Grilled Wild Salmon
with Fresh Tarragon Butter

This simple method for grilling salmon is the salmon recipe most requested at our house. The grilled fish is paired with the subtle flavor of fresh tarragon and Walla Walla sweet onions that have been slowly cooked in lemon butter. We like the flavor of the fish when it is cooked directly on the grill, but it can also be cooked on a sheet of heavy-duty foil. If you use the latter method, grill the fish, skin-side-down, on the foil and do not turn the fish over while it is cooking. When the fish is served, the skin will stick to the foil, making it easy to serve pieces of the fillet.

½ cup chopped Walla Walla
   sweet onion
2 tablespoons chopped
   parsley
8 tablespoons (½ cup)
   butter or margarine
1 teaspoon minced fresh
   tarragon, or ½ teaspoon
   crushed dried tarragon

2 tablespoons lemon juice
1 (3-pound) Chinook, silver, or
   sockeye salmon or steelhead
   fillet
Salt and pepper
2 lemon slices
2 sprigs fresh parsley

In a saucepan, cook the onion, parsley, butter, lemon juice, and tarragon over medium-low heat until the onion is tender, about 20 minutes. Brush fish with a small amount of the melted butter mixture to keep it from sticking to the grill, and sprinkle with salt and pepper. Put the fillet, skin-side-up, on a moderately hot grill and cook for 15 minutes. Turn the fillet over and carefully stack onion from the tarragon butter over the fish. Cook for another 10 minutes, basting with butter often. (The fish needs to be turned only once while cooking.) Serve grilled fish on a warm platter garnished with slices of lemon and sprigs of fresh parsley. Serves 4–6.

Dungeness Crabs and Blackberry Cobblers (Oregon)

Grilled Cedar Planked King Salmon

Southeast Alaskan natives long ago discovered the wonderful flavors that result when smoking and cooking seafood with wood. Cedar or alder are traditional favorites.

Grilling plank
2 king salmon steaks
1 tablespoon olive oil

½ teaspoon each salt and
** pepper**
Juice of 1 fresh lemon

Soak plank for at least 30 minutes. Lightly coat salmon with olive oil. Sprinkle both sides with salt and pepper. Place salmon on grilling plank and set on grill over indirect heat. Grill for approximately 20 minutes or until internal temperature reaches 145°.

Tip: Cover salmon with the grill lid or make a foil lid which will trap in and surround the salmon with more smoke.

Wild Alaska Seafood—Twice a Week (Alaska)

Grilled Citrus Salmon

1½ tablespoons freshly-
** squeezed lemon juice**
2 tablespoons olive oil
1 tablespoon butter
1 tablespoon Dijon mustard
4 garlic cloves, minced

2 dashes cayenne pepper
2 dashes salt
1 teaspoon dried basil
1 teaspoon dried dill
2 teaspoons capers
3 pounds fresh salmon fillets

In a small sauté pan over medium heat, combine lemon juice, olive oil, butter, mustard, garlic, pepper, salt, basil, dill, and capers. While stirring, bring to a boil. Reduce heat and simmer for 5 minutes.

While sauce is still hot, brush on fish. Place salmon fillets skin-side-down on a piece of heavy-duty foil with edges folded up, to make a pan. Pour remaining sauce evenly over fish. Place fish on grill and cover with a lid. Barbecue over medium-hot coals for 10–12 minutes, depending on thickness of fillets. Fish will be flaky and light pink in color when cooked. Yields 6 servings.

Note: May wrap fish in foil and bake in 350° oven for 15–20 minutes.

From Portland's Palate (Oregon)

Grilled Salmon Fillets

Over the years we have presented salmon to our guests in many forms. We now feel marinating and barbecuing salmon is the best way to retain its fresh flavor. The marinade and barbecuing technique we have developed is a "never-fail" method. The fish remains moist, and the fresh salmon flavor is unencumbered by rich sauce.

1 (4- to 5-pound) whole, fresh salmon, filleted (with head and tail on, 1 pound per person)
¼ cup vegetable oil

2 tablespoons lemon juice
3 tablespoons soy sauce
1 large garlic clove, minced
½ teaspoon dried thyme

Place salmon fillets in a glass or other non-corrosive baking pan. Combine oil, lemon juice, soy sauce, garlic, and thyme. Pour over salmon fillets. Marinate 1 hour, turning the fish occasionally.

Prepare the barbecue. Cover barbecue grate with aluminum foil. Remove the fillets from the baking pan, reserving marinade, and place skin-side-down on the foil. Basting with reserved marinade, grill fish over medium heat 20–25 minutes, until fish flakes easily with a fork. Do not turn fish.

When fillets are cooked, you should be able to transfer them to a serving platter, leaving the skin behind on the foil! Serves 4–5.

Thyme and the River (Oregon)

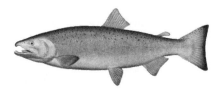

Pacific salmon are naturally found only in the northern Pacific Ocean, from California to Alaska. There are five different species of Pacific salmon: Chinook, Coho, Chum, Pink, and Sockeye. Pacific species account for all of the wild salmon caught in North America. Typically, salmon are anadromous: they are born in fresh water, migrate to the ocean, then return to fresh water to reproduce. Salmon natural history and human culture have closely intertwined for thousands of years. Whole economies were based on the salmon and the annual return of the salmon was a major cultural event. Native peoples around the Pacific Rim believed that these fish were a gift to be treated with respect, honored in ceremony, and celebrated in art. In recent years the lost relationship between salmon and humans has experienced a revival. "Salmon communities" once again welcome the fish's return to their home rivers with festivals and ceremonies.

Baked Dijon Salmon

This is a wonderful way to prepare fresh salmon fillets in the oven. Be sure to make extra; your family will be begging for more.

¼ cup butter, melted
3 tablespoons prepared Dijon-
  style mustard
1½ tablespoons honey
¼ cup dry bread crumbs
¼ cup finely chopped pecans

4 teaspoons chopped fresh
  parsley
4 (4-ounce) salmon fillets
Salt and pepper to taste
1 lemon for garnish

Preheat oven to 400°. In a small bowl, stir together butter, mustard, and honey. Set aside. In another bowl, mix together bread crumbs, pecans, and parsley.

Brush each salmon fillet lightly with honey-mustard mixture, and sprinkle top of fillets with bread crumb mixture. Bake salmon in pre-heated oven until it flakes easily with a fork, approximately 10–15 minutes. Season with salt and pepper, and garnish with a wedge of lemon. Makes 4 servings.

Allrecipes Tried & True Favorites (Washington)

Pecan-Crusted Salmon

1½ cups dry bread crumbs
½ cup crushed pecans
2 teaspoons garlic powder
6 (6-ounce) salmon fillets,
  about ¾ inch thick

6 teaspoons stoneground
  mustard
Pepper

Preheat oven to 425°. In a small bowl, combine bread crumbs, pecans, and garlic powder together. Place salmon fillets in a lightly oiled, oblong baking dish. Spread 1 teaspoon mustard on each fillet. Evenly sprinkle bread crumb mixture over each salmon fillet and sea-son with pepper. Bake 10–15 minutes, depending on the thickness, until salmon is slightly opaque and topping is lightly browned. Transfer to a platter and serve. Yields 6 servings.

Drop the Hook, Let's Eat (Alaska)

Salmon with Basil Cream Sauce

1 (2-pound) salmon fillet, cut into 6 (5⅓-ounce) fillets
1½ tablespoons unsalted butter
1 clove garlic, peeled and minced
3 shallots, peeled and minced
1½ cups chopped fresh basil
¼ cup chopped fresh parsley
¾ cup dry white wine
⅓ cup half-and-half
1 tablespoon lemon juice
¼ teaspoon white pepper
¼ teaspoon salt

Sear salmon in melted butter over medium-high heat on each side for 2 to 3 minutes. Remove and keep warm. Turn heat to low and sauté garlic with shallots for about 5 minutes. Add rest of ingredients to pan and cook on medium heat until sauce is reduced by half. Taste for seasoning, adding more pepper and salt as needed.

To serve, reheat fish gently in sauce until it flakes. The sauce is a nice green color. Spoon around fish on plates.

Note: The fish can be prepared up to 3 hours ahead, then reheated, uncovered, over low heat for 10 minutes. Serves 6.

Cooking with Herbs (California)

Alaska Salmon Nuggets

1 tablespoon finely minced celery
1 tablespoon finely minced onion
1 tablespoon butter, melted
1½ cups cooked, flaked salmon (or canned salmon)
½ cup cooked, mashed potatoes
¼ teaspoon salt
⅛ teaspoon pepper
1 teaspoon Worcestershire
1 egg, well beaten
¼ pound processed cheese
1 cup finely sifted bread crumbs

Colorlessly fry celery and onions in butter over low heat until they turn clear. Place fish and potatoes in a bowl and mash them. Add celery, onion, salt, pepper, Worcestershire, and egg. Mix thoroughly. Roll the mixture into balls the size of walnuts. Cut cheese into ¼-inch cubes. Roll these in palms of hands until round. Push 1 piece of cheese into the center of each fish ball and reshape by rolling in hands again. Roll in sifted bread crumbs. Fry in deep fat, 375°, until golden brown.

The Original Great Alaska Cookbook (Alaska)

Annie's Salmon Patties

Make extra of these so you can have a fish sandwich the next day on a toasted bun with lettuce, tomato, thin slice of onion, cheese, dill pickle, mayonnaise, ketchup, or tartar sauce.

1 pint salmon (remove dark pieces but leave bones and liquid)
2½ cups very dry mashed potatoes
¼ cup diced onion
¼ cup diced celery
¼ cup diced green pepper

1½ tablespoons lemon juice
½ teaspoon lemon pepper
½ teaspoon garlic salt
4–6 shakes of hot sauce
1 egg
1 tablespoon mayonnaise
½ cup fine cracker crumbs

Mash the salmon into the potatoes. Add remaining ingredients. Form into patties (if mixture does not hold its shape, add a few more cracker crumbs to the mixture). Let set a few minutes and then form patties. If too dry, add another egg or a small amount of milk.

COATING:
1 or 2 sleeves of crackers, crushed fine
½ cup plain, fine bread crumbs

Place 1 cup cracker crumbs and bread crumbs in a large plastic bag. Place patties in the cracker crumbs inside the bag. Pat down and turn over bag very carefully and pat crumbs into patty. Remove to a cracker-crumb-sprinkled cookie sheet. Refrigerate for 2 hours. (At this point, you can freeze the patties for 3 months; thaw in fridge before using.) Fry in ½ inch vegetable oil in a large cast-iron skillet, 2 at a time. Remove to warm platter. Makes about 6 patties.

Grannie Annie's Cookin' Fish from Cold Alaskan Waters (Alaska)

Salmon Squares à la Janet

3 tablespoons butter or margarine
2 pounds salmon fillets, cut into 1-inch squares

1 teaspoon salt
½ teaspoon pepper
2 eggs, slightly beaten
Soda crackers, crushed

Heat butter or margarine in frying pan. Season salmon squares to taste. Dip salmon squares in beaten egg and then in cracker crumbs until all sides are coated. Brown in butter until cooked. Serve with lemon wedges and a sauce of your choice. Serves 6.

"Pacific"ally Salmon (Oregon)

Ginger Salmon with Kiwi Salsa

GINGER SALMON:

4 salmon fillets

2 tablespoons thinly sliced
   fresh gingerroot

2 tablespoons chopped green
   onions

Soy sauce

4 teaspoons vegetable oil
   (optional)

Rinse salmon fillets and pat dry. Arrange on a microwave-safe plate.
Sprinkle with sliced gingerroot and green onions. Top each with a
splash of soy sauce. Cover plate with plastic wrap, venting 1 edge.
Microwave on high for 7 minutes or until fish flakes easily. Heat oil
in a small microwave-safe dish on high for 30 seconds or until hot.
Drizzle hot oil over salmon.

KIWI SALSA:

6 ripe kiwifruit, peeled, diced

2 tablespoons minced red
   onion

½ teaspoon finely chopped
   jalapeño chile

2 tablespoons finely chopped
   fresh cilantro

2 teaspoons grated lime zest

2 tablespoons (or more) fresh
   lime juice

½ teaspoon (or more) salt

Mix kiwifruit, red onion, jalapeño, cilantro, lime zest, lime juice, and
salt in a bowl. Add more lime juice or salt, if desired. Serve with
Ginger Salmon. Yields 4 servings.

Note: You may substitute pineapple in place of kiwifruit if kiwifruit is not
in season. May also serve the salsa with chicken or tortilla chips.

Cooking from the Coast to the Cascades (Oregon)

Honey Mustard Salmon

2 tablespoons honey
1 teaspoon Dijon mustard

Approximately 2 pounds salmon

Mix honey and mustard well. Place foil on barbeque grill. Poke holes
in foil approximately 3 inches apart. Place salmon on foil. Baste
salmon several times with honey and mustard mixture. Turn salmon
over and baste several times. Cook fish until done (when it flakes).

Fresh-Water Fish Cookbook (Oregon)

Halibut Stuffed with Alaskan Crab

CAPER BUTTER:

¼ pound butter, softened
2 tablespoons chopped capers
1 tablespoon chopped shallots

2 tablespoons lemon juice
1 teaspoon chopped, fresh dill
1 teaspoon Dijon mustard

Mix butter with capers, shallots, lemon juice, dill, and mustard. Set aside.

STUFFING AND HALIBUT:

2 slices bacon, chopped fine
1 tablespoon butter
2 stalks celery, diced
¼ cup dried onion
½ cup sliced mushrooms
¼ pound crabmeat, flaked
Salt to taste

Pepper to taste
1 teaspoon chopped fresh thyme
1 teaspoon chopped fresh parsley
1 egg
1 pound halibut fillet or steak

Sauté bacon in butter until brown. Add celery, onion, and mushrooms. When tender, add crab, salt, pepper, and herbs. Remove from heat and mix in egg. Set aside to cool. Cut a pocket in halibut and stuff with crab mixture. Grill until halibut flakes. Top with Caper Butter. Serves 2.

Alaska Shrimp & Crab Recipes (Alaska)

Halibut Steak with Sauce

1–1½ pounds halibut steak
Salt and pepper
1 small onion, sliced and
   separated into rings
⅓ stick butter, melted

½ cup sour cream
Juice of ½ lemon
½ cup grated Cheddar cheese
Parsley flakes
Garlic salt

Place halibut steaks in a baking dish and sprinkle with salt and pepper. Place rings of onion on top of steaks. Combine melted butter, sour cream, and lemon juice. Mix by hand and pour over steaks. Place cheese over fish/sauce. Garnish with parsley flakes and garlic salt. Bake at 350°, uncovered, for 30 minutes.

Grade A Recipes (Oregon)

Halibut Almandine

Flour
Salt and pepper
2 pounds halibut fillets
½ cup butter, melted, divided
1 can peaches, drained
½ cup blanched almonds
2 tablespoons lemon juice

Season flour with salt and pepper to taste. Dip halibut in butter, then in seasoned flour. Place halibut fillets in a greased baking pan and pour ½ the remaining butter over them. Bake at 350° for 20–25 minutes, or until fillets flake.

Sauté peaches and almonds in remaining butter. Add lemon juice. Spoon a peach and some juice over each fillet. Serves 4.

Alaskan Halibut Recipes (Alaska)

Halibut Enchiladas

4 ounces cream cheese,
  softened
¼ cup sour cream
¼ cup mayonnaise or more
1 small can sliced black olives
1 small can chopped Ortega
  peppers
½ medium onion, chopped
1½ cups flaked, baked halibut
  fillet (or more)
1½ cans enchilada sauce (hot
  or regular), divided
1 package flour or corn tortillas
2 cups grated cheese, divided

Cream cheese, sour cream, and mayonnaise. Add olives, peppers, onion, and halibut; mix well. Place 1 spoonful of enchilada sauce on each tortilla and enough filling to make a good sized enchilada. Put some cheese in each tortilla. Roll up and place in greased 9x13-inch pan, with ½ remaining enchilada sauce on bottom. Put remaining cheese over the top of the enchiladas and pour the remaining sauce over the entire casserole. Bake at 350° for 45 minutes or until heated through and cheese is melted.

Pelican, Alaska: Alaskan Recipe Cookbook (Alaska)

Baked Snapper
with Ginger Salsa

Fresh 'ōpakapaka (snapper) from Kona waters is the star of this easy, succulent dish.

GINGER SALSA:

3 medium tomatoes, peeled
and diced

2 tablespoons chopped
scallions

2 tablespoons chopped fresh
cilantro

2 tablespoons diced jicama

3 tablespoons fresh lime juice,
divided

2–3 teaspoons minced
Hawaiian chili pepper

2 teaspoons peeled and minced
fresh ginger

Combine tomatoes, scallions, cilantro, jicama, 2 tablespoons lime juice, chili pepper, and ginger in bowl. Cover and let sit for at least one hour.

4 (6-ounce) fresh red snapper
fillets

1 cup dry white wine

Preheat oven to 425°. Place snapper fillets in a shallow pan and cover with wine and remaining one tablespoon lime juice. Cover pan with aluminum foil and bake for 25 minutes or until fish flakes easily with a fork. Arrange fish on serving plate and spoon Ginger Salsa on top. Serves 4.

Kona on My Plate (Hawaii)

Kaua'i Fillet of Sole

4 fish fillets (about 1 pound)
Salt and pepper
2 tablespoons lime juice,
divided
Flour for dredging
3 or 4 tablespoons butter

¼ cup heavy cream
1 avocado, peeled, and sliced
¼ cup coarsely chopped
macadamia nuts
Lime wedges

Sprinkle fish with salt and pepper and 1 tablespoon lime juice; let stand 10 minutes. Dredge with flour. Sauté in butter 1–3 minutes on each side until nicely browned. Remove to warm platter, sprinkle with remaining lime juice. Keep warm.

To the pan, add cream and bring to rapid boil, scraping brown particles free; spoon over fish. Top with avocado slices, macadamia nuts, and lime wedges. Serves 2.

Cook 'em Up Kaua'i (Hawaii)

Baked Mahi

8 mahimahi fillets
8 tablespoons mayonnaise
8 tablespoons lime juice

8 dill sprigs
Black pepper
Lime wedges

Pat fillets dry. Place in aluminum foil, smear top with mayonnaise and dribble over with lime juice. Add sprigs of dill and sprinkle with pepper before sealing the edges of foil. Bake in preheated 350° oven for 20 minutes. Unwrap; garnish with lime wedges. Serves 6–8.

Favorite Island Cookery Book V (Hawaii)

Grilled Mahi Mahi with Mango Salsa

MANGO SALSA:

3 tablespoons lime juice
1 tablespoon fish sauce or fish extract
1 teaspoon sugar
2 tablespoons sliced green onions
1½ cups chopped tomatoes
2 ripe but firm mangos, peeled and diced

1 cup chopped Walla Walla or other sweet onions
2 tablespoons chopped fresh cilantro
1 or 2 jalapeño peppers, chopped, or 1 teaspoon crushed red pepper
1 teaspoon minced garlic

Combine lime juice, fish sauce, and sugar in a large bowl. Stir until sugar dissolves. Add remaining salsa ingredients, mix, cover and refrigerate for 30 minutes. Stir well before serving.

FISH:
2 pounds Mahi Mahi

Grill Mahi Mahi over medium-hot coals until fish flakes easily, about 15 minutes. Serve Mango Salsa over fish. Serves 4.

Note: Fish sauce can be found in the International section of many supermarkets. Try this recipe with any firm white fish such as halibut, cod, or red snapper.

Gold'n Delicious (Washington)

Grandpa's Scalloped Clams and Potatoes

6 cups thinly sliced potatoes
⅓ cup flour
½ cup chopped onion
1½ teaspoons salt or to taste
⅛ teaspoon pepper
½ teaspoon granulated onion
   or powdered onion

1½ cups chopped razor or
   other clams
1 cup water
1 cup evaporated milk
1 tablespoon butter or
   margarine

Dust potatoes with flour. Mix remaining ingredients (including all the flour) together, except milk and butter. Place in greased 2½-quart casserole dish with cover. Pour milk on top and dot with butter. Cook in 350° oven 1¼ hours, covered, and 15 minutes, uncovered, or until potatoes are almost done.

Note: May use clam nectar in place of milk and/or water.

What's Cookin' in the Kenai Peninsula (*Alaska*)

Northwest Clam Bake

6 dozen clams (steamers)
12 small onions
6 medium potatoes
6 ears of corn in the husks

3 Dungeness crabs, cleaned
Lemon wedges
Melted butter or margarine

Wash clam shells thoroughly. Peel onions; parboil for 15 minutes along with the potatoes. Drain. Remove corn silk and replace husks. Cut 12 pieces of cheesecloth and 12 pieces of heavy-duty aluminum foil, 18x36 inches each. Place 2 pieces of cheesecloth on top of 2 pieces of foil. Place 2 onions, a potato, an ear of corn, 1 dozen clams and ½ Dungeness crab on cheesecloth. Tie opposite corners of the cheesecloth together. Pour 1 cup of water over the package. Bring foil up over the food and close all edges with tight double fold. Make 6 packages. Place packages on grill, about 4 inches from hot coals. Cover with hood or aluminum foil. Cook for 45–60 minutes, or until onions and potatoes are cooked. Serve with lemon wedges and butter.

Clam Dishes and Rock Fishes (*Oregon*)

Baked Scallops

This recipe is deceptively simple to make and the results are wonderful.

1 pound scallops, raw
½ cup cream or half-and-half
Salt and pepper to taste

Dash of nutmeg
1 cup cracker crumbs, divided
1½ tablespoons butter, melted

Mix scallops with the cream. Add salt, pepper, nutmeg and most of the cracker crumbs. Place in baking dish and cover with remaining cracker crumbs and sprinkle with melted butter. Bake in preheated 375° oven for 25 minutes.

What's Cooking in Sisters (Oregon)

Oregon Seafood Stir-fry

¾ pound sole
¼ pound scallops
⅓ pound shrimp
2 teaspoons cornstarch
¼ cup white wine
1½ tablespoons soy sauce
¾ cup orange juice
2 tablespoons vegetable oil

2 teaspoons grated ginger root
1 tablespoon minced garlic
2 ounces pea pods
1 medium red pepper, thinly
  sliced
½ cup sliced green onions
½ teaspoon sesame oil
½ pound Oriental noodles

Rinse fish and shellfish briefly with cold water; pat dry with paper towels. Cut sole into large chunks. Combine cornstarch, wine, soy sauce, and orange juice. Add fish chunks and marinate in refrigerator 30 minutes. Drain fish, reserving marinade.

Heat oil in skillet; add ginger and garlic. Sauté 5–10 seconds. Add fish chunks and stir-fry for 4 minutes, or until medium-rare. Add scallops, vegetables, and sesame oil; stir-fry 2 minutes. Add shrimp and continue cooking just until sauce thickens. Serve immediately over Oriental noodles.

Scallops and Sole Food (Oregon)

Orange Broiled Shark

Shark steaks
Undiluted orange juice
  concentrate
Tequila (optional)

Onion rings
Bell pepper, cut into rings
Toasted, sliced almonds

The ingredients aren't given in specific quantities because you adjust to the amount of shark steak you have. Marinate shark steaks in orange juice concentrate overnight in refrigerator, adding tequila (to taste) if desired. A jigger or 2 is plenty. Place marinated shark in baking dish and decorate with rings of onion and bell pepper. Sprinkle with almonds. Broil about 7–9 minutes in preheated oven until meat flakes easily. Watch carefully to avoid burning. Turn and broil about 3 minutes on other side. Serve immediately on bed of rice.

Variation: As an alternate recipe, use a can of frozen piña colada drink concentrate and garnish with toasted coconut.

The Wild and Free Cookbook (Washington)

WIKIPEDIA.COM

Haystack Rock at Cannon Beach, Oregon, is 235 feet high. Climbing "The Rock" is prohibited because it is a sanctuary harboring four types of birds. The surrounding tide pools and marine life are also protected. Three smaller, adjacent rock formations to the south of Haystack Rock are collectively called "The Needles."

Oyster Stuffing

¼ cup butter
2 small onions, chopped
1 bunch celery, chopped
1 tablespoon chopped garlic
4 cups chicken stock
1 quart shucked oysters,
   halved if large, liquor
   reserved

¼ cup chopped parsley
6–8 cups bread cubes
1 tablespoon ground sage
1 tablespoon dried thyme
Salt and pepper
1 cup grated Parmesan cheese

Heat butter in a large saucepan over medium heat and sauté onions, celery, and garlic for about 5 minutes or until limp. Add chicken stock and oyster liquor. Boil to reduce by ⅓, then add oysters and parsley. Return just to a boil, then immediately take the pan from the heat. Add bread cubes, enough to make a moist dressing but not wet. Add sage, thyme, and salt and pepper to taste, then stir in Parmesan cheese. Put stuffing in a large, buttered baking dish and bake at 350° until heated through and somewhat crusty on top and sides, 15–20 minutes. Makes about 10 cups.

Recipe by Chef Eric Jenkins,
Duncan Law Seafood Consumer Center, Astoria, Oregon
Heaven on the Half Shell (Washington)

CAKES

Mount Rainier dominates the horizon of the Seattle-Tacoma area of Washington, where it is known fondly as "The Mountain." With 26 major glaciers and 35 square miles of permanent snowfields, it is the most heavily glaciated peak in the lower 48 states. The mountain and surrounding area are protected within Mount Rainier National Park, established in 1899.

'Ono Coconut Cake

3 cups cake flour
1½ cups sugar
5 teaspoons baking powder
½ teaspoon salt
8 egg whites

1½ cups fresh coconut milk
   (if not available, use canned)
1½ cups freshly grated
   coconut (or packaged)

Sift flour, sugar, and baking powder together. Add salt to egg whites and beat until stiff but not too dry. Add coconut milk to dry ingredients and beat till smooth. Fold in coconut and egg whites. Put into 2 (9-inch) cake pans that have been greased and floured. Bake for 40–45 minutes at 350°. Cool.

Frost with white frosting and sprinkle generously with additional freshly grated coconut.

Friends and Celebrities Cookbook II (Hawaii)

Kulik Cream Cake

2 cups sugar
1 stick margarine, softened
⅓ cup shortening
5 eggs, yolks and whites
  separated

1 teaspoon baking soda
1 cup buttermilk
2¼ cups flour
1 small can flaked coconut
1 teaspoon vanilla

Preheat oven to 350°. Grease and flour 3 (9-inch) cake pans. Cream together sugar, margarine, and shortening. Add egg yolks, one at a time, beating well after each one (reserve egg whites). Add baking soda to buttermilk, then alternately add flour and buttermilk to creamed mixture. Stir in coconut. Beat egg whites until stiff and fold into mixture. Add vanilla. Pour into 3 prepared cake pans. Bake at 350° for 25 minutes.

ICING:

1 (8-ounce) package cream
  cheese, softened
1 stick butter or margarine,
  softened

1 pound powdered sugar, sifted
1 teaspoon vanilla
1 cup chopped pecans

Cream together cream cheese and margarine, beating until smooth. Add powdered sugar and vanilla, and beat until light and fluffy. Stir in pecans. Spread on cooled cake layers. Serves 16.

Best Recipes of Alaska's Fishing Lodges (Alaska)

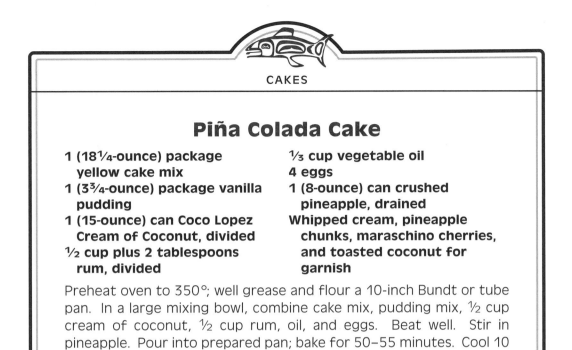

Piña Colada Cake

1 (18¼-ounce) package
  yellow cake mix
1 (3¾-ounce) package vanilla
  pudding
1 (15-ounce) can Coco Lopez
  Cream of Coconut, divided
½ cup plus 2 tablespoons
  rum, divided

⅓ cup vegetable oil
4 eggs
1 (8-ounce) can crushed
  pineapple, drained
Whipped cream, pineapple
  chunks, maraschino cherries,
  and toasted coconut for
  garnish

Preheat oven to 350°; well grease and flour a 10-inch Bundt or tube pan. In a large mixing bowl, combine cake mix, pudding mix, ½ cup cream of coconut, ½ cup rum, oil, and eggs. Beat well. Stir in pineapple. Pour into prepared pan; bake for 50–55 minutes. Cool 10 minutes.

With a table knife or skewer, poke holes about 1 inch apart in cake almost to the bottom. Combine remaining cream of coconut and remaining 2 tablespoons rum; slowly spoon over cake. Chill thoroughly. Store in refrigerator. Garnish as desired. Serves 12.

Dd's Table Talk (Hawaii)

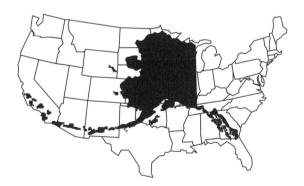

Alaska contains 586,412 square miles and is one-fifth the size of the Lower 48 states, 488 times larger than Rhode Island, two and a half times larger than Texas, and larger than the next three largest states in the U.S. combined. East to west (including the Aleutian Islands), Alaska measures 2,400 miles—roughly the distance between Savannah, Georgia, and Santa Barbara, California.

Blue Ribbon Carrot Cake

An extremely moist, rich cake.

BUTTERMILK GLAZE:

1 cup granulated sugar
½ teaspoon baking soda
½ cup buttermilk
¼ cup (½ stick) butter
1 tablespoon light corn syrup
1 teaspoon vanilla extract

In small saucepan over high heat, combine sugar, baking soda, buttermilk, butter, and corn syrup. Bring to a boil. Cook 5 minutes, stirring occasionally. Remove from heat and stir in vanilla. Set aside until cake is baked.

CAKE:

2 cups all-purpose flour
2 teaspoons baking soda
2 teaspoons cinnamon
½ teaspoon salt
3 eggs
¾ cup vegetable oil
¾ cup buttermilk
2 cups granulated sugar
2 teaspoons vanilla extract
1 (8-ounce) can crushed
   pineapple, drained
2 cups grated carrots
3½ ounces shredded coconut
1 cup seedless raisins
1 cup coarsely chopped walnuts

Generously grease a 9x13-inch baking pan or 2 (9-inch) cake pans. Sift flour, baking soda, cinnamon, and salt together; set aside. In a large bowl, beat eggs. Add oil, buttermilk, sugar, and vanilla and mix well. Add flour mixture, pineapple, carrots, coconut, raisins, and walnuts and stir well. Pour into prepared pan. Bake 45–55 minutes or until a toothpick inserted in the center comes out clean.

Remove cake from oven and slowly pour Buttermilk Glaze over the hot cake. Cool cake in pan until Glaze is totally absorbed, about 15 minutes.

FROSTING:

¼ cup (½ stick) butter,
   room temperature
1 (8-ounce) package cream
   cheese, room temperature
1 teaspoon vanilla extract
2 cups powdered sugar
1 teaspoon freshly squeezed
   orange juice
1 teaspoon grated orange peel

In a large bowl, cream butter and cream cheese until fluffy. Add vanilla, powdered sugar, orange juice, and orange peel. Mix until smooth. Frost cake and refrigerate until Frosting is set. Serve cake chilled. Yields 20–24 servings.

From Portland's Palate (Oregon)

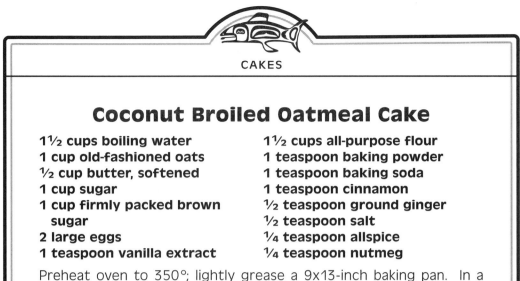

Coconut Broiled Oatmeal Cake

1½ cups boiling water
1 cup old-fashioned oats
½ cup butter, softened
1 cup sugar
1 cup firmly packed brown
 sugar
2 large eggs
1 teaspoon vanilla extract

1½ cups all-purpose flour
1 teaspoon baking powder
1 teaspoon baking soda
1 teaspoon cinnamon
½ teaspoon ground ginger
½ teaspoon salt
¼ teaspoon allspice
¼ teaspoon nutmeg

Preheat oven to 350°; lightly grease a 9x13-inch baking pan. In a mixing bowl, combine water and oats; let stand 15 minutes. In a mixing bowl, cream together butter and sugars. Add eggs and extract. Stir in oats and remaining ingredients. Pour mixture into prepared pan; bake 30–35 minutes. Serves 12.

FROSTING:
½ cup butter, melted
1 cup firmly packed brown
 sugar

6 tablespoons cream
1 cup chopped walnuts
1 cup flaked coconut

In a mixing bowl, combine ingredients. Spread onto hot cake. Place under broiler until bubbly.

Dd's Table Talk II (Hawaii)

Shanna's Birthday Cake

(Turtle Cake)

¾ cup butter or margarine
1 (14-ounce) package caramels
½ can condensed milk (not evaporated)
1 package German chocolate cake mix
2 cups chopped nuts, divided
1 cup chocolate chips

Melt butter, caramels, and condensed milk over low heat and set aside. Mix cake as directed on package. Pour half of batter into greased 9x13-inch pan. Bake 15 minutes at 350°. Pour caramel mixture over baked cake. Add 1 cup nuts and chocolate chips. Pour rest of batter over this and sprinkle remaining 1 cup nuts on top. Bake for an additional 20 minutes.

Recipes from the Paris of the Pacific—Sitka, Alaska (Alaska)

Potato Caramel Cake

2 cups light brown sugar
4 eggs, separated
⅔ cup shortening
½ cup sweet milk
3 squares chocolate, melted
1 cup hot potatoes, riced
2 cups pastry flour, divided
½ teaspoon salt
2 teaspoons baking powder
1 teaspoon cloves
1 teaspoon cinnamon
1 teaspoon nutmeg
1 cup chopped nuts

Cream together the light brown sugar, egg yolks, and shortening. Add milk, melted chocolate (beaten in while hot), and hot riced potatoes. Reserve ¼ cup flour for nuts. Add remaining flour, salt, baking powder, and spices sifted together; fold in the floured nuts. Beat egg whites until stiff; fold into mixture. Pour into 3 greased and floured layer cake pans, and bake at 350° for 25 minutes. Make Filling.

FILLING:
1 cup thin cream
1½ cups butter
2 cups brown sugar
1 teaspoon vanilla

Cook cream, butter, and sugar together until it forms a soft ball in cold water; remove from heat, add vanilla, and beat until creamy. When cool, spread between cake layers and on top.

Alaska Gold Rush Cook Book (Alaska)

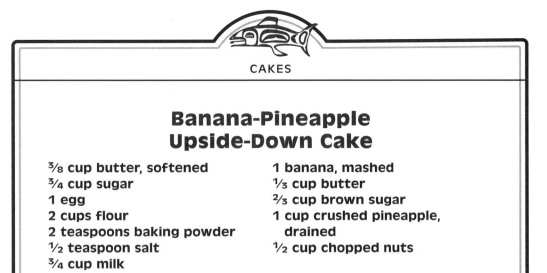
Banana-Pineapple Upside-Down Cake

3/8 cup butter, softened
3/4 cup sugar
1 egg
2 cups flour
2 teaspoons baking powder
1/2 teaspoon salt
3/4 cup milk

1 banana, mashed
1/3 cup butter
2/3 cup brown sugar
1 cup crushed pineapple, drained
1/2 cup chopped nuts

Cream 3/8 cup butter and sugar; add beaten egg. Sift flour, baking powder, and salt; add gradually with milk to butter mixture. Fold in mashed banana. Melt 1/3 cup butter in 8-inch-square pan or small tube pan. Sprinkle brown sugar over butter; add well-drained crushed pineapple and chopped nuts. Pour batter over this mixture and bake in 350° preheated oven for 25–30 minutes. Serves 6–8.

Cook 'em Up Kaua'i (Hawaii)

Alaska Blueberry Special Cake

1 yellow cake mix
1 large package lemon pie filling

1 (12-ounce) carton Cool Whip

Mix cake according to package directions. Bake in jellyroll pan. Cool. Mix lemon pie filling according to package directions (or make from scratch). Top cooled cake with lemon pie filling; cover with Cool Whip. Serve with Blueberry Sauce.

BLUEBERRY SAUCE:
2/3 cup brown sugar
1 tablespoon cornstarch
Dash of salt

2/3 cup water
2 cups fresh or frozen blueberries

Cook all ingredients except blueberries until thick. Add blueberries. Return to boil. Chill. Serve over cake.

Pelican, Alaska: Alaskan Recipe Cookbook (Alaska)

Blueberry-Raspberry Upside-Down Cake

I bake this wonderfully moist cake in my 9-inch cast-iron frying pan—the heavy pan keeps the butter from burning and the handle makes it easy to flip the cake upside down when it is done. It can be served warm from the oven for dessert or as a coffee cake for a brunch, but once it has cooled, the cake needs to be tightly wrapped in plastic wrap—it will get more moist the longer it sits.

7 tablespoons butter, divided
1 cup brown sugar
2 eggs
1 cup sugar
½ cup milk
¼ teaspoon salt
1 cup all-purpose flour
1 teaspoon baking powder
1 pint fresh raspberries
1 pint fresh blueberries
1 pint (2 cups) heavy cream
¼ cup powdered sugar
1 teaspoon vanilla

Preheat oven to 375°. Melt 5 tablespoons butter in a heavy skillet and stir in brown sugar. Cook over medium heat until sugar dissolves. Keep warm over low heat. Beat eggs and sugar together until light, about 4 minutes. Melt remaining 2 tablespoons butter in milk over low heat or in microwave, on high, for 1 minute. Sift together salt, flour, and baking powder. Add dry ingredients and warm milk to beaten eggs and sugar. Stir brown sugar and butter mixture in a cast-iron skillet and sprinkle raspberries and blueberries over it. Pour batter over berries and bake cake for 45 minutes, or until a toothpick inserted in center of cake comes out clean.

As soon as it is done, carefully turn cake upside down onto a large platter with a lip, to catch the juices. Whip cream with powdered sugar and vanilla. Serve cake warm with a dollop of whipped cream. Makes 8 servings.

Dungeness Crabs and Blackberry Cobblers (Oregon)

Strawberry Cream Cake

1 white cake mix
1 (8-ounce) package cream
    cheese, softened
2 cups powdered sugar
2 cups Cool Whip

2 cups frozen strawberries (or
    huckleberries, raspberries,
    etc.)
½ cup sugar
3 tablespoons cornstarch

Mix cake mix as directed on package and bake in a 9x13-inch pan. Cool. Whip cream cheese and powdered sugar; fold in Cool Whip. Spread over cooled cake. Combine strawberries, ½ cup sugar, and cornstarch in saucepan. Cook until thickened, cool slightly, and spread over cream mixture. Refrigerate until ready to serve.

Recipes from Our Friends (Washington)

Peach Refrigerator Cake

FILLING:
1 (13-ounce) can evaporated
    milk
1 (26-ounce) can sliced
    peaches, undrained

½ cup sugar
1 (3-ounce) box orange Jell-O
1 envelope unflavored gelatin

Put can of evaporated milk in freezer. Heat peaches with syrup and sugar and remove from heat. Add Jell-O and mix well. Add gelatin which has been softened in ¼ cup water. Cool. Beat icy cold can of evaporated milk until whipped. Fold into peach mixture gradually.

1 large chiffon cake   **Whipped cream**

Coat a 9x13-inch pan generously with butter. Break cake into bite-size pieces. Put in buttered pan. Layer cake pieces and Filling, starting with cake first. Frost with whipped cream. Chill.

Favorite Island Cookery Book I (Hawaii)

Huckleberry Dump Cake

1 quart huckleberries
1 cup sugar
2 tablespoons cornstarch
¼ teaspoon almond extract

1 box white or sour cream cake
  mix
1 stick margarine
1 cup chopped nuts

Put huckleberries in greased 9x13-inch pan. Mix sugar and cornstarch and put over berries. Sprinkle with almond extract. Sprinkle cake mix on top. Cut margarine in pieces and put on top of cake mix along with chopped nuts. Bake 40–45 minutes at 350°.

Our Best Home Cooking (Washington)

Fresh Apple Bundt Cake

CAKE:

3 cups flour
1 teaspoon salt
1 teaspoon baking soda
3 cups diced, peeled apples
1 cup chopped nuts

2 cups sugar
1 cup vegetable oil
2 eggs
1 teaspoon vanilla

Sift together flour, salt, and baking soda. Add rest of ingredients and mix together until blended. Spread into a greased and floured tube pan. Bake 1 hour and 15 minutes at 350°.

TOPPING:

½ cup butter, melted
¼ cup sugar
1 tablespoon corn syrup

1 teaspoon vanilla
Powdered sugar for sprinkling
  on top (optional)

Combine all ingredients except powdered sugar, and pour Topping down sides of hot cake while still in pan. Cool 30 minutes; remove from pan. Sprinkle top with powdered sugar, if desired.

Marilyn Thomas: The Homemaker Baker's Favorite Recipes (California)

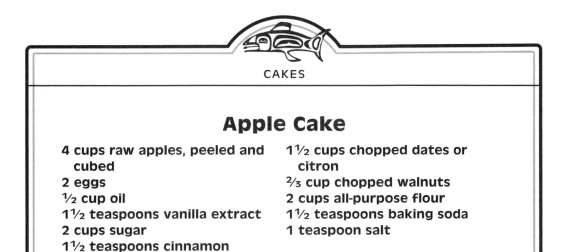

Apple Cake

4 cups raw apples, peeled and cubed

2 eggs

½ cup oil

1½ teaspoons vanilla extract

2 cups sugar

1½ teaspoons cinnamon

1½ cups chopped dates or citron

⅔ cup chopped walnuts

2 cups all-purpose flour

1½ teaspoons baking soda

1 teaspoon salt

Preheat oven to 350°. Place cubed apples in bowl. Break eggs over them and mix well. Add oil, vanilla, sugar, cinnamon, dates, and walnuts and stir together. Sift flour, baking soda, and salt together and add to apple mixture. Mix with wooden spoon until flour mixture is thoroughly blended into apple mixture. Pour batter into greased 9x13-inch baking pan and bake for 45 minutes. Serve warm or cold with Grand Marnier Whipped Cream.

GRAND MARNIER WHIPPED CREAM:

1 cup whipping cream

2 tablespoons Grand Marnier

1 tablespoon powdered sugar or to taste

Whip cream in bowl until stiff. Slowly beat in Grand Marnier and powdered sugar until blended.

Skagit Valley Fare (Washington)

Microsoft Corporation is a multinational computer technology corporation that develops, manufactures, licenses, and supports a wide range of software products for computing devices. Headquartered in Redmond, Washington, its most profitable products are the Microsoft Windows operating system and the Microsoft Office suite of productivity software as well as home entertainment products such as the Xbox video game console, and the Zune mp3 player.

The Best Rhubarb Cake

All rhubarb cakes are good, but this is the best!!!

¼ cup shortening
¼ cup vegetable oil
1½ cups brown sugar
1 egg
1 teaspoon vanilla
1 teaspoon baking soda
¼ teaspoon salt

1 cup buttermilk or sour milk
  (1 teaspoon vinegar in a cup
  of milk)
2 cups flour
1½–2 cups diced rhubarb
1 cup chopped walnuts
  (optional)

Cream shortening and oil with brown sugar. Add egg and vanilla. Cream until very fluffy. While this is mixing; combine baking soda, salt, and flour in a separate bowl. Alternate buttermilk and flour mixture into the creamy mixture; mix slowly until fully incorporated. Stop mixer and fold in rhubarb and nuts, if using. Pour into a greased 9x13-inch cake pan and sprinkle with Topping. Bake in 350° oven for 45 minutes.

TOPPING:

¼ cup brown sugar
¼ cup white sugar

1 teaspoon cinnamon

Mix with a fork and sprinkle on top of the unbaked cake.

Variation: Instead of rhubarb, you may substitute same amount of chopped apples, dried apricots, peaches, etc.

Grannie Annie's Cookin' at the Homestead (Alaska)

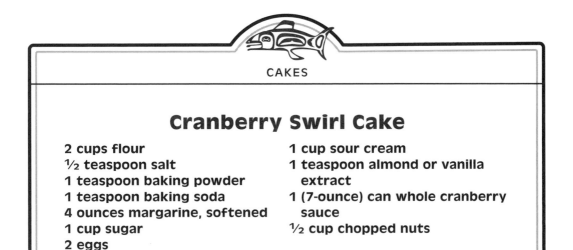

Cranberry Swirl Cake

2 cups flour
½ teaspoon salt
1 teaspoon baking powder
1 teaspoon baking soda
4 ounces margarine, softened
1 cup sugar
2 eggs
1 cup sour cream
1 teaspoon almond or vanilla
 extract
1 (7-ounce) can whole cranberry
 sauce
½ cup chopped nuts

Preheat oven to 350°. Sift together dry ingredients; set aside. In a large bowl, cream margarine; add sugar gradually. Add unbeaten eggs, one at a time, with mixer at medium speed. Reduce mixer speed and alternately add dry ingredients and sour cream, ending with dry ingredients. Add flavoring.

Grease an 8-inch tube pan. Put ⅓ of batter in bottom of pan; swirl ⅓ of the whole cranberry sauce into pan. Add another layer of batter and more cranberry sauce. Add remaining batter; swirl the remaining cranberry sauce on top. Sprinkle nuts on top. Bake for 55 minutes.

TOPPING:

¾ cup powdered sugar
1 tablespoon warm water
½ teaspoon almond or vanilla
 extract

While cake bakes, mix together Topping ingredients in small bowl; set aside. Let cake cool in pan for 10 minutes. Remove carefully cake from pan and drizzle Topping over it. Serves 10.

California Kosher (California)

Earthquakes in California are common occurrences (photo from the 2006 San Francisco earth-quake), as the state is located in a major fault zone known as the San Andreas Fault. It is esti-mated there are approximately 500,000 detectable seismic tremors in California annually, though most of them are so small that they are not felt. Alaska has more earthquake activity than any other region in North America. Approximately 52% of all earthquakes in the United States have occurred in Alaska. Seven of the ten largest earthquakes in the United States occurred in Alaska.

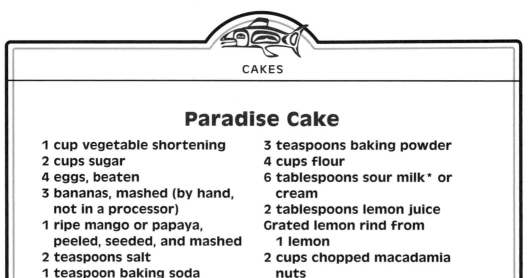

Paradise Cake

1 cup vegetable shortening
2 cups sugar
4 eggs, beaten
3 bananas, mashed (by hand, not in a processor)
1 ripe mango or papaya, peeled, seeded, and mashed
2 teaspoons salt
1 teaspoon baking soda
3 teaspoons baking powder
4 cups flour
6 tablespoons sour milk* or cream
2 tablespoons lemon juice
Grated lemon rind from 1 lemon
2 cups chopped macadamia nuts

Cream shortening and sugar. Add beaten eggs, bananas, and mango or papaya. Sift salt, baking soda, baking powder, and flour, and add to fruit mixture with milk, lemon juice, rind, and nuts. Mix well and turn into a well-greased Bundt pan. Bake at 350° for one hour. Cool in pan.

*Make sour milk by adding one tablespoon lemon juice to regular milk and mixing.

TOPPING:

1 (8-ounce) package cream cheese, room temperature
2 cups whipped cream topping
½ (6-ounce) can unsweetened pineapple juice
1 cup ground macadamia nuts

Mix cream cheese and whipped cream topping. Add pineapple juice slowly until reaching a light consistency, about half the can. Top cooled cake with mixture and sprinkle with nuts. May be made a day ahead.

Hawaii's Best Tropical Food & Drinks (Hawaii)

Almond Buttercream Cake

1 box Duncan Hines butter
  cake mix
1 stick margarine
3 eggs
⅔ cup water
1 large package vanilla pudding
  (not instant)

2 cups milk, divided
2 sticks unsalted butter, room
  temperature
1 (3¾-ounce) package sliced
  almonds
2 tablespoons butter
4 tablespoons sugar

Combine cake mix, margarine, eggs, and water until well blended. Bake in an angel cake tube pan according to directions on box. Let stand at least 4 hours.

Combine pudding mix and ⅓ cup milk. Mix until smooth. Bring remaining 1⅔ cups milk to a boil in a medium saucepan. Take off heat and combine with pudding mixture. Return to heat and bring to a full boil, stirring constantly. Cool 3–4 hours. Place a sheet of wax paper over top of pudding during cooling to prevent the formation of a skin.

To make buttercream, blend unsalted butter with electric mixer until creamy. Gradually add vanilla pudding to mixture by tablespoonful until all is used. (It is very important that pudding and butter are at room temperature or buttercream will curdle.)

To prepare toasted almonds, melt 2 tablespoons of butter over medium heat in a large frying pan. Stir in almonds and cook until they start to become golden. Add 4 tablespoons sugar and continue stirring until the sugar is melted and almonds are golden brown. Cool on wax paper.

To assemble cake: Cut into 3 layers using a sharp knife. Fill each layer with buttercream, reserving enough for top and sides. Reassemble and frost top and sides with buttercream. Cover completely with almonds. Serves 12.

Symphony of Flavors (California)

French Almond Cake

Fantastic!

1 cup (8 ounces) almond paste, room temperature
3 eggs
⅔ cup sugar
½ cup butter, softened
¼ cup cake flour
½ teaspoon baking powder
¼ teaspoon salt
Sliced almonds (optional)
Powdered sugar (optional)
Fresh berries or berry sauce (optional)
Whipped cream (optional)

Preheat oven to 350°. Grease and flour a 9-inch springform pan. Beat almond paste until soft and pliable. Add eggs, one at a time. Beat in the sugar. Add butter and beat until the batter is well creamed.

Sift together dry ingredients. Stir into creamed mixture. Pour into the prepared pan. (Sliced almonds may be sprinkled on top.) Bake for 40–45 minutes. Cool.

Serve sprinkled with powdered sugar and fresh berries on the side, or with berry sauce and whipped cream.

Albertina's Exceptional Recipes (Oregon)

Crazy Chocolate Cake

3 cups flour
2 cups sugar
½ teaspoon salt
2 teaspoons baking soda
5 heaping tablespoons cocoa
¾ cup cooking oil
2 tablespoons vinegar
2 cups cold water

Mix all ingredients together. Bake in greased and floured 9x13-inch pan (or 2 round cake pans) at 350° for 35–40 minutes.

We're Cookin' Now (Alaska)

Italian Swirl Cheesecake

This cheesecake keeps well in refrigerator and also freezes well.

CHOCOLATE NUT CRUST:

¾ cup chocolate wafer
  crumbs (10 wafers)
¾ cup finely chopped
  almonds

2 tablespoons sugar
3 tablespoons melted butter

Preheat oven to 350°. Mix chocolate wafer crumbs, nuts, and sugar together. Put in bottom of 9-inch springform pan. Pour melted butter over top and use a fork to blend mixture and press into bottom of pan. Cook 15–20 minutes until lightly browned. Remove and cool slightly. Reduce oven to 325°.

CHEESECAKE:

2 (8-ounce) packages cream
  cheese
1 cup sugar, divided
2 tablespoons flour
2 tablespoons vanilla

6 eggs, separated
1 cup sour cream
3 ounces semisweet chocolate
2 tablespoons amaretto

In food processor or with electric mixer, beat cream cheese until soft. Beat in ¾ cup of sugar, flour, and vanilla. Mix until well blended. Beat in egg yolks and sour cream. In a separate bowl, beat egg whites and ¼ cup sugar until soft peaks form. Fold egg whites into cream cheese mixture. Pour ⅔ of batter into baked crust. Melt chocolate with amaretto in top of double boiler. Add to remaining batter. Gently blend. Starting at outside edge, pour chocolate batter onto white batter in a swirl pattern, ending up in middle of pan.

   Place in 325° oven for 50 minutes. Turn the oven off. Prop door open 2–3 inches and let cheesecake sit for 2 hours. Remove to rack to cool. Chill before serving. I usually serve this with chocolate sauce.

The Old Yacht Club Inn Cookbook (California)

Kahlúa Fantasy Chocolate Cheesecake

CHOCOLATE CRUMB CRUST:

1⅓ cups chocolate wafer
  crumbs

¼ cup softened butter
1 tablespoon sugar

Mix and press into springform pan.

CHEESECAKE:

1½ cups semisweet chocolate
  pieces
¼ cup Kahlúa
2 tablespoons butter
2 eggs, beaten

⅓ cup sugar
¼ teaspoon salt
1 cup sour cream
2 (8-ounce) packages cream
  cheese, softened

In small saucepan over medium heat, melt chocolate with Kahlua and butter. Stir until smooth. Set aside. In bowl, combine eggs, sugar, and salt. Add sour cream and blend well. Add cream cheese and beat until smooth. Gradually blend in chocolate mixture. Turn into prepared crust. Bake at 350° for 40 minutes or until filling is barely set in center. Remove from oven and let stand at room temperature for 1 hour; then refrigerate several hours or overnight before serving.

Pig Out (Washington)

Cherry Mini-Cheesecakes

24 vanilla wafers
2 (8-ounce) packages cream
  cheese
¾ cup sugar

2 eggs
1 teaspoon vanilla
1 can cherry pie filling

Fill 24 muffin cups with cupcake liners; add wafers to liners. Beat cream cheese, sugar, eggs, and vanilla together; fill liners about half full. Bake at 350° for 15 minutes; cool. Add 2 or 3 spoonfuls of cherry pie filling on top. Refrigerate.

Christmas in Washington Cook Book (Washington)

Apple Bake Cheesecakes

An easy and elegant dessert.

FILLING:

1 (8-ounce) package cream
  cheese, room temperature
1 large egg
½ cup sugar

1 teaspoon vanilla
1 teaspoon finely grated lemon
  zest

Preheat oven to 350°. Combine all ingredients in a food processor and process until smooth. Transfer into a bowl. Cover and refrigerate.

APPLES:

8 medium-sized dessert apples
  (Criterion, Rome, Golden
  Delicious or Honeycrisp)

⅔ cup honey
8 cookies (vanilla wafers, ginger
  snaps, biscotti, etc.)

Core apples, being careful not to cut through all the way to the bottom. Spoon out core in sections and scoop out most, but not all of the flesh. Put apples in a baking dish and spoon 1½–2 tablespoons of the Filling into each cavity. Pour enough warm water or cider into the dish to reach a level of ½–¾ inch. Cover with foil and place the pan in the lower third of the oven and bake 30–40 minutes or until the apples are fork-tender. Remove from oven (the Filling will be soft). Serve warm, or for a traditional cheesecake consistency, refrigerate for at least 2 hours. If chilled, remove from refrigerator 1 hour before serving. Drizzle honey over apples and crumble cookies over top. Serves 8.

Recipe by Mt. Hood Organic Farms
***The Fruit Loop Cookbook* (*Oregon*)**

Boysenberry Swirl Cheesecake with a Hazelnut Crust

Many pioneers of Irish and British descent settled in the Pacific Northwest, and cheesecake recipes were part of their heritage. It was natural for them to make use of indigenous nuts and berries; this recipe reflects that kind of adaptation. In this recipe I use the intensely flavorful boysenberry—the commercial blackberry I consider number one for flavor. It's a cross between a wild blackberry, a raspberry, and a loganberry and features the best of each berry.

CRUST:

8 tablespoons (½ cup) butter, softened

1 cup all-purpose flour

½ cup finely ground, roasted hazelnuts

½ cup sugar

Put all ingredients in a bowl and blend with a fork or pulse 8–10 times in a food processor. Put mixture in an 11-inch springform pan and pat crust into bottom and sides of pan. Chill crust in refrigerator while preparing filling.

FILLING:

3 (8-ounce) packages cream cheese, softened

2 cups sugar

3 eggs

1½ cups fresh or frozen boysenberries (or any variety of blackberry or raspberry), thawed and drained

Preheat oven to 375°. Using a mixer, blend cream cheese, sugar, and eggs together until smooth. Run berries through a food mill or purée them in a blender or food processor and push them through a sieve to remove seeds.

Layer half the cheese mixture over crust, then spread on all the puréed berries. Carefully add remaining cheese filling over berries and cut through batter with a knife, using a circular motion, to create swirls. Bake for 45–50 minutes. Remove from oven and let cool to room temperature. Chill in refrigerator for 3–4 hours before serving. Serves 8–10.

Dungeness Crabs and Blackberry Cobblers (Oregon)

Liliko'i Cheesecake

CRUST:

1⅔ cups graham cracker crumbs (or 22 squares finely rolled)

3 tablespoons honey
¼ cup butter or margarine, softened

Mix together crumbs, honey, and margarine, and press firmly into a 9-inch springform pan.

CHEESECAKE:

1 envelope or 1 tablespoon gelatin (unflavored)
½ cup liliko'i (passion fruit) juice, divided

½–¾ cup sugar
½ cup boiling water
2 (8-ounce) packages cream cheese, softened

In a large bowl, soften gelatin in a little of the fruit juice; mix in sugar. Add boiling water and remaining liliko'i juice, and stir until gelatin is completely dissolved. With electric mixer, beat in cream cheese until smooth. Pour into Crust; chill until firm (about 2 hours). Makes about 8 servings.

Note: For a sweeter cake, use ¾ cup sugar. Passion fruit juice comes frozen.

Cook 'em Up Kaua'i (Hawaii)

White Chocolate Cheesecake with Raspberry Sauce

CRUST:

2 cups finely ground
  shortbread cookie crumbs
½ cup ground almonds,
  toasted

3 tablespoons sugar
¾ stick butter, melted

Preheat oven to 350°. Combine all crust ingredients. Press on bottom and sides of 10-inch springform pan. Bake 10 minutes. Reduce heat to 325°.

FILLING:

6 ounces white chocolate,
  finely chopped
4 (8-ounce) packages cream
  cheese, room temperature
¾ cup sugar, divided

1 teaspoon vanilla
½ teaspoon almond extract
5 large eggs
3 tablespoons flour

Melt chocolate in top of double boiler over hot, but not boiling water; cool. Beat cream cheese, ½ cup sugar, vanilla, and almond extract until smooth. Beat in eggs one at a time. Mix flour and remaining ¼ cup sugar, add to cheese mixture and beat until incorporated. Stir 1 cup of mixture into cooled chocolate. Mix in remaining Filling. Pour Filling over Crust. Bake for 45 minutes or until center of Filling moves slightly when side of pan is tapped. Cool and refrigerate.

TOPPING:

1 (14-ounce) package frozen
  raspberries, thawed and
  drained

⅓ cup light corn syrup

Purée raspberries in food processor; slowly add corn syrup. Press through sieve to remove seeds. Refrigerate until serving time. To serve, spoon a tablespoon of Topping over each slice. Serves 12.

A Slice of Santa Barbara (California)

COOKIES and CANDIES

Located in northeast Oregon, Hells Canyon is North America's deepest river-carved gorge. At 7,800 feet deep, it is one-third of a mile deeper than the Grand Canyon and five miles narrower. Walls of the canyon are like a museum displaying 3,000-year-old pictographs and petroglyphs, evidence of the Indians' early settlements.

Peanut Butter-Chocolate Chip Cookies

1 cup creamy peanut butter
1 cup sugar
2 large eggs

1 cup semisweet chocolate chips

It's no mistake—there's no flour or butter in these cookies. Heat oven to 350°; mix peanut butter, sugar, and eggs in a medium bowl with a wooden spoon until blended. Stir in chocolate chips. Drop rounded teaspoonfuls 2 inches apart on ungreased cookie sheet. Bake 10–12 minutes or until bottom of cookies are lightly browned. Cool on cookie sheet 2 minutes before removing to a wire rack to cool completely. Makes approximately 2 dozen. You may substitute raisins or coarsely chopped peanuts for some of the chocolate chips.

A Taste of Heaven (Washington)

Butterfinger Cookies

These great cookies never last long.

½ cup butter, softened
¾ cup sugar
⅔ cup brown sugar
2 egg whites
1¼ cups chunky peanut butter

1½ teaspoons vanilla
1 cup all-purpose flour
½ teaspoon baking soda
¼ teaspoon salt
5 (2.1-ounce) Butterfinger candy bars, chopped

Preheat oven to 350°. In a mixing bowl, cream butter and sugars. Add egg whites. Beat well. Blend in peanut butter and vanilla. Combine flour, baking soda, and salt and add to cream mixture. Mix well. Stir in candy bars. Shape into 1½-inch balls and place on greased cookie sheet. Bake for 10–12 minutes or until golden brown. Cool on wire racks. Makes 4 dozen.

Recipe by Bryan Price, Pitching Coach, Seattle Mariners
Home Plates (Washington)

Snow-Cap Cookies

In some circles, these rich, chewy cookies are known as chocolate crinkles because each cookie acquires a crinkled white topping during the baking process. In this recipe, dark chocolate and espresso make the contrast even greater, giving the cookies a snow-capped appearance and a superb flavor. If you're a real chocolate lover, try adding semisweet chocolate chips to the dough before chilling. You won't be sorry.

4 tablespoons unsalted butter
2 ounces unsweetened chocolate
2 eggs, room temperature
1 teaspoon vanilla extract
1 tablespoon instant espresso powder

1 cup granulated sugar
1 cup all-purpose flour
1 teaspoon baking powder
¼ teaspoon salt
½ cup sifted powdered sugar

In small saucepan, melt butter and chocolate over low heat. Stir to blend and set aside to cool slightly.

In medium bowl combine eggs, vanilla, espresso powder, and granulated sugar. Using an electric mixer on medium speed, beat until light and fluffy, about 3 minutes. In another bowl, whisk together flour, baking powder, and salt. Alternately blend dry ingredients and chocolate mixture into egg mixture in 3 increments. Cover and refrigerate until firm, at least 3 hours.

Preheat oven to 350°. Shape chilled dough into 1-inch balls and roll in powdered sugar to form a thick coat. Place about 2 inches apart on an ungreased baking sheet. Bake until set, about 15 minutes. Transfer to wire rack and let cool completely. Makes about 2½ dozen cookies.

The New Complete Coffee Book (Oregon)

Almond Frosties

2¼ cups all-purpose flour
½ teaspoon salt
1 cup butter, softened

3 tablespoons granulated sugar
1 teaspoon almond extract

Preheat oven to 350°. Combine flour and salt in medium bowl. Beat butter, sugar, and almond extract in mixer bowl until light and fluffy. At low speed, beat in dry ingredients until blended. Shape dough into 1-inch balls. Place on ungreased cookie sheets. Flatten slightly to ¾ inch thick. Bake 15–17 minutes until golden. Cool on wire rack.

FROSTING:
1½ cups confectioners' sugar
2 tablespoons unsweetened
  cocoa
½ teaspoon vanilla extract

2–3 tablespoons hot water

½ cup slivered almonds,
  toasted

Combine confectioners' sugar, cocoa, and vanilla in bowl. Stir in water until spreadable. Frost cookies; top each with almonds. Makes 3 dozen.

Taste of Fillmore (California)

Lemon Frosted Pecan Cookies

1 cup unsalted butter
¾ cup powdered sugar
1½ cups flour

¾ cup cornstarch
2 tablespoons milk
¾ cup chopped pecans

Mix butter, sugar, flour, cornstarch, and milk until well blended. Chill. Place small spoonful of chopped pecans 2 inches apart on ungreased cookie sheet. Place small balls of dough on pecans and flatten. Bake at 350° for 12–15 minutes. Cool.

FROSTING:
2½ cups powdered sugar
1 tablespoon soft butter

3 tablespoons fresh lemon juice

Mix Frosting ingredients, and frost cookies.

Rainy Day Treats and Sunny Temptations (Oregon)

Pecan Pie Cookies

PECAN FILLING:

½ cup powdered sugar
¼ cup butter or margarine

3 tablespoons dark corn syrup
½ cup chopped pecans

Combine sugar, butter or margarine, and corn syrup in saucepan; stir to blend. Cook over medium heat, stirring occasionally, until mixture reaches a full boil. Remove from heat; stir in pecans. Cool. Roll ½ teaspoon balls and put in freezer.

COOKIE:

1 cup butter or margarine
½ cup sugar
½ cup dark corn syrup

2 eggs, separated
2½ cups unsifted all-purpose
flour

Cream butter or margarine and sugar on low speed in large bowl of electric mixer. Add corn syrup and egg yolks; beat until thoroughly blended. Stir in flour gradually. Chill several hours. Beat egg whites slightly. Using one tablespoonful of dough for each cookie, roll into balls. Brush very lightly with egg white. Place on greased cookie sheet, leaving a 2-inch space between each cookie. Bake at 375° for 5 minutes. Remove from oven.

Press a frozen Pecan Filling ball into the center of each cookie. Return to oven; bake 5 minutes longer or until lightly browned. Cool 5 minutes on cookie sheet. Remove; cool completely on rack. Makes about 4 dozen.

Recipes, Recipes, Recipes! (Oregon)

Date Pinwheel Cookies

1 cup finely cut dates
1½ cups packed brown sugar,
    divided
⅓ cup plus ¼ cup evaporated
    milk, divided
½ cup chopped nuts

1 tablespoon lemon juice
1¾ cups flour
¾ teaspoon baking soda
½ cup shortening
¾ teaspoon salt
¼ teaspoon grated lemon rind

In a mixing bowl, combine dates, ½ cup brown sugar, and ⅓ cup milk. Cook over medium heat in a saucepan until very thick. Remove from heat then add nuts and lemon juice. Set aside to cool.

In a separate bowl, sift together flour and soda. Set aside. In another bowl, combine shortening, salt, lemon rind, 1 cup brown sugar and ¼ cup milk. Stir in flour mixture and mix until well blended. Divide dough into 2 or 3 balls. With a floured rolling pin, flatten each ball into a 12-inch square (use wax paper if too soft). Spread with cooled date mixture over the squares. Roll each into a log and chill until firm. Cut into ½-inch slices. Bake on greased cookie sheet at 375° for 10 minutes or until done.

Note: Prepared dough logs can be frozen until ready to slice and bake.

Grandma Jean's Rainy Day Recipes (Oregon)

Low-Bush Cranberry Pinwheels

DOUGH:

1½ cups flour	¾ cup sugar
¼ teaspoon baking powder	1 large egg
½ teaspoon salt	1 teaspoon grated orange peel
½ cup butter, softened	1 teaspoon vanilla extract

Mix together the flour, baking powder, and salt; set aside. Cream butter and sugar. Add egg, orange peel and vanilla extract to butter mixture. Add flour mixture gradually and mix well. Place dough on plastic wrap and flatten out slightly into a square. Wrap and refrigerate 4–6 hours. Remove dough and roll on a piece of floured wax paper into a 10-inch square. Place on a flat pan and place back in refrigerator and chill.

FILLING:

½ cup frozen low-bush cranberries	3 tablespoons brown sugar
½ cup walnuts	2½ teaspoons canned milk
1 tablespoon grated orange peel	

In mini-blender, or meat grinder, process cranberries and walnuts. Remove and place in a small dish; add grated orange peel. Set aside. Mix brown sugar and canned milk. Spread sugar mixture on Dough, leaving a ½-inch space on 2 of the edges. Spread the berry mixture evenly over the sugar mixture. Roll tightly, starting with the plain edge, in a jellyroll fashion. Place the rolled log on plastic wrap; cover and place in the freezer overnight or until you are ready to bake.

Remove cookie roll and allow to stand at room temperature for 5 minutes. With serrated knife, cut ¼-inch slices and place on greased cookie sheet. Bake in oven at 375° for 12–14 minutes. Remove from oven and let cookies set a few minutes before removing.

What's Cookin' in the Kenai Peninsula (Alaska)

Big, Big Sugar Cookies

2 cups sugar
1 cup margarine, softened
2 eggs
1 teaspoon lemon extract
4¾ cups flour, divided
2 teaspoons cream of tartar
2 teaspoons baking soda
½ teaspoon salt
½ teaspoon nutmeg
1 cup sour cream
Raisins or maraschino cherries
   (optional)

Beat the sugar and margarine together. Add eggs and lemon extract; cream together. Combine 4 cups flour, cream of tartar, baking soda, salt, and nutmeg and add to sugar/egg mixture alternately with sour cream. Then add about ¾ cup more flour to stiffen dough. Put dough on a floured board and roll ½ inch thick. Use more flour as needed.

Use floured rim of a wide-mouthed jar or bowl to cut cookies about 4 inches in diameter. Place each cookie on a greased cookie sheet about 2 inches apart. Sprinkle with sugar before baking. Add a raisin or chunk of maraschino cherry in center of cookie, if desired. Bake at 350° for 15 minutes. Makes 4 dozen.

33 Days Hath September (Alaska)

Alaska Mining-Camp Oatmeal Cookies

1 cup butter
1 cup white sugar
1 cup brown sugar
2 eggs, beaten
1½ cups flour
1 teaspoon baking soda
½ teaspoon salt
3 cups old-fashioned oatmeal
1 teaspoon vanilla

Mix together butter and sugars; add beaten eggs. Add remaining ingredients and mix well. Drop by teaspoon onto greased cookie sheet. Bake 8–10 minutes at 375°.

Pioneers of Alaska Auxiliary #8 (Alaska)

Guava Crispies

¾ cup butter, divided
⅓ cup guava jelly
2 tablespoons lemon juice
2 tablespoons sugar
¼ teaspoon salt
1 egg yolk, slightly beaten
¼ cup chopped macadamia
   nuts

1 cup flour
½ teaspoon salt
½ teaspoon baking soda
½ cup brown sugar
1 cup quick oats

Combine ¼ cup butter, guava jelly, lemon juice, sugar, and salt in the top of a double boiler. Heat until the guava jelly has dissolved. Stir a part of this into slightly beaten yolk, then return the egg mixture to the rest of the jelly mixture. Heat and stir until the mixture thickens. Add nuts. Remove from heat and cool.

Sift flour, salt, and soda over brown sugar and remaining ½ cup butter. Cut together with 2 knives until coarse crumbs form. Add oatmeal and mix well. Pat half of the mixture into the bottom of a 9-inch-square pan. Spread guava mixture on top and sprinkle remaining oatmeal mixture on top. Bake in a 350° oven for 25 minutes. Cool and cut into squares. Makes 3 dozen.

Joys of Hawaiian Cooking (Hawaii)

Coconut Macadamia Nut Crisps

¾ cup butter, softened
¾ cup sugar
½ cup firmly packed brown
   sugar
1 large egg
1 teaspoon vanilla extract
2 cups all-purpose flour

1 teaspoon baking powder
1 teaspoon baking soda
½ teaspoon salt
1 cup chopped macadamia nuts
1 cup old-fashioned oats
½ cup flaked coconut

Preheat oven to 375°; lightly grease baking sheets. In a mixing bowl, cream together butter and sugars until fluffy. Add egg and extract. Stir in remaining ingredients until well blended. Drop by teaspoonfuls 1 inch apart on prepared sheets. Bake 8–10 minutes until edges are brown. Makes 5 dozen.

Dd's Table Talk II (Hawaii)

Frost Bites

Orange spiced oatmeal cookies dipped in white chocolate.

3 tablespoons orange juice
¾ cup raisins
½ cup margarine, at room temperature
¾ cup sugar
1 large egg
2 teaspoons grated orange peel

1 cup flour
1 teaspoon baking soda
1½ cups rolled oats
9 ounces (1½ boxes) Nestle Toll House Premier White Baking Bars

In a small bowl, combine orange juice and raisins. Let stand several hours or overnight. In a large bowl, beat margarine and sugar until fluffy. Beat in egg and orange peel. In another bowl, combine flour and baking soda; stir into butter mixture. Add raisins, any soaking liquid that may be left in bowl, and oats. Mix well.

Drop dough by rounded teaspoonfuls onto ungreased baking sheets, spacing 2 inches apart; flatten slightly. Bake at 350° for 10–12 minutes. Transfer to racks and cool completely.

Follow melting directions on box of white chocolate, using either microwave or double boiler method. When cookies are completely cool, dip ⅓ of cookie in white chocolate. Set on waxed paper-lined baking sheets. Chill until chocolate is firm. Yields about 3 dozen.

Sharing Our Best (Washington)

A glacier is a accumulation of ice, snow, water, rock, and sediment that moves under the influence of gravity. The density of ice causes it to absorb all light and reflect only blue, thus giving glaciers their blue/white appearance. Alaska has more than 100,000 glaciers covering approximately 30,000 square miles of land—5% of the state. The longest glacier in Alaska is the Bering Glacier at more than 100 miles long. The largest glacier is the Malaspina Glacier at 850 square miles. Washington contains more glaciers than the other 47 contiguous states combined.

White Chocolate Coconut Cookies

These are especially light and heavenly cookies with a distinctively coconut-y flavor.

1 cup butter, softened
1 cup white sugar
2 large eggs
1 teaspoon rum extract or
  dark rum
3 cups all-purpose flour

½ teaspoon baking soda
1 teaspoon salt
1 cup shredded coconut
1 (12-ounce) package white
  chocolate chips

Preheat oven to 350°. Oil baking sheet. Cream together butter and sugar until light. Add eggs and rum extract or rum. Sift together flour, soda, and salt, and gradually mix into egg-butter mixture. Fold in coconut and white chocolate chips.

Drop mounds of dough onto oiled baking sheet. Bake for 35–40 minutes in 350° oven. Remove cookie sheet from oven and let cool. Variation: Add ½ cup chopped, dried pineapple to coconut mixture for a piña colada cookie.

Sugar and Spice–Cookies Made with Love (Hawaii)

Cornflake Macaroons

2 eggs, well beaten
½ cup sugar
¼ cup brown sugar
1 teaspoon vanilla

2 cups cornflakes
1 cup angel flake coconut
½ cup chopped nuts

Beat eggs; add sugars and vanilla and beat until light lemon in color. Add remaining ingredients, drop onto parchment-lined cookie sheet, and bake at 350° for 10–12 minutes. It's important to line your cookie sheet with parchment paper, as these macaroons will stick. Don't remove cookies until cool. Makes approximately 2 dozen medium-size cookies.

Cooking Pure & Simple (California)

Grandma Lizzie's Ginger Cookies

'Member the day of the cookie jar? Is the spicy fragrance of ginger or molasses cookies only a faded memory? These are more than cookies as they will rekindle your memories of your grandmother.

1 cup sugar
1 cup butter (no substitute)
1 cup molasses
1 egg
1 tablespoon vinegar

1 teaspoon ginger
1 teaspoon baking soda
A little hot water
4 cups flour

Mix all ingredients together and chill. Roll out to your own desired thickness and cut to shapes for the occasion. Bake at 375° for 7–10 minutes.

Sleigh Bells and Sugarplums (Washington)

Grandma Ost's Soft
Brer Rabbit Ginger Cookies

6–8 cups flour, divided
1 teaspoon salt
1½ teaspoons cinnamon
2 tablespoons ginger
¼ teaspoon nutmeg
1 cup shortening

1 cup sugar
1 egg
2 cups molasses
2 tablespoons vinegar
4 teaspoons baking soda
1 cup boiling water

Sift 6 cups of flour with salt and spices. Cream shortening and sugar. Add egg. Beat all together until light. Add molasses and vinegar, then sifted dry ingredients. Lastly, add baking soda dissolved in boiling water. If necessary, add more flour to make a soft dough. Drop by teaspoonfuls on greased cookie sheet. Sprinkle with sugar. Bake 8–10 minutes in a moderate (350°) oven. Makes 100 plump, spongy cookies.

Nome Centennial Cookbook 1898-1998 (Alaska)

Cranberry Almond Biscotti

1¼ cups dried cranberries
2 eggs
¾ cup sugar, plus extra for topping
½ cup oil
2 tablespoons orange zest
1 teaspoon cinnamon

1¼ teaspoons baking powder
1 teaspoon vanilla
¾ teaspoon almond extract
¼ teaspoon salt
2 cups flour
1 cup slivered blanched almonds, pounded

Preheat the oven to 350°. Place the dried cranberries in a bowl and cover with hot water. Let sit for 10 minutes.

In a large mixing bowl, combine the eggs, ¾ cup sugar, oil, zest, cinnamon, baking powder, vanilla, almond extract and salt. Whisk to blend. Drain the cranberries. Add the flour, cranberries and pounded almonds to the above mixture and stir to form dough. Place on heavily floured board and knead until smooth. Add more flour, if necessary. Knead only about 20 turns and divide the dough in half. Form each half into a log, 2 inches in diameter. Place logs on ungreased cookie sheets. Sprinkle tops with sugar. Bake for 25 minutes or until golden brown and firm to touch. Remove logs from oven, but leave oven on. Cut while warm with a large chopping knife. Cut slices diagonally ½ inch thick. Return slices with cut side down and bake 25 minutes or until cookie turns brown. Transfer to wire racks to cool. Makes 2 dozen.

Sounds Tasty! (California)

©PHIL COBLENTZ/ SAN FRANCISCO CONVENTION & VISITORS BUREAU

Alcatraz Island, commonly referred to as simply Alcatraz or locally as The Rock, is a small island located in the middle of San Francisco Bay in California. It served as a lighthouse, then a military fortification, then a military prison followed by a federal prison until 1963. It became a national recreation area in 1972. The entire Alcatraz Island was listed on the National Register of Historic Places in 1976, and was further declared a National Historic Landmark in 1986.

Russian Tea Cakes

1 cup butter, softened
½ cup powdered sugar
1 teaspoon vanilla extract
2½ cups all-purpose flour

¼ teaspoon salt
¾ cup finely chopped pecans
Powdered sugar for rolling

Cream together butter, sugar, and vanilla. Stir together flour and salt. Blend with butter mixture. Stir in pecans. Chill dough thoroughly (at least 2 hours).

Preheat oven to 400°. Roll chilled dough into 1-inch balls and place on greased cookie sheet. Bake for 10–12 minutes until set, but not brown. Cool slightly, and roll warm cookies in powdered sugar. Allow to cool completely, and roll in powdered sugar again. Yields 48 cookies.

Alaska's Gourmet Breakfasts (Alaska)

Raspberry Shortbread

¾ cup butter (no substitute)
½ cup sugar

1 teaspoon vanilla
2 cups flour

Cream butter and sugar. Add vanilla, then flour. Press in greased 9-inch-square pan. Bake at 325° for 40 minutes. Remove.

TOPPING:

1 cup raspberry jam
1 teaspoon almond extract

½ cup chopped almonds

Mix jam with almond extract and smooth over shortbread; sprinkle with almonds. Bake another 15 minutes. Cool and cut.

Rainy Day Treats and Sunny Temptations (Oregon)

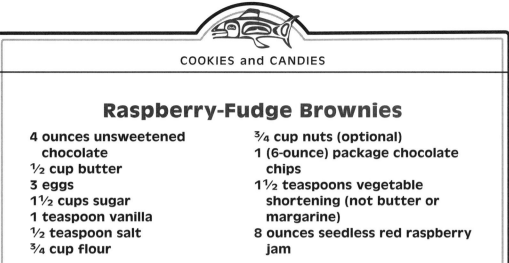

Raspberry-Fudge Brownies

4 ounces unsweetened
  chocolate
½ cup butter
3 eggs
1½ cups sugar
1 teaspoon vanilla
½ teaspoon salt
¾ cup flour

¾ cup nuts (optional)
1 (6-ounce) package chocolate
  chips
1½ teaspoons vegetable
  shortening (not butter or
  margarine)
8 ounces seedless red raspberry
  jam

Melt unsweetened chocolate and butter in top of double boiler or in microwave oven. Beat eggs until foamy. Add sugar and beat only a few seconds. Add vanilla, salt, and chocolate mixture, being careful not to overbeat. Mix in flour; add nuts. Turn into greased and floured 9-inch square pan. Bake at 350° for 30 minutes. (Toothpick should be barely clean when inserted in center of cake; cake will be moist.)

While brownies cool, melt chocolate chips with vegetable short-ening. Spread raspberry jam over brownies in pan, then melted chocolate chips over the jam. Cool in refrigerator before cutting into pieces. Yields 18 (1½ x 3-inch) brownies.

Only in California (California)

German Chocolate Bars

1 package German chocolate
  cake mix
⅔ cup butter

1 cup chocolate chips
1 container pecan frosting
½ cup milk

Mix cake mix together with butter. Divide it in half and spread half in a 9x13-inch pan; bake at 350° for 10 minutes. Remove from oven; sprinkle with chocolate chips. Drop frosting by teaspoonfuls on top of chocolate chips. Combine milk with reserved batter and drop on top of frosting by teaspoonfuls. Bake at 350° for 30–35 minutes, or until top appears dry. Cool completely before cutting.

Western Washington Oncology Cook Book (Washington)

Alaskan Brownies

Not to be confused with Alaskan grizzlies. . . .

1½ cups semisweet chocolate chips, divided
1 cup butter
4 eggs
2 cups sugar
2 tablespoons vanilla extract
1 tablespoon Frangelico Hazelnut Liqueur (optional)

1½ cups unbleached white flour
1 tablespoon ground dark coffee
1 cup chopped walnuts or ground hazelnuts

Preheat oven to 350°. Grease a 9x13-inch baking pan. In double boiler, melt 1 cup chocolate chips and butter. In bowl, cream eggs, sugar, and melted chocolate mixture. Add vanilla and Frangelico, if using. Add flour, coffee, nuts, and remaining ½ cup chocolate chips; stir until blended. Pour into baking pan. Bake for 30–35 minutes until center is done. Cool. Frost, if desired. Yields 16–20 servings.

Note: Hazelnuts may be ground in a coffee grinder.

FROSTING:
2 cups powdered sugar
¼ cup butter, softened
¼ cup unsweetened cocoa powder

1 teaspoon vanilla extract
1 tablespoon hazelnut liqueur (optional)
2–3 tablespoons milk

Blend ingredients together until smooth.

Drop the Hook, Let's Eat (Alaska)

Hawaii is the only state that grows coffee. The 10-day Kona Coffee Cultural Festival in Kona, started in 1970, is recognized as the oldest product festival in Hawaii, and is the only coffee festival in the United States. Kona coffee is only grown on the Big Island of Hawaii, and any coffee claiming to be Kona coffee must be at least 10% pure Kona.

Hawaiian Caramac Brownie Wedges

CRUST:

2 cups ground Oreo cookies
2 tablespoons melted butter
½ cup semisweet chocolate
  chips
½ cup chopped macadamia
  nuts
20 caramels
2 tablespoons heavy cream

Preheat oven to 350°. Spray a 9-inch springform pan with nonstick spray. Combine cookie crumbs and butter. Press into bottom of pan. Bake for 15 minutes. Remove from oven and sprinkle with chocolate chips and nuts. Combine caramels with cream in a microwave-safe bowl. Microwave on high 1 minute. Drizzle over nuts and refrigerate while preparing Brownie.

BROWNIE:

¾ cup unsalted butter
4 ounces unsweetened
  chocolate, chopped
3 tablespoons macadamia nut
  liqueur, or 2 tablespoons
  crème de cacao
3 large eggs
2 cups sugar
1 cup flour
¼ teaspoon salt
¾ cup chopped semisweet
  chocolate

Melt butter and unsweetened chocolate in large saucepan, stirring until smooth. Remove from heat. Whisk in liqueur, eggs, and sugar. Stir in flour, salt, and semisweet chocolate. Pour over crust. Bake until wooden pick inserted in center comes out with moist crumbs, 60–65 minutes. Cool on rack. Refrigerate until firm. Remove from pan; cut into wedges. Brownies will be thick and fudgy, not like cake.

GANACHE:

½ pint heavy whipping cream
10 ounces high-quality
  semisweet chocolate,
  chopped

Heat whipping cream in medium saucepan until hot. Add chocolate and stir until completely blended. Pour Ganache over top and sides of each wedge, covering completely. Refrigerate until set. Decorate with chocolate hibiscus leaves, macadamia nuts, and caramel drizzle, if desired.

Fair's Fare (*California*)

Caramel-Cream Cheese Apple Bars

PASTRY:

3 cups flour
¼ cup sugar
1¼ teaspoons salt
1 stick plus 2 tablespoons
  butter

¼ cup cooking oil
1 egg
¼ cup water

Combine flour, sugar, and salt. Cut in butter and mix well. In separate bowl blend together oil, egg, and water. Blend both mixtures together and form into a square. Place on 17x11-inch piece of foil that has been sprayed with Pam. Roll Pastry to fit foil and place on cookie sheet. Flute edges of crust.

APPLE FILLING:

5 cups sliced, peeled apples
¼ cup flour

3 tablespoons lemon juice
1 cup sugar

Place all ingredients in mixing bowl and blend well. Spread Apple Filling evenly over Pastry.

CREAM CHEESE TOPPING:

1 (8-ounce) package cream
  cheese, softened
¼ cup sugar

1 egg
¾ cup chopped walnuts

Blend all ingredients together except walnuts and whip until smooth. Set aside.

CARAMEL TOPPING:

½ pound caramels

¼ cup cream or canned milk

Combine milk and caramels in double boiler. Heat until caramels melt and are blended with milk. Spread a portion of Cream Cheese Topping in a 1½-inch wide strip the length of the Pastry. Spread a portion of the caramel in the same manner next to the cream cheese. Continue this alternating pattern until the entire top of the Apple Filling is covered. Sprinkle with chopped walnuts. Bake at 375° for 35 minutes. Let cool and cut into squares to serve. Makes about 16 squares.

Marilyn Thomas: The Homemaker Baker's Favorite Recipes (California)

Judy's Macadamia Nut Bars

These easy-to-make cookies are some of the most addictively delicious morsels you can imagine. Macadamia nuts give a taste of Hawaiian crunch and flavor. This recipe, from a special family friend, is a winner.

FILLING:

2 eggs
1 teaspoon vanilla
1¼ cups brown sugar
2 tablespoons flour
¼ teaspoon baking powder
¼ teaspoon salt

½ cup flaked coconut
1 (3½-ounce) can (1 cup)
   toasted macadamia nuts,
   coarsely chopped
Powdered sugar for topping

Beat the eggs, vanilla, and brown sugar together until smooth. Sift flour with baking powder and salt; stir into egg mixture and blend well. Fold in coconut and nuts to complete the Filling.

BUTTER CRUST:

½ cup butter
¼ cup sugar

1 cup flour

Blend butter, sugar, and flour together with a fork to make a crumbly texture. Press into a 9-inch-square pan. Bake at 350° for 20 minutes or until light brown. Remove from the oven.

   Gently spread Filling over crust. Bake an additional 25 minutes at 350°. Remove from oven and place on a rack. Sprinkle with powdered sugar. Cool 5 minutes, then cut with a knife into desired size squares. For a romantic dessert, serve with chilled champagne!

Honolulu Hawaii Cooking (Hawaii)

The macadamia was introduced into Hawaii from Australia about 1881 where it was used as an ornamental plant and for reforestation. The Mauna Loa Macadamia Nut Corporation in Hilo, Hawaii, is the world's largest processor of macadamia nuts. The first Mauna Loa macadamia nut plantation was planted in 1946, and the first commercial crop was harvested in 1956. The Hawaiian-produced macadamia established the nut internationally and has dominated the market. There is a limited but significant commercial production of the nuts in Southern California.

Almond Bars

This cookie has been a favorite in our family for over 30 years. When our daughter was married at the Seattle Yacht Club, these bars were requested in lieu of a cake.

CRUST:

¾ cup butter
½ cup sugar
1 egg

1 teaspoon vanilla
2¼ cups flour
½ teaspoon salt

Cream butter and sugar. Stir in the other ingredients. Press into a greased 9x13-inch pan.

ALMOND LAYER:

2 eggs
½ cup sugar
2 teaspoons butter

1 (8-ounce) can almond paste
1 teaspoon almond extract
¾ cup chopped almonds

Beat eggs with sugar; slowly add butter, almond paste, and almond extract. Pour over Crust and spread with nuts. Bake at 325° for 25–35 minutes or until a toothpick in center comes out clean. Cool. Cut into bars.

Extraordinary Cuisine for Sea & Shore (Washington)

Glacier Bear Bars

Easy, no-bake; pack for team trips or freeze, if they last that long.

2 cups white Karo syrup
2 cups packed brown sugar
2 cups peanut butter
4 cups cornflakes

6 cups Rice Krispies
2 cups chopped unsalted peanuts
Chocolate chips (optional)

Combine syrup and sugar and bring to a boil in a saucepan. Remove from heat; stir in peanut butter. Add cornflakes and Rice Krispies. Stir in peanuts until all are mixed. Press mixture into a 9x13-inch pan and allow to cool. "Frost" with melted chocolate chips or any chocolate icing, if desired. Cut into bars and enjoy. Cheer for the team!

Literary Tastes (Alaska)

Pineapple Squares

½ cup (1 stick) butter or margarine, softened
1⅓ cups sugar
4 eggs
1½ cups flour
1 teaspoon baking powder

½ teaspoon baking soda
¼ teaspoon salt
1 (20-ounce) can crushed pineapple, drained
Powdered sugar

Cream together butter and sugar with an electric mixer for 2 minutes on high speed. Mix in eggs. Add dry ingredients, except the powdered sugar, and mix.

Drain pineapple by pressing the top of the open can against the pineapple while draining the juice. Add pineapple to the ingredients in the bowl and stir with a spoon until blended. Pour batter into a greased, 9x13-inch pan and bake for 30–35 minutes at 350°. Cool; cut into 24 bars. Sprinkle with powdered sugar.

Editors' Extra: Don't throw the pineapple juice away. I like adding it to orange juice for a delicious drink.

Aunty Pua's Keiki Cookbook (Hawaii)

Easy Elegant Truffles

These are limited in flavors only by your imagination. When dipping, decorate truffle tops differently to indicate the center flavor. Have fun! These make wonderful, elegant gifts.

**2 (12-ounce) bags real
chocolate chips (semisweet,
milk, flavored or vanilla or
combination)
1 (8-ounce) package cream
cheese, room temperature**

**⅛ teaspoon salt
1 cup powdered sugar
1 tablespoon vanilla
Semisweet or milk chocolate for
dipping or almond bark in
chocolate or white**

Melt chocolate chips in top of large double boiler over barely sim-mering water until melted. Add cream cheese and stir until it is melted in. Remove from heat; add salt, powdered sugar, and vanilla, and beat by hand or with mixer to blend and smooth. Cover and cool to about room temperature. Form into truffle-size balls; chill until firm. Dip into melted chocolate or almond bark coating to cover. Chill until firm.

VARIATIONS:

Mocha: Dissolve 3 tablespoons instant coffee in the vanilla before adding.

Orange: Add grated rind of large orange.

Black Forest: Add ½ teaspoon almond extract in place of vanilla and stir in 3 tablespoons very finely chopped, well drained maraschi-no cherries.

Coconut: Use vanilla chips. Use 1 teaspoon coconut flavoring with vanilla; stir in 4 tablespoons very finely chopped coconut.

Toasted Almond: Vanilla chips, ½ teaspoon almond extract, 2 table-spoons very finely chopped toasted sliced almonds.

German Chocolate: Use milk chocolate chips, add 2 tablespoons very finely chopped coconut and 2 tablespoons very finely chopped toasted pecans.

Mint: Use mint flavored chocolate chips or add 1 teaspoon mint extract.

Raspberry: Use raspberry chocolate chips and stir in 2 tablespoons seedless raspberry jam.

Great Recipes from Redeemer's Fellowship (Oregon)

Almond Roca

2 cups butter
4 cups superfine sugar
2 cups whole almonds

4 cups semisweet chocolate
  chips, divided
2 cups finely ground walnuts

Melt butter in heavy saucepan over medium heat. Add sugar, stirring vigorously. Cook until caramel in color (or to 270° on candy thermometer), stirring constantly. Add almonds. Cook until medium brown in color (or to 290° on candy thermometer), stirring constantly. Pour onto buttered baking sheet. Top with 2 cups chocolate chips, spreading evenly. Sprinkle half the walnuts on top. Chill until set. Turn candy over. Melt 2 cups chocolate chips; spread over candy. Sprinkle with remaining walnuts. Let stand until set. Break into pieces. Yields 32 pieces.

California Gold (California)

Microwave Almond Roca

2 cups chopped almonds,
  divided
1 cup butter, plus some for pan

1 cup sugar
1 package real chocolate chips

Spread 1¼ cups almonds in buttered 9x13-inch pan. Cook 1 cup butter and sugar in microwave on high for 1 minute. Stir. Cook an additional 6–8 minutes on high, stirring every 2 minutes. Mixture will be caramelized in color. Pour immediately over almonds. (Don't be surprised if the butter/sugar mixture partially separates.) Pour chocolate chips on hot caramel mixture. When melted, spread evenly. Sprinkle with remaining nuts. Chill or freeze. Break in pieces to serve.

Favorite Recipes Cookbook (Oregon)

Chocolate Ball Candy

1 can condensed milk
1 cup butter
2 pounds powdered sugar,
  sifted
14 ounces flaked coconut

1 cup chopped nuts
1 (12-ounce) package chocolate
  chips
1 block paraffin

Heat milk and butter, stirring constantly, until butter melts. Remove from heat and slowly add sifted powdered sugar, coconut, and nuts. Cool. Roll into balls. Let stand until cold.

Melt chocolate chips and paraffin. Dip balls into chocolate and set on cookie sheet. Freezes well.

From Our Kitchen to Yours (Washington)

Stix 'n Stones

These were one of the sweet treat favorites in our home when our children were growing up. Actually, Dad enjoyed them the most.

1 (12-ounce) package
  butterscotch chips
2–3 cups Kix cereal

1 cup dry (oriental) noodles
1–1½ cups miniature
  marshmallows

Melt chips on low-medium burner or in the microwave. They will hold their shape until stirred, so test often or they may scorch. Add remaining 3 ingredients to melted chips, stir gently to coat well. Drop by large spoonfuls onto waxed paper; let cool.

We have added other cereals, other chips, and melted some of the marshmallow with the chips. Also try adding raisins, coconut, granola, nuts or M&M'S. Any flavor chip works well and cereals, too.

McNamee Family & Friends Cookbook (Washington)

PIES and OTHER DESSERTS

The best known existing cable car system is in San Francisco, California. The only moving National Historic Landmark in the United States, San Francisco's cable cars constitute the oldest and largest such system in permanent operation, and it is the only one to still operate with manually operated cars running in street traffic.

Alaskan Key Stout Pie

"I wrote this recipe for the 1998 Alaska Brewery Contest, and it won!"

CRUST:

¾ cup graham cracker
  crumbs
½ cup finely chopped pecans
¼ cup firmly packed, light
  brown sugar

¼ cup white sugar
½ stick (¼ cup) unsalted
  butter, melted and cooled

In a bowl, combine graham cracker crumbs, pecans, and sugars. Stir in butter. Press the mixture into bottom and ½ inch up side of a buttered, 9-inch springform pan. Bake 10 minutes at 325°. Cool, then chill for 1 hour before filling.

FILLING:

1 tablespoon cornstarch
½ tablespoon arrowroot
¼ teaspoon salt
5 egg yolks
4 egg whites, divided
½ cup fresh squeezed lime
  juice (1–2 limes; save a slice
  and zest for garnish)

½ cup Alaskan Stout Beer
  (or any stout beer)
1⅜ cup sugar, divided
1⅓ tablespoons plain gelatin
  softened in ⅓ cup water
1 cup whipping cream

Mix cornstarch, arrowroot, and salt together. In a large bowl, beat egg yolks until fluffy; blend in ½ of the egg whites, the lime juice, and Alaskan Stout. Add 1¼ cups of the sugar and the rest of cornstarch mixture. Put in double boiler and cook, stirring with wooden spoon, until thick. Remove from heat. Stir in gelatin. Cool in refrigerator, stirring frequently, especially if in metal bowl. Beat remaining egg whites in small bowl with remaining ⅛ cup sugar. Beat whipping cream in large bowl. Fold cooled yolk mixture and egg whites into whipped cream. Pour into crust. Chill.

TOPPING:

1½–2 cups sour cream
2 tablespoons sugar

2 tablespoons Alaskan Stout
  Beer (or any stout beer)

Mix ingredients. Spread over chilled pie. Garnish with lime slice and zest. Chill overnight.

Be Our Guest (Alaska)

Okinawan Sweet Potato Pie with Haupia Topping

A new favorite that combines the different textures of a light crust, dense sweet potato, and smooth haupia. A hands-down winner at any gathering.

CRUST:

4 tablespoons sugar
1½ cups flour
½ cup chopped nuts
(optional)

¾ cup margarine or butter
(1½ sticks)

Combine sugar, flour, and nuts. Cut margarine into flour mixture until texture is sandy. Press lightly into 9x13-inch pan. Bake at 325° for 20–25 minutes.

FILLING:

8 tablespoons butter or
margarine, softened
1 cup sugar
2 eggs, beaten
2 cups Okinawan sweet potato,
cooked and mashed

½ cup evaporated milk
1 teaspoon vanilla
¼ teaspoon salt

Beat butter and sugar. Add eggs and mix. Gradually mix in mashed sweet potatoes. Add evaporated milk, vanilla, and salt; mix well. Pour onto Crust. Bake at 350° for 30–35 minutes. Cool.

HAUPIA TOPPING:

½ cup sugar
½ cup cornstarch
1½ cups water

2 (12-ounce) cans frozen
coconut milk, thawed

Combine sugar and cornstarch; stir in water and blend well. Stir sugar mixture into coconut milk; cook and stir over low heat until thickened. Cool slightly. Pour coconut milk mixture (haupia) over the pie filling and refrigerate.

Hawai'i's Best Local Desserts (Hawaii)

Haupia is a traditional coconut milk-based Hawaiian dessert in Hawaii. Since World War II, it has become popular as a topping for white cake, especially at weddings. Although technically considered a pudding, the consistency of haupia closely approximates gelatin dessert and is usually served in blocks like gelatin. The traditional Hawaiian recipe for haupia calls for heated coconut milk to be mixed with ground Polynesian arrowroot until the mixture thickens. Due to the lack of availability of arrowroot starch, some modern recipes for haupia substitute cornstarch.

Haupia Pie

1 (10- to 12-ounce) can
  coconut milk
¼ cup sugar
¼ cup water

3 tablespoons cornstarch
1 (8-inch) prepared graham
  cracker crust

Put coconut milk and sugar in saucepan and heat. Measure water in a liquid measuring cup and add the cornstarch to it. Stir until smooth and add to the hot coconut milk. Cook on medium heat until mixture thickens, stirring constantly. Cool to room temperature and pour into prepared crust. Refrigerate at least 3 hours. Serves 6.

Aunty Pua's Keiki Cookbook (Hawaii)

Kona Coffee Ice Cream Pie

3 pints vanilla ice cream
1½ cups heavy cream,
  divided
½ cup coarsely chopped
  macadamia nuts
2 tablespoons coffee liqueur
2 tablespoons instant coffee

1 (9-inch) pastry shell, baked
4 egg whites
¼ teaspoon cream of tartar
½ cup sugar
Maraschino cherries for
  garnish

Soften 1 pint ice cream in a medium-size bowl. Beat ½ of the heavy cream in a small bowl until stiff. Fold into softened ice cream along with nuts and liqueur. If very soft, place in freezer until mixture holds its shape.

Soften remaining 2 pints ice cream in large bowl. Stir instant coffee into remaining heavy cream. Beat until stiff. Fold into remaining softened ice cream. Spread ⅔ coffee mixture in pastry shell. Make a depression in center. Spoon macadamia mixture into center. Mound remaining coffee mixture on top. Freeze overnight or until firm.

Beat egg whites and cream of tartar until foamy. Beat in sugar until meringue forms soft peaks. Cover ice cream filling with meringue and maraschino cherries in proportions desired. Chill.

Hawaii–Cooking with Aloha (Hawaii)

Fluffy Frozen Peanut Butter Pie

GRAHAM CRACKER CRUST:

12 graham crackers, crushed   **¼ cup butter, melted**
2 tablespoons sugar

Blend all ingredients together and press into a 9-inch pie plate. Bake in a 325° oven for 12–15 minutes.

FILLING:

8 ounces cream cheese   **1½–2 cups defrosted Cool**
1⅓ cups powdered sugar   **Whip**
Scant ½ cup peanut butter   **¼ cup finely chopped peanuts**
½ cup milk

Whip cream cheese at low speed until soft and fluffy. Beat in sugar and peanut butter. Slowly add milk. Fold in Cool Whip. Pour in shell and sprinkle with peanuts. Freeze. (Can easily be sliced while frozen.) Serves 6–8.

Children's Hospital Oakland Cookbook (California)

Washington Nut Pie

1 (9-inch) pie pastry   **1 cup dark Karo syrup**
3 eggs   **¼ teaspoon salt**
½ cup sugar   **1 teaspoon vanilla**
4 tablespoons butter, melted   **1 cup chopped pecans**

Line a 9-inch pie plate with pastry. Beat eggs; add sugar, butter, syrup, salt, and vanilla. Fold in nuts. Bake at 450° for 15 minutes, then reduce to 375° for 25–30 minutes. Be careful not to over-bake—should be like a custard.

Unser Tagelich Brot (The Staff of Life III) (Washington)

Chocolate Caramel Pecan Pie

CARAMEL SAUCE:

1 teaspoon butter
1 teaspoon flour
⅛ teaspoon salt
⅓ cup whipping cream

¼ cup sugar
¼ cup firmly packed brown
   sugar

In a glass bowl, melt butter. Stir in flour and salt. Stir in whipping cream. Add sugar and brown sugar. Mix well. Microwave on high until mixture boils; microwave at a boil for 2 minutes longer. Set aside.

FILLING:

⅔ cup sugar
½ teaspoon salt
⅓ cup butter, melted
1 cup light corn syrup
3 eggs

1 cup pecan halves
2 ounces unsweetened
   chocolate, melted
1 (9-inch) pie crust, unbaked

In a large bowl, combine sugar, salt, melted butter, corn syrup, and eggs. Beat well. Stir ½ cup of Filling mixture into Caramel Sauce; blend well. Set aside. Stir pecans and chocolate into remaining Filling mixture; blend well. Pour into crust-lined pan. Pour Caramel Sauce evenly over Filling. Bake at 375° for 45 minutes or until outer edge of Filling is set and center is partially set. Cool on wire rack. Serve with whipped cream.

Great Recipes from Redeemer's Fellowship (Oregon)

Alaska Mixed Berry Pie

1 cup sugar
4 tablespoons flour
¼ teaspoon salt
1½ cups huckleberries or
  blueberries

1½ cups salmonberries or
  cloudberries
Pie pastry for 9-inch pie shell,
  unbaked

Mix dry ingredients and pour over berries in shell. Use top crust or leave open-faced to serve with whipped cream. Bake 10 minutes at 450°, lower heat to 350° and bake 30 minutes longer, until golden brown.

Let's Taste Alaska (Alaska)

Northwest Huckleberry Pie

Native huckleberries are a summer treat for hikers throughout the timberline areas of the Pacific Northwest. These small, firm berries are a favorite of cooks and bears alike. If you are unable to find them, blueberries are a reasonable alternative.

1 (9-inch) pie crust, unbaked

FILLING:
¾ cup sugar
¼ cup all-purpose flour
½ teaspoon nutmeg
½ teaspoon cinnamon

5 cups peeled, cored, and thinly sliced tart apples
1 cup huckleberries or blueberries

TOPPING:
1 cup all-purpose flour
½ cup butter, cut into pieces

½ cup brown sugar

Press pie crust into a 9-inch pie plate and flute edges. Combine Filling ingredients and place in pie crust. Combine Topping ingredients and mix until crumbly. Sprinkle over pie filling. Bake at 375° for 50 minutes. Cover with aluminum foil for the last 10 minutes if top browns too quickly. Serves 8.

Gold'n Delicious (Washington)

Huckleberry-Cherry Pie

3 tablespoons quick-cooking tapioca
1 cup sugar
2 cups huckleberries
1 cup canned cherries

½ cup cherry juice
1 tablespoon lemon juice
2 (9-inch) pie shells
1 tablespoon butter

Combine tapioca, sugar, huckleberries, cherries, cherry juice, and lemon juice. Pour mixture into prepared 9-inch pie shell. Dot with butter and add top crust. Bake at 400° for 55 minutes.

Huckleberries and Crabmeat (Oregon)

Sour Cream Pear Pie

This is our most popular pear dessert at the Pear Party in September. Our daughter-in-law Linda, makes lots so everyone can sample.

PIE:

1 cup sour cream
1 egg
¾ cup sugar
1 teaspoon vanilla
¼ teaspoon salt

2 tablespoons flour
4 cups peeled and diced ripe pears
1 (9-inch) pie shell, unbaked

Preheat oven to 375°. Blend sour cream, egg, sugar, vanilla, salt, and flour until smooth. Fold in prepared pears. Pour into pie shell. Bake for 40 minutes. Sprinkle with Pecan Streusel Topping and bake another 10 minutes. Cool slightly and serve.

PECAN STREUSEL TOPPING:

¼ cup butter, cut in small pieces
¼ cup flour

¼ cup brown sugar
1 teaspoon cinnamon
¼ cup finely chopped pecans

Cut butter into combined flour, sugar, and cinnamon. Add pecans. Serves 6–8.

Recipe by Rasmussen Farms (Hood River)
The Fruit Loop Cookbook (Oregon)

LYN TOPINKA, U.S. DEPT OF THE INTERIOR

Each year around 10,000 climbers attempt to climb to the top of Mount Rainier with about fifty percent success. Most climbers require two to three days to reach the summit. Shown here behind Tacoma, Washington, it is the highest peak in the Cascade Range at 14,411 feet. Mount Rainier National Park became a national park in 1899.

Farmer's Market Caramel Apple Pie

A Market Fruit original and one of our most popular pies!

PIE:

**6–8 Granny Smith apples,
  peeled and sliced**
¾–1 cup sugar
¼ teaspoon cinnamon

1 (9-inch) pie shell, unbaked
**2 tablespoons margarine, cut
  into small pieces**

Preheat oven to 400°. Mix sliced apples with sugar and cinnamon. Pour apple mixture into pie shell. Dot with margarine.

TOPPING:

2 cups oats
¼ cup margarine

¼ cup brown sugar

Mix ingredients for Topping with a fork until crumbly. Spread evenly on top of apple mixture. Bake for 45–50 minutes, covering with foil the last 10–15 minutes. Serves 6–8.

The Fruit Loop Cookbook (Oregon)

My Secret Apple Pie

1¼ cups sugar
1¼ teaspoons cinnamon
½ teaspoon nutmeg
½ teaspoon salt
⅓ cup cornstarch

2 (9-inch) pie crusts, unbaked
6–7 cups sliced apples
¼ cup orange juice
¼ cup honey or maple syrup

Mix all dry ingredients in 1 gallon plastic bag. Line pan with crust. Add sliced apples to the plastic bag. Shake quickly to coat apples and dump immediately into crust. Mix orange juice and honey. Spread juice mixture over apples and seal on top crust. Sprinkle drops of water on crust and then a little sugar on the set spots. Cut a few vent holes in top and bake with edge of crust protected. Uncover edge for the final 10–15 minutes of baking. Bake at 425° for 70–75 minutes. The secret is out!

Taste of the Methow (Washington)

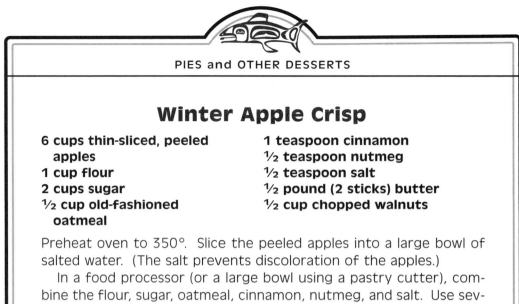

Winter Apple Crisp

6 cups thin-sliced, peeled
  apples
1 cup flour
2 cups sugar
½ cup old-fashioned
  oatmeal

1 teaspoon cinnamon
½ teaspoon nutmeg
½ teaspoon salt
½ pound (2 sticks) butter
½ cup chopped walnuts

Preheat oven to 350°. Slice the peeled apples into a large bowl of salted water. (The salt prevents discoloration of the apples.)

In a food processor (or a large bowl using a pastry cutter), combine the flour, sugar, oatmeal, cinnamon, nutmeg, and salt. Use several short bursts of the food processor to combine ingredients, then cut the hard butter into small cubes and drop it into the work bowl. Cut the butter in until it looks like coarse crumbs, then pulse or stir in the walnuts just to combine.

Lift the apples out of the water and mound into a 10-inch baking dish, packing them down as tightly as possible. Mound topping over the apples and press down to cover every bit of apples. Bake 30–45 minutes, waiting until there are apple juices bubbling out of the center of the top. Poke a knife into the center to check the doneness.

Alaska Cooking: Featuring Skagway (Alaska)

Apricot Crisp

Rich in vitamin A; easy because the fruit needs no peeling.

4 cups fresh apricots, cut in
  thin slices and chunks
¾ cup firmly packed brown
  sugar
½ cup whole-wheat flour

¾ cup rolled oats
¾ teaspoon ground cinnamon
¾ teaspoon ground nutmeg
⅓ cup margarine

Preheat oven to 375°. Place cut fruit in 8-inch square baking pan. Blend remaining ingredients with pastry knife. Spread mixture over fruit evenly. Bake about 30 minutes or until knife cuts fruit easily. Serve warm. Yields 6 (½ -cup) servings.

Taste California (California)

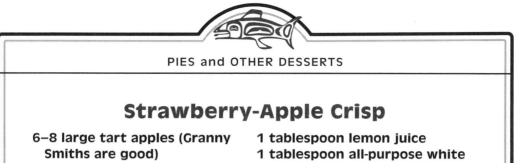

Strawberry-Apple Crisp

6–8 large tart apples (Granny
  Smiths are good)
1½–2 cups fresh strawberries
  or frozen, thawed with juice
2 tablespoons apple juice

1 tablespoon lemon juice
1 tablespoon all-purpose white
  flour
2 teaspoons cinnamon

Peel and core apples. Thinly slice apples lengthwise and place in a 9x13-inch baking dish. Add strawberries with juice, apple juice, and lemon juice. Sprinkle with flour and cinnamon and lightly toss in the baking dish.

TOPPING:

1½ cups old-fashioned rolled
  oats
¼ cup wheat germ, toasted
⅓ cup finely chopped pecans
Pinch of salt
1 teaspoon cinnamon

½ teaspoon nutmeg
2 tablespoons honey
¼ cup brown sugar
3 tablespoons melted butter or
  olive oil

In a medium bowl, combine all Topping ingredients and sprinkle evenly on top of apples and strawberries. Bake at 375° for 35–40 minutes, until apples are soft. Serve warm with non-fat frozen yogurt or ice cream. Mmm!

Note: Blackberries, raspberries, or peaches may be substituted for straw-berries.

Good Food for (Mostly) Good People Cookbook (Washington)

South of Eureka, California, along Highway 101, there are three redwood trees you can actually drive through—Leggett's Chandelier Drive-Thru Tree, the Tour-Thru Tree near Klamath, and the Shrine Drive-Thru Tree in Myers Flat. The legendary Giant Sequoia tree with a highway running through it, located in Yosemite National Park, fell in 1969.

Cobbler in a Shake

6–8 apples
¼ cup sugar, divided
1 teaspoon cinnamon
⅓ cup raisins (optional)

½ cup biscuit mix
2 eggs, beaten
1 cup milk

Butter a deep-dish pie plate and fill it with peeled, thinly sliced apples. Sprinkle with a mixture of ⅛ cup sugar and cinnamon. Scatter the raisins. In a quart jar, shake together biscuit mix, eggs, milk, and remaining sugar until they are evenly blended, and pour over apples. Bake at 375° for 35–45 minutes or until apples are tender.

A Taste of Heaven (Washington)

Three Berry Cobbler

We were sorry when this recipe was finished, since that meant we would no longer have it at our tasting sessions. Served warm and topped with frozen vanilla yogurt, it is an all-time favorite of our staff members. Frozen berries are available all year long, so you do not have to wait for summer to enjoy this great treat.

1 tablespoon margarine
½ cup whole-wheat flour
½ cup white flour
½ cup sugar
1½ teaspoons baking powder
¾ cup skim milk

3 cups fresh blueberries,
  blackberries, and red
  raspberries or 2 (12-ounce)
  bags frozen mixed
  berries, thawed 1½ hours

Preheat oven to 350°. Put margarine in an 8-inch-square baking pan and heat in oven to melt, about 2 minutes. Combine flours, sugar, baking powder, and milk. Pour batter over margarine, but do not mix. Put berries on top of batter (if using frozen berries, do not include juice). Bake 35 minutes (frozen berries will take 45–50 minutes) or until a wooden pick inserted in the center comes out clean. Makes 9 servings.

The New American Diet Cookbook (Oregon)

All American Apple Cobbler

6 apples, thinly sliced
½ cup sugar
1 teaspoon cinnamon
3 tablespoons water
**1 cup plus 1 tablespoon
  all-purpose flour, divided**

½ cup brown sugar
**½ cup butter or margarine,
  melted**

Combine apples, sugar, cinnamon, water, and 1 tablespoon flour in medium bowl; mix well. Place in a greased casserole. Combine remaining ingredients in a medium bowl; mix well. Place topping evenly over apples. Bake in preheated 350° oven for 45 minutes or until topping is slightly browned. Serves 8.

Pig Out (Oregon)

Blackberry Roll

We in Oregon are blessed with abundant blackberries and I am always looking for ways to utilize them. This is a great recipe.

2 cups flour
4 teaspoons baking powder
½ teaspoon salt
**¼ cup cold butter or
  margarine**
**1 cup grated sharp Cheddar
  cheese**

¾ cup milk
2½ cups fresh blackberries
**½ cup plus 2 tablespoons
  sugar, divided**
¼ cup brown sugar
½ teaspoon grated nutmeg

Preheat oven to 350°. In a mixing bowl, combine flour, baking powder, salt, and butter. Work until butter is fine crumbs. Blend in cheese and milk; do not overmix. Roll dough out lightly into a 10x12-inch rectangle, about ⅓ inch thick. Sprinkle blackberries on top, then add ½ cup white sugar, the brown sugar, and nutmeg.

Starting from the long edge, roll up dough like a jellyroll and transfer to a greased baking sheet, placing it seam-side-down. Pinch edges together and fold under. Pat roll into a tidy bundle and sprinkle remaining 2 tablespoons white sugar on top. Bake for 45 minutes or until the roll is golden brown. Slice and serve warm in bowls with cream. Serves 10.

Then 'til Now (Oregon)

Angel Lemon Delight

This pudding-cake is refreshing, different, and easy. In fact, it's just plain won-derful. Pretty served in shallow, glass bowls with stem strawberries on the side.

1½ cups sugar, divided
½ cup flour
¼ teaspoon salt
3 egg yolks
Juice and grated rind of
  2 large lemons

2 tablespoons butter, melted
1½ cups milk
3 egg whites

Preheat oven to 375°. Mix 1 cup sugar, flour, salt, egg yolks, juice and rind, butter, and milk together in order given. Beat until very smooth and creamy. Beat egg whites until stiff. Add ½ cup sugar and beat again. Fold into first set of ingredients. Pour into ungreased, shallow, 8x12-inch, glass baking dish. Set in a shallow roasting pan in 1 inch hot water. Bake, uncovered, for 40 minutes. Serve warm or cold. Serves 6–8.

The Overlake School Cookbook (Washington)

The Iditarod Trail Sled Dog Race, usually just called the Iditarod, is an annual sled dog race in Alaska, where mushers and teams of typically 16 dogs cover 1,161 miles in eight to fifteen days from Anchorage to Nome. The Iditarod began in 1973 as an event to test the best sled dog mushers and teams, evolving into the highly competitive race it is today. The current fastest winning time record was set in 2002 by Martin Buser with a time of 8 days, 22 hours, 46 min-utes, and 2 seconds. Teams frequently race through blizzards causing whiteout conditions, and sub-zero weather and gale-force winds which can cause the wind chill to reach -100 °F. The race is the most popular sporting event in Alaska, and the top mushers and their teams of dogs are local celebrities. While the yearly field of more than fifty mushers and about a thousand dogs is still largely Alaskan, competitors from fourteen countries have completed the event including the Swiss, Martin Buser, who became the first international winner in 1992.

Apple Bread Pudding
with Bourbon Sauce

8 cups sourdough or French bread (day old is best)
4 tablespoons butter
3 cups low-fat milk, scalded
1 cup brown sugar

1 cup apple pie filling
3 eggs, beaten
1 tablespoon vanilla extract
½ cup raisins

Butter bread and tear into small pieces. Place in a large bowl. Scald milk and then pour over bread to cover. Let soak for 30 minutes. Once bread has been soaking for about 15 minutes, preheat oven to 350°. Toss the brown sugar and apple pie filling. Add beaten eggs and vanilla and whisk together. Pour over bread mixture. Sprinkle raisins over top and lightly stir to blend. Scrape the mixture into a 2-quart baking dish, lightly oiled. Place the baking dish in a larger pan filled with hot water. Place the entire contents into oven. Bake for 60–70 minutes. You may want to loosely cover pudding with foil after 30 minutes of baking to prevent the top from burning. While Bread Pudding is baking, prepare the Bourbon Sauce.

BOURBON SAUCE:
6 tablespoons butter
1 large egg

¾ cup powdered sugar
3 tablespoons bourbon whiskey

Melt butter in a small saucepan. In a small bowl, beat egg, then beat in powdered sugar. Stir into melted butter and whisk mixture until it becomes hot. Do not boil. Remove from heat and let cool to room temperature, stirring occasionally. The sauce will thicken as it cools. Stir in the bourbon. Serve pudding hot or warm, spooning the sauce over each serving. Yields 8 servings.

Drop the Hook, Let's Eat (Alaska)

Bread Pudding with Chocolate Chips

Even better the next morning, cold, for breakfast, if you have any left!

8 cups stale, cubed bread
1 cup chocolate chips
4 cups scalded milk
1 cup sugar

4 eggs, slightly beaten
½ teaspoon salt
1 teaspoon cinnamon

Place cubed bread in a 9x13-inch baking dish. (You can try and dress it up with sourdough, etc., but the most inexpensive white bread, left on the counter to get stale, works the best.) Mix in chocolate chips. In a separate bowl, blend milk, sugar, eggs, salt, and cinnamon. Pour over bread. Place baking dish in a larger pan of hot water (1 inch) and bake at 350° for 40–45 minutes, until browned and knife inserted into middle comes out clean. Serve hot in a bowl with a little milk poured over the top, if desired (half our family likes it with milk, half just plain).

Taste of Fillmore (California)

Swedish Baked Rice Pudding

½ cup uncooked regular
  long-grain rice
2 tablespoons sugar
2 cups milk
1 tablespoon margarine or
  butter
6 eggs

1 cup sugar
1 teaspoon cinnamon
½ teaspoon salt
½ teaspoon nutmeg
½ cup raisins
2 cups milk
1 teaspoon vanilla

In medium pan (nonstick), combine rice, sugar, milk and butter. Bring to a boil. Reduce heat to low; cook 20–25 minutes or until thickened and creamy, stirring so as not to stick. Remove from heat and cool slightly. Grease an 8-inch-square baking dish.

In large bowl, beat eggs; stir in remaining pudding ingredients and rice mixture. Pour into greased pan. Bake at 350° for 55–60 minutes, until set. Serve warm with cream over each serving.
Note: May plump raisins by soaking in warm amaretto or water.

Nautical Niceaty's from Spokane Yacht Club (Washington)

Kona Coffee Chocolate Pôt de Crème

12 ounces Hawaiian semi-
sweet chocolate, finely
chopped
2 large eggs
½ teaspoon salt
1½ cups fresh milk

1 tablespoon Irish cream or
other liqueur
3 tablespoons instant Kona
coffee
Whipped cream and chocolate
shavings (optional)

Place first 3 ingredients in blender container. Scald together milk and liqueur over medium-high heat, stirring constantly. Remove from heat and stir in Kona coffee granules until dissolved. Add hot liquid to blender and immediately blend all ingredients for 5–8 seconds at high speed. Divide mixture among 8 small dessert ramekins or pôt de crème cups and chill until firm, at least 4 hours. Serve unadorned in traditional manner, or garnish with a dollop of slightly sweetened whipped cream and shaved chocolate. Almost any liqueur of choice is suitable for taste variations. Serves 8.

Kona on My Plate (Hawaii)

Vanilla Coconut Ball Treats

1½ cups sweetened coconut
shreds
1 stick butter
1 cup condensed milk

1 large Symphony candy bar
Vanilla ice cream
Chopped nuts (optional)

Brown coconut shreds under broiler until golden brown. Set aside and cool. Melt butter, then add milk and chocolate bar a piece at a time, and heat slowly until the consistency is creamy. Make ice cream into balls and roll in coconut shreds. Top each ball with chocolate sauce; serve immediately. Nuts of your choice can be added to the top of each vanilla ball, if desired.

Recipe by Fire Fighter 3 Brian Derby
Hawai'i's Favorite Firehouse Recipes *(Hawaii)*

Nut Tart with Apricot Cream

A superb nutty tart.

CRUST:

2 cups flour

¼ cup sugar

¾ cup butter

2 egg yolks, slightly beaten

Combine flour and sugar; cut in butter with pastry blender or food processor. Work in egg yolks with fork or continue in food processor just until dough holds together. Press evenly over ungreased bottom and sides of 11 or 12-inch tart pan with fluted sides and removable bottom. Bake at 325° for 10 minutes; color will be pale. Use hot or cold.

FILLING:

1½ cups whipping cream

1½ cups sugar

1 teaspoon grated orange rind

¼ teaspoon salt

2 cups coarsely chopped walnuts

¼ teaspoon vanilla

¼ teaspoon orange extract

Combine cream, sugar, rind, and salt in large saucepan. Bring to a boil, stirring constantly. Reduce heat to medium; continue cooking for 5 minutes, stirring often. Remove from heat; stir in nuts and extracts. Pour into pastry shell and bake at 375° until lightly browned, about 35 minutes for a 12-inch tart and 40 minutes for an 11-inch tart. Cool in pan on wire rack until just warm to touch. Remove sides, not bottom, and cool to room temperature. May be made a day ahead. Serve in slender wedges topped with Apricot Cream or whipped cream. May also be served unadorned.

APRICOT CREAM:

¼ pound dried apricots

1 cup orange juice

2 tablespoons sugar

2 tablespoons Grand Marnier

1 cup whipping cream

Snip apricots into quarters. Simmer apricots in orange juice until very soft, about 30 minutes. Remove from heat; add sugar, and stir until dissolved. Cool to lukewarm; purée in blender or food processor adding Grand Marnier. Chill. Whip cream, then gently fold in apricot purée. Chill until ready to serve. Leftover Apricot Cream is delicious frozen.

Favorite Recipes Cookbook (Oregon)

Fried Cream

Fried cream is a dessert with a long tradition in San Francisco. It is delicious, spectacular, and up to the final frying stage it can—in fact must—all be done in advance. It is worth the last-minute effort for the impressive results.

3 egg yolks
¼ cup sugar
1 tablespoon plus ¼ cup dark rum
Pinch of salt
5 tablespoons cornstarch
3 tablespoons milk

2 cups heavy cream, scalded and cooled
1 (½-inch) cinnamon stick
1 cup ground almonds
1 egg, beaten
1 cup zwieback crumbs
Oil for deep frying

Beat together egg yolks, sugar, 1 tablespoon rum, and salt until lightly thickened. Mix cornstarch and milk into smooth paste and add to egg yolk mixture. Stirring constantly, gradually add cream and cinnamon stick. Cook in the top of a double boiler over boiling water, stirring constantly, until thick and smooth. Remove cinnamon stick and pour cream mixture into a buttered shallow 9x13-inch pan to a depth of ¾ inch. Chill thoroughly.

Cut cream into diamond shapes and roll in ground almonds. Dip pieces in beaten egg, then roll in zwieback crumbs. Chill once more. Heat oil to a deep-fry stage and fry cream until lightly browned, then drain on paper towels and arrange on a heated serving platter. Heat ¼ cup rum in a small saucepan, ignite, and pour over cream. Serve immediately. Serves 6–8.

San Francisco à la Carte (California)

California's world famous San Diego Zoo is in Balboa Park and is one of the largest and most progressive zoos in the world with over 4,000 animals of more than 800 species. It is also one of the few zoos in the world that houses the giant panda. There are outdoor escalators and a "Skyfari" that takes you on an elevated ride across the park.

The San Diego Zoo also operates the San Diego Zoo's Wild Animal Park, which displays animals in a more expansive condition than at the zoo. Animals are regularly transferred between both parks, as well as other zoos around the world, usually due to Species Survival Plan recommendations.

Flour Tortilla Torte

1 (6-ounce) package semisweet chocolate bits
3 tablespoons powdered sugar, divided
2 cups sour cream, divided
4 (7- to 8-inch) flour tortillas
1–2 ounces milk chocolate

Melt semisweet chocolate in the top of a double boiler. Add 1 tablespoon powdered sugar and 1 cup sour cream. Stir thoroughly. Then cool mixture.

Set 1 flour tortilla on a serving plate and spread evenly with ⅓ of the chocolate mixture. Cover with another flour tortilla, another ⅓ chocolate mixture, a third tortilla, the rest of the chocolate mixture, and then the last tortilla. Blend the remaining sour cream with 2 tablespoons powdered sugar and spread evenly over the top and sides of the Tortilla Torte. Chill, covered with inverted bowl at least 8 hours, or as long as overnight.

Shave milk chocolate into curls using a vegetable peeler. Pile chocolate curls on top of Tortilla Torte. Cut in slim wedges with a sharp knife. Makes 8–12 servings.

Literary Tastes (Alaska)

Mocha Polka Walnut Torte

1 package brownie mix (or your own recipe)
2 eggs
¼ cup water
¾ cup coarsely chopped nuts
2 cups whipping cream
½ cup firmly packed brown sugar
2 tablespoons instant coffee
Walnut halves

Follow cake-like method for preparing brownie mix, adding eggs and water as directed; add nuts. Spoon into 2 greased 9-inch cake pans. Bake at 350° for 20 minutes. Turn onto racks to cool. Whip cream until it begins to thicken. Gradually add brown sugar and instant coffee. Continue beating until of spreading consistency. Spread between layers of torte and swirl over top and sides. Polka-dot with walnut halves. Chill overnight. This is very rich, so one torte serves 10–12.

Mammoth Really Cooks Book II (California)

Individual Baked Alaska

1 sponge cake or pound cake   **Vanilla or strawberry ice cream**

Cut cake into 4- or 5-inch rounds ½ inch thick. Place cut cake on wooden plank or foil-lined cookie sheet. Top each round with a scoop of ice cream, centering so a ½-inch rim of cake remains. Cover lightly with waxed paper and place in freezer until needed (up to 3 days) and Meringue is made.

MERINGUE:

3 egg whites   **⅓ cup super-fine sugar**
¼ teaspoon cream of tartar

Whip egg whites and cream of tartar until stiff; gradually adding sugar, continue to beat until very stiff peaks form. Heat oven to 450°. Remove cakes from freezer and quickly frost completely with Meringue.   Bake in hot oven about 5 minutes, or until light brown all over. With spatula, remove to serving dishes. Drizzle with Raspberry Topping. Also good with strawberry, blueberry or rhubarb sauce.

RASPBERRY TOPPING:

1½ cups raspberries, fresh   **¼ cup orange liqueur or juice**
  or thawed   **1 tablespoon cornstarch**
¼ cup sugar

Place in small saucepan. Cook over low heat until thickened. Cool.

Editors' Extra: If using a frozen pound cake, slice in thirds lengthwise. Using the bottom of a coffee or nut can as a guide, cut circle shapes in cake with a serrated knife to make six rounds.

A Cook's Tour of Alaska (Alaska)

Forty Below Cranberry Dessert

1 (12-ounce) package vanilla
  wafers, divided
2 eggs
1 cup powdered sugar
½ cup margarine, softened

2 cups ground cranberries
⅔ cup sugar
2 bananas, sliced
½ cup chopped nuts
1 cup whipped cream

Crush wafers. Line baking dish with ½ of wafers. Mix eggs, powdered sugar, and margarine. Spread over crumbs. Mix ground cranberries, sugar, and bananas. Spread over egg mixture. Sprinkle on chopped nuts. Spread whipped cream over nuts. Sprinkle remaining wafers on top. Refrigerate overnight. May serve with additional whipped cream. Serves 12.

Sharing Our Best (Alaska)

Mai Tai Sundae Sauce

1 (12-ounce) jar pineapple-
  mango jam, or peach jam
3 tablespoons butter
2 teaspoons lime juice

¼ cup orange marmalade
½ teaspoon each: cinnamon,
  cloves, and nutmeg
¼ cup rum

Combine all ingredients, except rum. Cook over low heat until smoothly blended. Add rum. Serve warm over ice cream (macadamia flavor is best). Bananas may also be added just before serving.

The Friends of 'Iolani Palace Cookbook (Hawaii)

Alaska ranks 47th in population by state with 686,293 people. Only North Dakota, Vermont, and Wyoming have fewer. By comparison, California ranks first among U.S. states in population with more than 36 million people. Taking a closer look, Alaska is home to 1.1 residents per square mile compared to California with 234.4. The rest of the nation averages 79.6 residents per square mile.

Baked Bananas in Orange Juice

We love bananas. It's an old family recipe.

6 medium firm bananas
1 medium orange
2 tablespoons orange juice
2 tablespoons lemon juice

⅓ cup sugar
Dash of ground cinnamon
Dash of ground nutmeg

Preheat oven to 350°. Peel bananas. Peel and chop orange. Arrange bananas and orange pieces in an 8x8-inch baking dish. In a small bowl combine juices, sugar, cinnamon, and nutmeg. Pour over fruit. Bake for 25–30 minutes until bananas are golden and tender. Serve hot with ice cream. Serves 6.

Recipe by Jay Buhner, Outfielder, Seattle Mariners
Starters & Closers (Washington)

Sautéed Bananas

Sautéed fruit makes a quick and easy dessert. I've used bananas here, but peaches, nectarines, pears, or thinly sliced apples also work well.

1 tablespoon butter
2–3 tablespoons sugar, or to taste
¼ cup rum, Cointreau or fruit juice

Zest and juice of 1 orange
4 bananas, peeled and sliced lengthwise

In an nonstick pan, heat butter, sugar, and liquids until sugar dissolves. Add bananas and cook on low to medium heat until barely soft. Serve warm, garnished with zest, alone or with whipped cream or ice cream. Serves 4.

The $5 Chef: How to Save Cash & Cook Fast (California)

Custard Igloo or Lemon Snow

2 tablespoons unflavored
  gelatin (2 envelopes)
½ cup cold water
2 cups very hot water
2 cups sugar

½ cup lemon juice
6 egg whites, beaten stiff
  (reserve yolks for Custard
  Sauce)
1 tablespoon grated lemon rind

In a large mixing bowl, soften gelatin in cold water; dissolve in hot water. Add sugar and stir until sugar is completely dissolved. Add lemon juice. Chill until partially set, or consistency of unbeaten egg whites (usually about 2 hours).

Beat until frothy (about 2 minutes), then fold in egg whites. Beat until gelatin will hold its shape (another 2 minutes); fold in lemon rind. Pour into mold and chill until firm. For "Custard Igloo" use round bowl for mold. When set, invert pudding to serving plate (use thin knife around edge, if necessary to loosen) which is several inches larger than bowl. Make ice block lines with thick custard sauce or pour sauce over. Serve with extra sauce.

CUSTARD SAUCE:

4 slightly beaten egg yolks
Dash of salt
5 tablespoons sugar

2 cups scalded milk
1 teaspoon vanilla

In top of double boiler, combine egg yolks, salt, and sugar. Gradually stir in scalded milk. Cook over gently boiling water until mixture coats spoon, stirring constantly (usually 2–3 minutes). Remove from heat, and stir in vanilla. Chill thoroughly.

Editors' Extra: This makes four igloos, so half a recipe is plenty for an average dessert.

A Cook's Tour of Alaska

The word igloo comes from the people of eastern and northern Canada and of Arctic Alaska. The dome-shaped house built of snow is rarely found in Alaska any more, except perhaps when mountain climbers and bush travelers build temporary shelters against the elements. An Alaskan igloo was traditionally a dome or Quonset-hut shaped structure built with sod and reinforced with driftwood and whale bones. "Igloo," or "iglu" in the Inupiaq (inOO΄pE-ak) language, simply means "house."

LIST of CONTRIBUTORS

PHOTO BY GWEN McKEE

Within hours during the attack on Pearl Harbor, 2,390 service men and women lost their lives; 1,177 of these casualties were from the battleship **U.S.S. Arizona.** Completed in 1961, the 184-foot-long U.S.S. Arizona Memorial was built over the remains of the sunken battleship.

Listed below are the cookbooks that have contributed recipes to this book, along with copyright, author, publisher, city, and state. The information in parentheses indicates the BEST OF THE BEST cookbook in which the recipe originally appeared.

Alaska Connections Cookbook III, Prince of Wales Island Chamber of Commerce, Craig, AK

Alaska Cooking: Featuring Skagway ©2001 Greatland Classic Sales, Tigard, OR

Alaska Gold Rush Cook Book ©2000 by Ron Wendt, Wasila, AK

Alaska Magazine's Cabin Cookbook ©1988 Alaska Publishing Properties, Inc., Augusta, GA

Alaska Shrimp & Crab Recipes ©1996, 2003 by Stuart Nibeck, Anchorage, AK

Alaska's Cooking Volume II, GFWC Anchorage Woman's Club, AK

Alaska's Gourmet Breakfasts, by Leicha Welton, Fairbanks, AK

The Alaskan Bootlegger's Bible, by Leon Kania, Wasilla, AK

Alaskan Halibut Recipes ©1989, 1996, 2003 by Stu Nibeck, Anchorage, AK

Albertina's Exceptional Recipes ©1996 Albertina's, Portland, OR

All About Crab ©2000 by Nancy Brannon, Florence, OR

All-Alaska Women in Timber Cookbook, Alaska Women in Timber, Ketchikan, AK

Allrecipes Tried & True Favorites ©2001 Allrecipes, Seattle, WA

Another Taste of Aloha ©1993 The Junior League of Honolulu, HI

Another Taste of Washington State ©2000 Tracy Winters, Greenburg, IN

Apples Etc. Cookbook ©1998 Santa Cruz, CA Chapter of Hadassah

The Art Lover's Cookbook: A Feast for the Eye, Fine Arts Museums of San Francisco, CA

Aunty Pua's Keiki Cookbook ©1991 by Ann Kondo Corum, Honolulu, HI

Be Our Guest, Juneau CVB, Juneau, AK

Begged, Borrowed and Stöllen Recipes, by Jean Ritter Smith, Eugene, OR

Best Recipes of Alaska's Fishing Lodges ©1997 by Adela Batin, Fairbanks, AK

Bounteous Blessings ©2001 by Frances A. Gillette, Yacolt, WA

The California Cookbook ©1994 Gulf Publishing Company, Houston, TX

California Country Cook Book ©1996 Golden West Publishers, Phoenix, AZ

California Gold ©1992 California State Grange, Sacramento, CA

California Home Cooking ©1997 by Michele Anna Jordan, Boston, MA

California Kosher ©1991 Women's League of Adat Ari El, North Hollywood, CA

California Sizzles ©1992 The Junior League of Pasadena, CA

California Wine Country Herbs and Spices Cookbook ©1994 by Kathleen DeVanna Fish, Monterey, CA

Celebrating California ©1995 Children's Home Society of California, Oakland, CA

The Chicken Cookbook, The Washington Fryer Commission, Renton, WA

Children's Hospital Oakland Cookbook, Chestnut Branch, Castro Valley, CA

Christian Bakers Cookbook, Christian Church of Burns, OR

Christmas in Washington Cookbook ©1995 Golden West Publishers, Phoenix, AZ

Clam Dishes and Rock Fishes, by Carol Cate, Winchester, OR

The Coastal Cook of West Marin ©1991 Riley and Company, Bolinas, CA

Coastal Flavors, American Assn. of University Women, Seaside, OR

Collection Extraordinaire, Assistance League of Eugene, OR

The Colophon Café Best Recipes ©1995 Mama Colophon, Inc., Bellingham, WA

The Colophon Café Best Vegetarian Recipes ©1998 Mama Colophon, Inc., Bellingham, WA

Cook 'em Up Kaua'i ©1993 Kauai Historical Society, Kauai, HI

Cook Book, Mary Martha Society of Redeemer Lutheran Church, Chico, CA

Cookin' with CASA, CASA Choices for Children, Yreka, CA

Cooking from the Coast to the Cascades ©2002 Junior League of Eugene, OR

Cooking on the Fault Line–Corralitos Style, Corralitos Valley Research and Educational Assn., Corralitos, CA

Cooking Pure & Simple ©1988 Kincaid House Publishing, Newport Beach, CA

Cooking Treasures of the Central Coast, International Quota Club of Morro Bay, Los Osos, CA

Cooking with Booze, by Evelyn Barbee, Fresno, CA

Cooking with Herbs ©1997 Quail Botanical Gardens Foundation, Inc., Encinitas, CA

Cooking with Love, by Diana Bishop, Roseburg, OR

Cooking with Mushrooms ©1997 by John Pisto, Monterey, CA

A Cook's Tour of Alaska ©1995 A Cooks Tour of Alaska, Anchorage, AK

Crime Stoppers: A Community Cookbook, Thurston County Crime Stoppers, Lacey, WA

Dd's Table Talk II, by Deirdre Kieko Todd, Mililani, HI

Dilley Family Favorites, Bible Church of Dilley, OR

Dining Door to Door in Naglee Park, The Campus Community Assn., San Jose, CA

Drop the Hook, Let's Eat, by Rachel Barth, Petersburg, AK

Dungeness Crabs and Blackberry Cobblers ©1991 Janie Hibler, Portland, OR

Durham's Favorite Recipes, Durham Woman's Club, Durham, CA

Eat More, Weigh Less Cookbook ©1995 by Terry Shintani, Mc.D., J. D., M.P. H., Honolulu, HI

Ethnic Foods of Hawaii ©2000 by Ann Kondo Corum, Honolulu, HI

Extraordinary Cuisine for Sea & Shore ©1990 Seattle Yacht Club, WA

Fair's Fare, Del Mar Fair, Del Mar, CA

Favorite Island Cookery Book I, Honpa Hongwanji Hawaii Betsuin, Honolulu, HI

Favorite Island Cookery Book V, Honpa Hongwanji Hawaii Betsuin, Honolulu, HI

Favorite Recipes from Alaska's Bed and Breakfasts, Fairbanks Assn. of B&B's, Fairbanks, AK

Favorite Recipes from Our Best Cooks, St. John Vianney Altar Society, Spokane, WA

. . . Fire Burn & Cauldron Bubble ©1998 by Julie Lugo Cerra, Culver City, CA

The $5 Chef: How to Save Cash & Cook Fast ©1991 by Marcie Rothman, San Diego, CA

Flavor it Greek! ©1999 Philoptochos Society of Holy Trinity Greek Orthodox Church, Portland, OR

Fresh-Water Fish Cookbook, by Dave Hopfer, Turner, OR

Friends and Celebrities Cookbook II, Castle Performing Arts Center, Kaneohe, HI

The Friends of 'Iolani Palace Cookbook ©1987 The Friends of 'Iolani Palace, Honolulu, HI

From My Heart for Yours, by Linda L. Smith, Lake Bay, WA

From Our Kitchen to Yours, by Jewel and Jeanette, Vader, WA

From Portland's Palate ©1992 Junior League of Portland, OR

The Fruit Loop Cookbook ©2001 Hood River County Fruit Loop, Hood River, OR

Glorious Soups and Breads! ©1994 by Nancy Brannon, Florence, OR

Gold'n Delicious ©1995 The Junior League of Spokane, WA

Good Food for (Mostly) Good People Cookbook, by Marla Emde, Spokane, WA

Grade A Recipes, Christ Lutheran School, Coos Bay, OR

Grandma Jean's Rainy Day Recipes, by Kristina Y. McMorris, Portland, OR

Grannie Annie's Cookin' at the Homestead, by Ann Berg, Kenai, AK

Grannie Annie's Cookin' Fish from Cold Alaskan Waters, Ann Berg, Kenai, AK

Grannie Annie's Cookin' on the Wood Stove, by Ann Berg, Kenai, AK

Great Recipes from Redeemer's Fellowship, Redeemer's Fellowship, Roseburg, OR

The Great Vegetarian Cookbook ©1994 by Kathleen DeVanna Fish, Monterey, CA

Harvest Feast, Christ Church Women's Group, Puyallup, WA

Hawaii—Cooking with Aloha ©1981, 1984 by Elvira Monroe, Gerturde Margah, Theoni Pappas, San Carlos, CA

Hawaii Tropical Rum Drinks & Cuisine ©2001 Mutual Publishing, Honolulu, HI

Hawaii's Best Local Desserts, by Jean Watanabe Hee, Honolulu, HI

Hawaii's Best Local Dishes ©2002 Mutual Publishing, Honolulu, HI

Hawaii's Best Tropical Food & Drinks, Booklines Hawaii, Ltd., Honolulu, HI

Hawaii's Favorite Firehouse Recipes, Filmworks Press, Honolulu, HI

Hawaii's Favorite Pineapple Recipes ©2002 Mutual Publishing, Honolulu, HI

Hawaii's Spam Cookbook ©1987 by Ann Kondo Corum, Honolulu, HI

Hawaiian Country Tables ©1998 The Bess Press, Inc., Honolulu, HI

Heaven on the Half Shell ©2001 University of Washington, Seattle, WA

Heavenly Fare, Presbyterian Women of Montesano Presbyterian Church, Montesano, WA

Heavenly Temptations, St. Anne's Catholic School, Grants Pass, OR

The 'Hole Cake Doughnut Book, by Alice Matthews Jones, Coos Bay, OR

Home Plates, Seattle Mariners Wives and Mariners Care, Seattle, WA

Honolulu Hawaii Cooking ©1991 by Betty Evans, Hermosa Beach, CA

How to Use Hawaiian Fruit ©1974 Petroglyph Press, Hilo, HI

Huckleberries and Crabmeat, by Carol Cate, Winchester, OR

International Garlic Festival Cookbook ©1994 Caryl I. Simpson/Garlic Festival, Gilroy, CA

Jan Townsend Going Home ©1996 by Janice Lynn Townsend, Auburn, CA

Joys of Hawaiian Cooking ©1977 Petroglyph Press, Hilo, HI

Just for the Halibut ©1988 Flatfish Publications, King Salmon, AK

Kau Kau Kitchen ©1986 by Dana Black Yuen, Kailua, HI

Kay's Kitchen, Kay Gundersen, Ketchikan, AK

Kona on My Plate ©2002 Kona Outdoor Circle Foundation, Kona, HI

La Jolla Cooks Again, La Jolla Country Day School, La Jolla, CA

LaConner Palates ©1998 by Patricia Flynn and Patricia McClane, Oak Harbor, WA

The Lazy Gourmet ©1987 by Valerie Bates, Whittier, CA

Let's Taste Alaska, by Mary Carey, Trapper Creek, AK

Liberty Lake Community Cookbook, The Friends of Pavalion Park, Liberty Lake, WA

License to Cook Alaska Style ©2001 Penfield Press, Iowa City, IA

Literary Tastes, Friends of the Haines Borough Public Library, Haines, AK

Little Dave's Seafood Cookbook ©1998 by David J. Harvey, Los Angeles, CA

A Little San Francisco Cookbook ©1992 Chronicle Books, San Francisco, CA

Look What's Cooking, Oregon Farm Bureau Federation Women's Advisory Council, Salem, OR

Mammoth Really Cooks Book II, Mammoth Hospital Auxiliary, Mammoth Lakes, CA

Manna by the Sea, St. Peter the Fisherman Lutheran Women's Missionary League, Lincoln

Marilyn Thomas: The Homemaker Baker's Favorite Recipes ©1990 Marilyn Thomas, Camino, CA

Mariners Mix'n and Fix'n Grand Slam Style, Seattle Mariners Wives and Mariners Care, Seattle, WA

McNamee Family & Friends Cookbook, by Terri L. McNamee-Snyder, Colville, WA

Mendocino Mornings ©1996 by Arlene and Jim Moorehead, Mendocino, CA

Methodist Pie, United Methodist Church, Sitka, AK

The Miller Cookbook, by Carrie Gingerich, Shedd, OR

Monterey's Cookin' Pisto Style ©1994 by John Pisto, Monterey, CA

Moose & Caribou Recipes of Alaska ©1992, 1997 by Stuart Nibeck, Anchorage, AK

Moose in the Pot Cookbook, Burchell High School, Wasilla, AK

Moose Racks, Bear Tracks, and Other Alaska Kidsnacks ©1999 by Alice Bugni, Seattle, WA

Multnomah Falls Lodge Cook Book, Multnomah Falls Lodge Company, Troutdale, OR

Nautical Niceaty's from Spokane Yacht Club, Spokan Yacht Club, Spokan, WA

The New American Diet Cookbook ©2000 by Sonja L. Conner, M.S., R.D. and William E. Connor, M.D., Portland, OR

The New Complete Coffee Book ©2001 by Sara Perry, San Francisco, CA

New Covenant Kitchens, by Jell Neff, Grass Valley, CA

The 99¢ a Meal Cookbook ©1996 Loompanics Unlimited, Port Townsend, WA

Nome Centennial Cookbook 1898–1989 ©1996 by Kay Hansen, Homer, AK

Northwest Garlic Festival Cookbook, Ocean Park Chamber of Commerce, Ocean Park, WA

Nuggets, Nibbles and Nostalgia, Kern County Museum Foundation, Bakersfield, CA

The Old Yacht Club Inn Cookbook, by Nancy Donaldson, Santa Barbara, CA

Only in California ©Children's Home Society of California, Oakland, CA

Oregon Cook Book ©1995 Golden West Publishers, Phoenix, AZ

Oregon Farmers' Markets Cookbook and Guide ©1998 by Kris Wetherbee, Oakland, OR

The Organic Gourmet ©1995 by Barbara L. Kahn, Berkeley, CA

The Original Great Alaska Cookbook ©1997 Star-Byte, Inc., Hatfield, PA

Our Best Home Cooking ©1993 Pend Oreille County Historical Society, Newport, WA

Our Burnt Offerings, Presbyterian Women–First Presbyterian Church, Vancouver, WA

Our Favorite Recipes, Elliott Prairie Community Church, Woodburn, OR

The Overlake School Cookbook ©1984 The Overlake School, Bellevue, WA

"Pacific"ally Salmon, by Carol Cates, Winchester, OR

Panhandle Pat's Fifty Years, by Patricia Emel, Seabeck, WA

Paradise Preserves ©1987 by Yvonne Neely Armitage, Kailua, HI

Pelican, Alaska: Alaskan Recipe Cookbook, Pelican Citizen's Emergency Travel Fund, Pelican, AK

Pig Out, White Eagle Grange # 683, Pilot Rock, OR

Pioneers of Alaska Auxiliary #8, by Kitty Hensley House, North Pole, AK

Pupus from Paradise, Assistance League of Hawaii, Honolulu, HI

Quick & Healthy Volume II (ScaleDown) ©1995 by Brenda J. Ponichtera, R. D.,The Dalles, OR

Rainy Day Treats and Sunny Temptations, Medical Faculty Aux. of the Oregon Health and Science University, Portland, OR

Recipes, Recipes, Recipes!, Easter Seals Oregon, Eugene, OR

Recipes and Remembering, by Dorothy J. O'Neal, Eugene, OR

Recipes from Our Friends ©2001 Friends of Whitman County Library, Colfax, WA

Recipes from the Paris of the Pacific, Europe '97, Sitka, AK

Recipes to Remember, St. Joseph Hospital & Long Term Care, Chewelah, WA

Rogue River Rendezvous ©1992 The Junior Service League of Jackson County, Medford, OR

Sagebrush Surprises Cookbook, National Historic Oregon Trail Interpretive Center, Baker City, OR

San Francisco à la Carte ©1979 The Junior League of San Francisco, CA

San Francisco Flavors ©1999 Junior League of San Francisco, CA

San Francisco's Cooking Secrets ©1994 Kathleen DeVanna Fish, Monterey, CA

San Juan Classics II Cookbook ©1998 by Dawn Ashbach and Janice Veal, Anacrotes, WA

San Ramon's Secret Recipes, San Ramon Library Foundation, San Ramon, CA

Savor the Flavor of Oregon ©1990 The Junior League of Eugene, OR

Scallops and Sole Food, by Carol Cates, Winchester, OR

Seasoned with Words ©1998 Oregon Writers Colony, Portland, OR

Seasons: Food for Thought and Celebration, Christ Episcopal Church, Los Altos, CA

Serving Up Oregon ©2000 Serving Oregon, Salem, OR

Sharing Our Best ©1996 Eagle Historical Society & Museums, Eagle, AK

Shrimp Shack, Irene Theofanis, Punalu'u, O'ahu, HI

Simply Whidbey ©1991 by Laura Moore and Deborah Skinner, Oak Harbor, WA

Six Ingredients or Less ©2001 by Carlean Johnson, Gig Harbor, WA

Skagit Valley Fare ©1996 Lavone Newell, Mt. Vernon, WA

Sleigh Bells and Sugarplums ©1992 by Frances A. Gillette and Daughters, Yacolt, WA

A Slice of Santa Barbara ©1991 Junior League of Santa Barbara, CA

Sounds Tasty!, KAZU-FM, Pacific Grove, CA

Starters & Closers, Seattle Mariners Wives and Care, Seattle, WA

The Steinbeck House Cookbook ©The Valley Guild, Monterey, CA

Sugar and Spice–Cookies Made with Love, by Kelimia Mednick, Honolulu, HI

Summertime Treats ©1999 by Sara Perry, San Francisco, CA

Symphony of Flavors, Associates of the Redlands Bowl, Redlands, CA

Tailgate Party Cookbook ©1990 The Bess Press, Inc., Honolulu, HI

Taste California ©1993 California Dietetic Assn., Playa del Rey, CA

A Taste of Aloha ©1983 The Junior League of Honolulu, HI

Taste of Fillmore, Fillmore Christian Academy, Fillmore, CA

A Taste of Heaven, Grand Coulee United Methodist Women, Mansfield, WA

A Taste of Oregon ©1980 Junior League of Eugene, OR

A Taste of Sitka, Alaska, The Sitka Girls Basketball Team, Sitka, AK

Taste of the Methow, Methow Valley United Methodist Women, Twisp, WA

A Taste of Tillamook, Tillamook Chamber of Commerce, OR

Tastefully Oregon ©1996 Oregon Dietetic Association, Portland, OR

The Tastes and Tales of Moiliili, Moiliili Community Center, Honolulu, HI

Tasty Treats from Tenakee Springs, Alaska ©1968, 1993 Circulation Service, Inc., Tenakee Springs, AK

Then 'til Now, by Dorothy J. O'Neal, Eugene, OR

33 Days Hath September, by Karen Cauble, Fairbanks, AK

Thyme and the River ©1988 Steamboat Inn, Idleyld Park, OR

Thyme & the River, Too ©1988 Steamboat Inn, Idleyld Park, OR

Treasured Recipes, Western Welcome Newcomers, Grants Pass, OR

Treasured Recipes, St. Joseph of Cupertino Parish and School, Cupertino, CA

Unser Tagelich Brot, Odessa Memorial Hospital Auxiliary, Odessa, WA

Upper Kenia River Inn Breakfast Cookbook, by Peggy J. Givens, Cooper Landing, AK

Wandering & Feasting ©1996 Board of Regents of Washington State University, Pullman, WA

Washington Cook Book ©1994 Golden West Publishers, Phoenix, AZ

Washington Farmer's Markets Cookbook and Guide ©2000 by Kris Wetherbee, Oakland, OR

We, the Women of Hawaii Cookbook ©1986 We, The Women of Hawaii, Kailua, HI

We're Cookin' Now, Sitka Emblem Club #142, Sitka, AK

Western Washington Oncology Cook Book, by Diane Fisher, Olympia, WA

What's Cookin' in the Kenai Peninsula, Holy Assumption Russian Orthodox Church, Kenai, AK

What's Cooking??, St. Gerard Guild, Beaverton, OR

What's Cooking in Sisters, Friends of Sisters Library, Sisters, OR

What's for Dinner?, by Brenda Abelein & Kelly Wilkerson, Portland, OR

The When You Live in Hawaii You Get Very Creative During Passover Cookbook, Congregation of Ma'arav, Hololulu, HI

Wild Alaska Seafood–Twice a Week ©2003 by Evie Hansen, Richmond Beach, WA

The Wild and Free Cookbook ©1996 by Tom Squier, Port Townsend, WA

Your Favorite Recipes, Mukilteo Presbyterian Church, Mukilteo, WA

INDEX

Alaskans have evolved into the "flyingest" people in the nation. With well over 10,000 registered pilots, roughly one in every 58 Alaskans has a license to fly. It's no wonder, since many towns and cities here are not accessible by road.